KNOWLEDGE IS POWER
MY LIFE ON CORONATION STREET

KEN MORLEY

WITH

CHARLES YATES

BLAKE

Published by Blake Publishing Ltd,
3 Bramber Court, 2 Bramber Road, London W14 9PB

Published in hardback 1995

ISBN 1 85782 1521

British Library Cataloguing-in-Publication Data:
A catalogue record for this book is available
from the British Library.

Typeset by James Wright

Printed in England by Clays Ltd, St Ives plc

1 3 5 7 9 10 8 6 4 2

Text copyright © Ken Morley 1995

Contents

With Thanks

To Mother for having me, to my wife Sue for putting up with me, to Peter and Monica Smith for helping me, to *The Sun*'s Editor, Stuart Higgins; Deputy Editor, Neil Wallis; and computer wizard, Brigham Green, for their support; and to Charles Yates for making it fast, funny and I hope a right riveting read.

And finally to my son, Roger, for giving me so much pleasure and reminding me that I am, if nothing else, a wonderful, kind, caring, considerate, thoughtful human being, etc., etc., etc...

1

Leave or Die

'Here Comes the Bride': the organ music echoed round the church. It was the biggest day of my professional life. I, Reg Holdsworth, was to take Maureen Naylor and make an honest woman out of her. Millions tuned in and saw the soap wedding of the decade. It was all beaming smiles and Holdsworth charm.

The joy of the occasion jumped at you from the screen. The cast put on a tremendous display of overwhelming happiness. Even 'Poison' Ivy Brennan was at the wedding, smiling radiantly with the beginnings of her new lips.

The viewers' eyes at this point, though, weren't focused on any facial surgery — all were glued to the bride and groom. But what the fans didn't know was that those magical scenes, full of smiles and loving glances, had nearly been the final straw that snapped the camel's back. I was almost on my knees. By the end of the week we'd been on location for five days and when I walked out of the church with Maureen, my beloved, I was so exhausted I could hardly keep my eyes open, let alone consummate my nuptials.

I had spent five years on the top soap on television. I'd performed in front of the most beautiful women in the world, both on and off the box. The money was good, the scripts were good, the girls were good, the men were even better and I wanted more. But the one thing I didn't want more of was the skin that was hanging off my face.

Not only had I worked myself to death on the *Street*, but I'd galloped round Britain and the globe grabbing as much cash as I could. My personal appearances had become a way of life. As a member of a pop group said to me: 'You've got five years, Reg, and then you're going to have to take it easy, because if you don't you're going to be very dead.' Well, there I was five years on and married on screen to the marvellous Maureen.

The only problem was that instead of the skin being on my eyelids, it was now hanging down my face. I looked in the mirror and thought I was going to need plastic surgery. But after what happened to Lynne when she had her lips done again the following month, I must admit I was very glad I hadn't seriously considered the surgeon's knife. As a well-known surgeon apparently said: 'I don't know what's worse, a slack face or a slack bum, but the charge is the same.'

The wedding was filmed on the New Year bank holiday 1994 and I had spent my second Christmas running with my nose buried in scripts. From 8 a.m. to 7 p.m. through the entire festive season I was learning my lines. It was my second Christmas hard at it, and it was too much. I had a baby son and a wife, but my head was stuck in scripts all day, every day. When it wasn't, I was at work. That Christmas I had a mind-numbing forty-seven pages of dialogue to learn, so my wife Sue and I had just one night out together.

The wedding day may have been Reggie's finest hour, but I was a physical and emotional wreck as a result of it. I had aged almost overnight. My hair was falling out, my already burgeoning stomach was in danger of reaching my knees and I was definitely feeling worn out.

Lynne Perrie told me not long after I started that I'd knacker myself working on *Coronation Street*. She said: 'You push yourself and push yourself, but you don't realize that the mechanics of the body just shut down. I once went to bed on Friday, woke at twelve noon on Saturday, nodded off again and didn't wake until Sunday morning. I still felt tired, and after breakfast I went back to bed and didn't wake until Monday morning. And that was without the help of a bottle of booze.' After doing those wedding scenes I believed her.

Later, Sue warned me: 'If you keep on working like this it will kill you.' No male in my family has ever lived beyond sixty-five. That gave me another twelve years and I didn't want to spend them all doing six days a week, fifty-two weeks a year on the *Street*. Much as I loved it, I loved living more.

That's why I told the producer: 'I have to stop this Bettabuys stuff — it's really wearing me down.' I left Bettabuys because I wanted to stay alive. We were doing three episodes a week and between ten and sixteen scenes on a Sunday at Bettabuys. It was a huge amount of work. I had done the equivalent of nearly 200 episodes. Most actors don't do more than ten episodes for a series a year, so I had crammed in nearly twenty years' work in just a few years on *Coronation Street*.

I replayed a tape of Reg recently and you can see the deterioration. I was ageing on the screen before your very eyes. Towards the end I was looking like death. The old batteries were running down. I am a high-burn actor and give the job everything. I had some great times in Bettabuys, but boy, oh boy, was it hard work.

EastEnders beware! They have only been on a three-episodes-a-week caper for a short while, but give them all a couple of years and they'll be falling off their perches. It is a punishing schedule. With Reg being so verbose, it somehow seemed worse for me. Stuck in a study from 7 p.m. to 10 p.m. each and every night learning lines.

I was going to leave twelve months before; in spring 1994 I had handed in my ticket. As a result of the phenomenal popularity of Reg, I had been offered a whole series of very interesting projects. Impresarios, TV chiefs and agents were trying ever so hard to entice me away from *Coronation Street*. Since Bettabuys had come to an end, we had flogged the mother-in-law joke to death and old Reggie seemed to be going off the boil.

I decided the time was right to move on. My feet were itching. In May I was ready to give the company notice that I was leaving at the end of my contract, which expired on 31 July. But just as I was about to chuck the towel in, Eva Pope, who played temptress Tanya Pooley, did the same thing. Everyone was shell-shocked that she was leaving after such a short space of time. She had been there less than twelve months. She was very professional and drop-dead gorgeous. It was a dream to find a woman with such enormous talent and stunning looks.

She had a tremendous spirit and was a great laugh. Everybody felt it was a great loss. She had reinvigorated the Rovers Return. Her storylines with Des Barnes, Raquel Wolstenhulme, Bet Gilroy and Charlie Whelan were absolutely amazing. I hear she's now pregnant and expecting a Christmas baby. I wish her all the best. But back then her announcement pre-empted mine, so I decided to hold off revealing my plans for a week.

I was about to resign again when Anne Kirkbride, who plays Deirdre Rachid, returned after winning her personal cancer battle. Once again, I held off making my own announcement.

I had by this point started discussing with International Artists the prospect of doing a big-money panto in Bradford in the winter of 1994. These discussions leaked to the press and a journalist approached me over it. I admitted that I was considering leaving, but asked him not to write anything until I had approached Granada TV the next week.

But a story appeared in the *News of the World* talking of envy, jealousy, backbiting and greed among the cast. None of it was true, and it had appeared the day before I was going to tell Granada. I wasn't best pleased, and neither were my bosses.

But such was the popularity of Holdsworth, who was described as a national institution by the press, that a team of up to two dozen journalists arrived on my doorstep. I was under siege. I went out for a ride on my bicycle and the press hordes photographed every pedal movement.

The producer Sue Pritchard called me to say that she

was cancelling her holiday so she could sort out the situation. I told her she needn't do that and we'd discuss it when she came back.

Then I had another call, summoning me to a meeting with the executive producer Carolyn Reynolds and Andrea Wonfor, who is now Granada TV's managing director. It was suggested that we meet somewhere quiet and possibly dark. A date was set for a meeting upon my return from the Isle of Man, where my friend, Kevin Kennedy, and I had been invited by the Isle of Man tourist board to help with some promotion for the famous TT motorbike races in June. The *Daily Star* newspaper had organized the trip.

I jetted off, leaving hordes of press men hanging round the streets of Chorley. I'd instructed my mother Phyllis, wife Sue, our son Roger, who was three-and-a-half, and our pet dogs not to say a word to any journalists.

In the heyday of Hollywood, the film studios introduced the stars to the press and encouraged a working relationship. It worked for both sides, with the exception of big, big scandals, which are always bound to come out anyway. As Hugh Grant discovered on Sunset Boulevard, if you're an actor and get caught with a hooker you must expect big headlines as well as big lips. Fortunately the journalists on my doorstep weren't there because I'd been caught with my pants down. Let's face it, Randy Reg hardly ever had them up at one stage.

But, for the moment, I had left the press pack behind and the *Daily Star* team were delighted to have a superb scoop on their hands. I told them I couldn't discuss any of the newspaper revelations. But they were still rubbing their hands that they would get some great exclusive photographs that would be the envy of Fleet Street.

But unbeknown to us, the rest of the press were flying out to the island. *The Sun* had sent a team over late at night. They were trawling hotel bars, nightclubs and casinos, searching for us until four in the morning. They even camped outside our hotel from 6 a.m. They had a long wait, because we weren't going anywhere for several hours.

When we left the hotel in a convoy of cars we were

unaware that *The Sun*'s vehicle was trailing us. They tracked us for miles round the island. They even parked at a discreet distance when we pulled into a motorbike museum for a *Daily Star* photo shoot. They craftily bided their time as Kevin and I changed into 1920s motorcycle outfits, before jumping on a couple of vintage machines.

The next day *The Sun* splashed a photo of myself and Kevin riding the motorbikes all over the front page in colour. We were holding hands, and the clever headline was 'HANG ON REG'. The message from *The Sun*'s millions of readers was that they didn't want Reg to quit the *Street*. The strength of public feeling was obviously something I had to consider.

My meeting with two of the most powerful women at Granada Television was scheduled upon my return. The meeting was very pleasant and congenial. It was put to me that instead of going off to some other TV company to do other programmes, why didn't I do them with Granada? There was a logic behind this — after all Granada is one of the biggest and best television companies in the world. As a result of this, I cancelled the £100,000-plus panto. I also cancelled another programme I was going to do with another TV company and scrapped an advertising campaign I had lined up.

The agreement was that the pilot for this Granada programme would be made by May 1995. Reggie was back in business for another year. But as we now know, nothing was to be forthcoming as the year went on. Meanwhile, in the green room my fellow thespians were doing great donkey impersonations. This old fool had been taken for a mule. Well, as they say, if the cap fits wear it and mine had ears on it. I had been taken for a jackass. As one actor put it: 'What's your new pilot called, luv? *Death of a Donkey*?'

At the end of March 1995, there was a run-in with the management when I failed to appear at a photo session for the *Street*'s special thirty-fifth anniversary cast portrait. Other members of the cast had cancelled holidays to be there, but I was heading off for a TV appearance on the very day it was happening. The Granada press office had okayed my TV appearance and even provided clips for the *Kirsty* chat show, broadcast on Scottish telly.

It was possibly my fault for not noticing the date, and nobody alerted me to it as I set off for Scotland. I was arriving in Glasgow when I received the phone call asking: 'Where are you, Ken? And can you be in the studios in ten minutes?' I replied: 'Not in this car.' I was literally 200 miles away. I did get a great deal of slagging from the producer for not being there. I felt this was another nail in the proverbial coffin.

Yet again I was beginning to feel I was being tarred with the troublemaker's brush. The black sheep of the family. The one who always stepped out of line and had to be coshed. One gets very fed up of that particular approach. When I wasn't there for the portrait, people started muttering about me being off opening yet another supermarket, but in reality I was doing a job that Granada had approved and even helped arrange.

It was a case of the left hand not knowing what the right hand was doing. And I was getting slapped in the face by both of them. But the truth of the matter is I have given my all to Granada in the last six years. During that time Sue and I haven't been out to the theatre, to the cinema or anywhere else with each other, because I have been working so hard at the job and the personal appearances that I felt I had to do for the fans.

With all this in mind, there was only one more ingredient needed to make up my mind about leaving. That was when I came home from work one night earlier this year utterly exhausted. I had a pile of scripts under my arm and my mind was already on the scenes I had to learn. And there was a lot of demand to make personal appearances because Reg was such a popular character. I find it very hard to say no to fans and it is even harder saying no to the cash.

Roger ran up to me that night and said: 'Daddy, Daddy, do you want to see my new train set?' I should have walked through to the lounge and played with him, but I shut myself in my study to learn my lines. Roger started to cry outside and I heard him ask Sue: 'Why can't Daddy play with me any more?' I felt dreadful — it was the most gut-wrenching sound for any dad to hear.

Then Sue walked in and said: 'Can't you give him just half

an hour? He'll only be four once and you're missing out.' I remembered my own dad was always working when I was younger. I recalled the way I resented him for years as a result of this absence. I realized I didn't want Roger going the same way. I looked down at the scripts and thought, 'No, no, this is not the way.'

Instead of learning my lines early that night, I sat down and played with Roger and his trains. I knew then that I had to leave the *Street*. As soon as I made that decision, I felt as if a monstrous burden had been lifted from my shoulders. When I told Sue, she said: 'I am so glad. We can go back to where we left off. And you can be a husband and a dad.'

I'm not leaving the *Street* because of money, or rows with the show's makers. It is because I want to play football with my boy, take my family to the seaside, walk the dog — everything other people take for granted.

So this summer I made it clear I was on my bike for real. Scripts for the pilot sitcom *Flash Harry* had been sent to me, but in the words of the late, great Max Wall: 'I had never had such a great time without laughing.' I sent the script back to underline my displeasure. I then asked several people in Granada for their view on the script.

The question-and-answer sessions were better than the script itself. I would say, 'What do you think?' and they would say, 'Well, I don't know, what do you think?' And then I would say, 'I think it's a load of crap' and they would say, 'Yes, it's a load of crap.' It had taken somebody months to come up with this carefully crafted load of crap. Granada's comedy division had apparently undergone a temporary sense of humour by-pass.

By now twelve months had passed and we still didn't have a pilot. But I did have another fabulous offer of well in excess of £100,000 for a month in panto — as much as I earned at Granada in a year. I was told I couldn't take the time off to do the show. Granada has a rule that no *Coronation Street* star can take the time off to appear in panto, so I felt I had to leave the soap.

Rules are rules, and if you sign the contract you have to

accept them and I did. But that doesn't mean the rule is right, or even that it makes economic sense. Why lose a money-spinner like old Reggie for the sake of some antiquated rule carried over from another time?

I was perfectly within my rights to leave on 31 July, but I offered to stay on so the scriptwriters could write Reg out properly. I thought this company had done an enormous amount for me and I owed them a great deal. Granada created Reg Holdsworth and Bettabuys and gave a lot of people, including myself, a lot of fun. Staying for three months was the least I could do. I wanted to say thank you to the wonderfully talented team who put the programme on our screens.

This also led me up towards Christmas, which suited me fine as I was going to sign a contract to appear as a madcap brother and sister, Muddles and Puddles, in the panto *Sleeping Beauty* at the Sunderland Empire theatre. There was a lot of tosh in the papers that I was being fired or given a three-month contract as a punishment. It was never the case. I was fed up with some of the treatment, true, and was leaving. I'd felt I was getting it from all sides, although some of it was humorous.

But criticism is criticism and I found myself being regarded as something of a risk, a maverick who wouldn't tow the line. Quite right. I am a maverick, a freelance, an easy rider — call it what you want. At the end of the day, ambition is the name of the game. And as Holdsworth would say, you've got to go onwards and upwards.

Before I announced my departure, I discovered via the usual Granada grapevine that Julie Goodyear was to quit — a sensational departure after twenty-five stunning years. I immediately called the production office. I asked two questions. The first was: 'Is it true Julie is leaving?' The second was: 'Do you intend to put Reggie in the Rovers?'

'No ... no ... and definitely no,' were the answers. On hearing those words, I told the agent I was leaving. Not jumping on anybody's toes this time, just leaving. Imagine my surprise after these point-blank denials when the next day the papers declared: 'JULIE GOODYEAR QUITS THE STREET'.

The newspapers had a field day. 'CORONATION STREET IN

CRISIS' the headlines screamed. But both Julie and I know that the show will survive without us. On the day my decision to go hit the papers, she rang me up to wish me all the best. We'd had our disagreements, as you'll find out, but at the end of the day we were both big enough to remain pals.

Another phone call I got that day was from Kevin Kennedy, who said: 'So you've finally gone and done it?' I said: 'Yes — because I want to live to be fifty-seven like my dad and play with my money on the carpet.' Kevin appreciated this, because he had endlessly played out my demise with the line: 'Hi, I'm Ken Morley and I've made a million pppppppurgh.' At which point he would fall to the floor clutching his chest. He was right: I had to do it for the sake of my health. As the saying goes, many a true word is spoken in jest.

I've just said my father died at fifty-seven, and not many males on the Morley side have got much past that. Talking about an early grave, another contributory factor to my quitting was the fact I'd had an operation to remove a cancerous growth from my neck. It was the size of a fingernail and was spotted by *Coronation Street* make-up artists, who persuaded me to see the doctor immediately.

It was identified as a type of skin cancer known as basal cell carcinoma, and it can prove fatal if left untreated. It was the most terrifying experience of my life. I thought my number was up. I kept thinking, 'I'm only in my early fifties and I've got cancer and could die.' Medics described me as a very lucky man. It could have eaten into my windpipe.

The lump had been there on my neck for three years. It grew bigger in that time, but because it wasn't painful I ignored it. When the consultant saw me he took me into theatre immediately and removed it. He was brilliant and left only a tiny scar, which needed just five stitches. But it was still terrifying. They took the growth away and had it analysed. I was horrified when they called me three days later as I was driving and told me in a jocular manner: 'Oh by the way, it was cancerous.' Up until that moment nobody had mentioned the big C.

I had to pull the car over — I was shaking that much. There

is something about that word that strikes fear into you. I wiped my face with my hankie because the sweat was just pouring off it. Now I regularly check my face and neck in case the thing comes back. Every day now is so important to me. It is only after an experience like this that you realize how precious life is. It slaps everything sharply in context.

It's a bit sad really, because the production office and in particular Carolyn Reynolds, the executive producer, very kindly ordered and paid for the medical treatment. Yet I've ended up leaving. Being bald and fat is one thing, being dead is something else. Like it or not, my future at *Coronation Street* would have been lots of hard work, followed by lots of feeling knackered, followed by lots of being dead.

But we're rushing ahead. Before covering my death, let's go back to the very beginning. I'd love nothing more than to give you a full running commentary of the conception, but I was never privy to that. So you'll have to make do with my birth.

2

Fat and Round

The day was dull and grey, but into the grim world there came a shining light. Yes, it was my bald head. It was 6 a.m. on 17 January 1943 when, kicking and screaming, I appeared, almost blinding the midwife with the gleam from my scalp. The doctor had said: 'This is a tricky one. It's coming out sideways.' And from that unconventional start I was set to continue in a similar fashion through life, ploughing my own furrow, walking my own plank and beavering away as best I could.

The world was at war when I arrived and Adolf Hitler was having a profound effect on all our lives. But little did the Nazi hordes know that another little dictator was being born deep in the heart of Lancashire — in Chorley District Hospital to be exact. The hairless bonce, the little round belly, were nearly half a century later set to make their own impact on the nation in the shape of Randy Reg Holdsworth, the formidable, frightening and often foolhardy Beast of Bettabuys.

But for now we had best begin at the beginning with the birth of Kenneth William Morley. On the same day one of Britain's great leaders, Lloyd George, was celebrating his eightieth birthday with hundreds of congratulatory telegrams from around the globe. The following day the Soviet army broke the sixteen-month siege of the city of Leningrad. The Huns were on the run. Meanwhile, I lay in my cot with runs of my own. And in those days, lest we forget, there were no disposable nappies. My rear was wrapped in towelling and all the washing was done by hand.

Obviously I was a beautiful baby. The first and only child of engineer Frank and his darling bride Phyllis — Mum and Dad, as they later became affectionately known to me. Back then it wasn't just me who was short; my father was short, food was short and even my mother was going short.

The Second World War meant suffering for millions. It was madness, mayhem and bloodshed on a huge scale. But the brutal conflict brought my parents together. Try as he might, Dad wasn't permitted to shed his blood overseas for King and Country. As an engineer he had a reserved occupation and was deemed more useful at home making the weapons. Mother was simultaneously called up to help the war effort. She had the option of working in a munitions factory or she could have joined the vast Land Army of women digging for victory by farming the land.

Mum opted for Leyland Motors, and there in the midst of tank making she found true love — in the small but perfectly formed shape of Frank. He grabbed her attention almost immediately by smearing her overalls in oil after she'd hung them up at the end of a gruelling shift. Mother returned the next morning and slipped into them before feeling the clammy axle grease on the flesh of her arms. Mother immediately screamed and in proper Mills and Boon style Frank stood across the production line chortling at his wizard wheeze. What the Morleys didn't know about romance wasn't worth knowing.

Phyllis was horrified by Frank's pranks. Another favourite of my father's was putting lubricant on the machine handles so the girls couldn't keep their grip. He was a wag. Apparently his teasing and larking about annoyed Mum so much that she even went home and told her father about the factory fool who was making her life a misery. Her father — Preston cattle dealer Israel Owen — owned the town's Napier Hotel and café on the market. Luckily, he saw the funny side.

Somehow Frank turned the sticky situation round to his advantage. In no time he was wooing Phyllis for all he was worth, which wasn't a lot in those days. Now that I think about it, he never was worth much financially at any time in his life, but there's more to life than loot. So his quick wit and handsome features, which remain a family trait, soon had her hooked. He cycled her home every day en route to his parents' terraced house about ten miles away in Oswaldtwistle, Lancashire.

The courtship was going strong for twelve months when Frank eventually took the plunge and asked Phyllis's father for his daughter's hand in marriage. At the time it probably seemed like a mistake to Frank, who was told in no uncertain terms that twenty-seven-year-old Phyllis was too young to wed and was anyway perfectly happy at home with him. But Phyllis persuaded Israel otherwise.

And the happy couple got hitched, with my grandfather's threat that he'd swing for Frank if he upset Phyllis still ringing in their ears. Their big day was 6 August 1941, which was, strangely enough, a Wednesday. The wedding had to be midweek, because Israel's business commitments meant he was grafting the rest of the time. Mother says I take after my grandfather in the graft department. I, like him, don't like to stop once I've got going.

Mother, bless her, looked magnificent on her special day. Her beautiful bridal gown was bought from Maidens store in Chorley with coupons from her ration book. It was the last dress in town. Later in the War, Mother was to weep when she parted with it. She gave it away after a lady called and asked to buy it off her for her own wedding day. Mum refused to sell at any price, but the local girl, who was set to marry an American GI, started crying. Kind-hearted Mother was touched by her bawling and handed over the dress as a favour after she let the girl try it on for size and discovered it fitted like a glove. After the wedding the couple went to the States and Mother hasn't seen her ornate gown since.

The fact that she no longer has the wedding dress makes the photographs from that day priceless in our family. Even now, looking back at the old pictures of her and Frank and their friends in all their finery can take you back in time. One of my favourites of the wedding shows my parents flanked by my grandfather Israel on my mother's side, Dad's best man Richard beside him and Mum's bridesmaids Elsie Whitter and Molly Thompson. It is hard to imagine that as they tied the knot in St John's Church at Whittle-le-Woods, near Chorley, the Japanese were preparing to invade Saigon and war in the Pacific was looming. Just four months later, on 7 December, they bombed Pearl Harbor, bringing America into the conflict.

Yet in Whittle-le-Woods the big event was the wedding. After it, my family went for their wedding reception to a place called, curiously enough, Rimmer's Cafe, which features in its own right later in my life, though thankfully later it changed its name to Hill's Bakery. It was the place I first found employment. But I'll tell you about the hilarious and sometimes horrifying antics at that place later.

It was seventeen months after the wedding when I joined the family. It was two in the morning when the labour pains started for Mother in the bedroom of the tiny bungalow in Watkin Road, Whittle-le-Woods, a house her father had bought as a present for the newly-weds. Israel had a car and would happily have driven the pair to the hospital — except he'd been out celebrating that day and was incapacitated.

Fortunately, Frank knew just what to do ... he legged it straight out the front door. Mother hadn't heard him say he was going for the doctor and must have thought the daft sod had disappeared. But he returned shortly with family friend Dr Hugh Milligan, who lived up the road in nearby Shaw Hill. He took one look at Mother and bundled her into the back of his car, saying: 'For God's sake don't push down, woman, or you'll have the baby on the back seat.'

The five-minute drive up the bumpy road to the hospital must have helped hurry me along, because Sister Lee, the midwife, dashed Mum straight into the delivery room after answering the doctor's thumping knock on the solid oak front door. Mother was in agony, but I was oblivious to the pain. Cocooned safely in the watery womb that had been my home for nine months, I must have suddenly decided I was better off in than out and stayed put. Eventually, after a great struggle, and with my mother shouting for the midwife to go away, I made my first bow, as described earlier.

Before I popped out, my still half-sloshed grandfather had arrived at the hospital to help his daughter escape her torturers, as it appeared to him. He was only persuaded by Dr Milligan to leave the professionals to do the job after making a real song and dance, even storming into the delivery room.

Despite the early drama, I weighed in at a respectable 7lbs 3oz. At the time I was quite a bonny baby. Mum tells me that I had the pot belly and the bald head even then. And when my hair arrived the strands were as fair as fair could be — in recent years they've returned to that colour and I've still only got a few of them. Needless to say, I just kept getting heavier, although my present-day weight is one of the most closely-guarded secrets on *Coronation Street*. But as the saying goes, there are no fat dead folk — you're just dead!

Mother haemorrhaged during the delivery and in those days that was much more dangerous than it is today. Her problems at the birth meant I was destined to be an only child — so I grew up a real one-off. Frank had to leave the delivery room to go and make some more tanks, but Israel got to hold his grandson. My arrival gave him the ideal excuse to go and get inebriated again, by indulging in the ancient custom of wetting the baby's head.

Years later, when working as an actor and filming an episode of the hit TV show *Bulman* up near the Trough of Bowland, I met an old farmer who knew my grandfather. This fellow and his wife came into the pub at Whitewell, north of Preston, and we got chatting. During the conversation I mentioned Israel Owen, who always wore a bowler hat. Straight away recognition shot across their faces and they started to tell me what a good lad he was.

The old fellow said he'd never forgotten the time the pair of them went to a livestock auction in nearby Clitheroe and got absolutely pie-eyed. They'd bought a lorry-load of sheep and somehow managed to drive the stock back to his farm after twilight. The lady took up the story at this point, telling how the pair of them made a dreadful racket and asked her to give them a hand into the house. She refused, replying that they hadn't needed a hand to get into the state they were in so they could sort themselves out.

The old chap, with a twinkle in his eye, then picked up the tale, telling how both of them were too sozzled to stand and ended up falling fully dressed into the mud and dung, where they slept the night. The pair of them apparently woke at five the next morning with the engine on the truck still running and a stack of sheep to unload. Grinning from ear to ear, the old bloke recalled how, despite their massive hangovers, they got the job done. Then, it was on to the next jape.

To this day, I'm just like my grandfather — I work hard and I play hard. And don't we all drop in the manure from time to time? But back at birth I was apparently normal. However, Father, with his droll Lancashire wit, was rumoured to have said: 'Put it on top of the wardrobe, love — it'll come down when it's ready.' In them days you didn't have 'new men'; mothers brought up the children and the blokes went to work to bring home the bacon.

In the war years, of course, bacon, and for that matter pork of any description, was in very short supply. My mother tells a marvellous story of how one of my uncles came running into her terraced house with half a pig on his shoulder, chucked it into the cellar and ran out of the front door. Shortly afterwards, a policeman arrived asking after the pig, not my uncle, but the slab of meat. The Morley clan, tight-lipped, shook their heads in disbelief. The bobby went on his way and they had bacon for tea. A triumph in the face of adversity. A rum lot, my relatives, but deep down the salt of the earth.

I come from true working-class stock. On my mother's side, the Owen clan hailed from Staffordshire and before that from Wales. The Morleys, on the other hand, were originally from Cumbria and Scotland. Both sides converged on Lancashire in search of work when the industrial revolution started at the end of the eighteenth century. The dark satanic mills were stocked with many Morleys — a breed of bright artisans. They were craftsmen or engineers and my father followed in those footsteps, because when he was a lad in the 1920s there was an order and the Morleys knew their place.

My grandparents, on Father's side, inhabited a primitive terraced house in Oswaldtwistle. The home was basic, with no carpets, a stone sink, one cold-water tap, gas lamps, a coal fire, a tin bath and an outside non-flushing toilet. The lavatory was known as a 'tippler', and worked on the principle of having two buckets tied on a rod. When you dropped your own personal bombs into a bucket, the waste fell down a large hole into the sewer below. Very, very basic.

But we were comparatively fortunate, living in Whittle-le-Woods in the rolling countryside. Farm produce was all round us and a trip to the local farmer often secured a chicken and eggs for tea. In the cities they weren't quite so lucky during the war. Children regularly suffered from malnutrition. And trips to the doctor or the dentist were really too expensive for the average working man. Sadly, this seems to be a situation that is returning.

Our home then was this small bungalow named Durlston — no number, just the name. Funnily enough, it is only 150 yards from the sprawling mansion, well OK then, large detached bungalow I own today. But it was like living on another planet in the 1940s. Modern machines that we all take for granted were non-existent. Mother washed the clothes in a tub and then put them through a mangle. Kids today only get to see mangles in museums, what with electric washing machines and spin and tumble dryers. But, for the record, Mother was rather proud of her new-fangled mangle. It was very flashy for the time. It came from the Co-op and was housed inside a table. You lifted the tin tabletop and the rubber mangle rollers popped up. To squeeze the water out of the washing, you fed the clothes between the rollers and then turned a handle at the side to drag the fabric through. It was very heavy work, but married women with children had a lot to put up with in those days.

My mother, in particular, had a lot to put up with, because she had me. I was to prove a bit of a handful, because as an infant I went down with pneumonia. Another family in Chorley had a youngster with the condition at the same time as me. That poor little baby never pulled through, so that should give younger readers an idea of just how serious pneumonia was back then. Mum insisted on nursing me at home, but that put an enormous strain on her.

One day Dr Milligan called and found her collapsed with tiredness, yet still in a sitting position beside my cot. He put his foot down and insisted my father take time off work or he'd have Mother as ill as me. He gave him a note for the time off and thankfully I rallied round and pulled through. My mum still thinks of that other family in Chorley who so tragically lost their child.

Yet all over Britain mothers were losing sons as the war against the Nazis and the Japanese carried on. My second name, William, was given to me in memory of a great-uncle who lost his life in the 1914–18 war, but unbeknown to Mum and Dad the family was to lose another Billy in the Second World War: my Uncle William, Mum's cousin, who died along with thousands of other prisoners of war working on the Burma railway. The Japanese refusal to compensate families of those who suffered in that atrocious arena of warfare still leaves me sick. This year's fiftieth anniversary of VJ Day and for that matter, the VE Day commemoration, made me think back to the enormous sacrifice so many men and women made overseas in the fight for our freedom.

But even back home in the 1940s the Luftwaffe was bombing our biggest cities and military factories. Chorley was only bombed lightly during the war, but was made a target by the proximity of Leyland, where the tanks were manufactured, and the sprawling Euxton ammunition factory. The Royal Ordnance Factory at Euxton was second to London's Woolwich Arsenal as a strategic bombing target. It was one of the biggest munitions plants in Britain and the men and women who worked there regularly lost their lives in accidents on the production line.

The plant was purpose-built within two years at great speed, because at the start Britain simply wasn't ready for warfare. The factory was partly underground and disguised with ornamental lakes and imitation farms, so that from the air it looked like any other piece of open countryside scattered with farm buildings. A direct hit by the Germans would have obliterated not only the factory, but half the town of Chorley.

The slightest mistake by the staff would blow up a whole workshed and kill the workers inside. But with it being wartime there was a complete block on any information coming out. The tank factory at Leyland was regularly visited by the Luftwaffe. The workers would hide inside huge tyres to escape being wounded.

After work father, as a reservist, was part of the Home Guard and from what he told me about his outfit the lads were just like those in Captain Mainwaring's *Dad's Army* platoon that we all know and love from the television. The Chorley reserve army were equipped with some ancient carbine rifles that legend had it had last seen active service in the Boer War. In fact, they were Canadian Ross rifles of First World War vintage. But the most amazing part of his story about Chorley's finest shock troops was the fact that they had just six bullets between them. Ammunition was in such short supply that that was literally all they had to go round. I remember thinking years later just how lucky we were that the Germans never decided on a parachute drop on Whittle-le-Woods.

On my mother's side my grandfather Owen was the only other immediate member of the family to be called up for military service, and that was in the First World War. He was an engineer, but he managed to join the Royal Flying Corps — the forerunner of the modern-day Royal Air Force. He got his wings in 1918, but only managed to fly over Dover and the British ports before the end of the war was declared and the Versailles Treaty signed.

He was lucky — fliers in the First World War didn't have a great life expectancy, particularly as our lot didn't have parachutes. Our Government feared the chaps might not give their all if they had the option of bailing out. The Germans, on the other hand, gave the men in their flying machines a chance to survive after being shot down. As the old saying goes, he who fights and runs away lives to fight another day.

As I've already mentioned, my own life was on the line at one point as a result of pneumonia. But before I got that dreadful bout of sickness my mum had saved up for a special treat: a photo session starring her six-month-old son. Photographic film was another item in short supply during the war years, so the nearest studio where she could take me to have the snaps done was in Preston. Mum packed a picnic and put me under her arm for the trek to Phil Waine's studio on Friargate in the town. I was a natural in front of the camera, but at that early age nobody knew just how things were going to develop.

The pictures came out fine. Forty-eight years later, when my own son Roger was born, the resemblance was uncanny. As a babe I looked just like my father and I'm delighted to say that a generation down the line the enormously handsome Morley gene is still in evidence.

Anyhow, when I was a baby time flew, although my own personal development seemed to stand still. My mother tells me I was a slow starter when it came to walking and talking. I lay back and developed my belly with lack of exercise for the first couple of years of life. It was only when I was two that I stopped crawling — although years later at Granada TV this early practice proved invaluable as I took the role of Reginald.

My early attempts at walking caused much mirth in the family until Mother realized I was balancing on the outsides of my feet. She whisked me down to the doctor's. Sensibly, he told her to give it a while and swap my sandals for lace-up shoes before getting me referred to a specialist. My grandfather stepped in at this point and took me off to a cattle auction to meet his friend the leatherman, who made clogs among his other traditional wares, such as saddles and bridles for horses.

The clogs he created for me were something else. They had rubber on the soles and fancy bits of brass on them. I'm told I wore them right up to schooldays and only stopped then because I wanted shoes on like all the other kids — one of the few occasions in my life that I've made a point about conforming.

Like most people, I don't remember a great deal about my

early years. My first living memory was as a toddler flying down a mud road not 100 yards from where I live today. I recall someone shouting in the background trying to warn me to keep away from the road at the bottom of the hill as that was where the tanks from the factory thundered by. At the age of three-and-a-half I was blissfully unaware of the danger. I didn't get crushed by the tanks, but I did get a mauling from my mum and dad for doing something potentially very dangerous. Maulings became a way of life for the young Morley.

By this time the war had ended. I have no recollection of the street parties or the bunting that was everywhere when the wondrous news that the war was over was announced. The ration books remained and normality was still some way off. Some might say I never achieved it, but I'm not going to comment on that.

One awful shortage during the war, as far as kids were concerned, was the lack of toys. No factory made them, because they were all churning out armaments. And we hadn't even heard of Taiwan in those days. Instead of playing with toys as a toddler I would play make-believe games. It was like stage school at nursery age — I'd be pretending, as all kids do.

Nobody before me in my family had ever been on the stage. And as a child I had no aspirations to acting. Sure, I clowned round and dressed up, but show me a child who hasn't done that. The only time I came anywhere near making a stage appearance was when I was taken to the circus at Blackpool when I was about four. It was shortly after the war and I'd been taken there by my mum and Aunty Alice as a big treat.

Now Aunty Alice came from the village of Brinscall, near Chorley, and like many women she had lost her intended in the war. As a result of the fighting there weren't that many men to go round. She died a spinster — it was very sad, but there were lots like her. Well, during our trip to the circus the ringmaster kept saying he was going to take Aunty away.

He'd picked on her as one of the single women in the audience and was telling everyone he loved her as part of his act. He had no idea of the heartbreak she had been through, but I became fiercely protective. I'm told I got very upset and started shouting at him and my mother. 'You can't have Aunty Alice, you can't have Aunty Alice. She's with us,' I was yelling at this chap. Apparently I put my arms round her and didn't bat an eyelid at the whole audience looking at me. I just kept on telling him to go away — looking back, it probably was my first public appearance. More to the point, I never got paid. Perhaps I should send off an invoice to Blackpool's Tower Circus for services rendered. My mother tells me my performance had them rolling in the aisles. Now what was the going rate in 1946?

But joking apart, at about the same time I had my first girlfriend. Well, not really. She was just the girl next door or nearby, a lovely lass called Kathleen Durkan who played out with me in the street in our barefoot days. My mother tells me that Kathleen used to suck a soother and that I was forever wanting to taste it. I thought her dummy was a sweet, but Mum made sure I never took it off her. I must have looked daft enough without a large piece of plastic stuck in my mouth. She went to school before me and after she'd gone I was ever so lonely.

Mum says I used to hang about outside the local secondary school during this period longing to go there. Clinging to the fence, I watched the children doing their physical education lessons. Then one day she went outside for me and I'd vanished. She was frantic until she spotted me through the railings doing my exercises beside the teacher in front of all the other children. Another unpaid performance.

The teacher said I was sweet and would have had me help her every day, but Mother was steadfast about me not going to school until I was five. I was her little lad and she looked after me as such. She was ever so protective of me. They say you're always a little boy so long as your mother's alive. Well she's eighty-one now and still going strong, so I suppose that's one of the reasons I'm still a big kid at heart.

During this pre-school period I indulged in my one and only pilfering session: I strolled into the doorway of the local Catholic church and picked up a basket that was lying on the ground. Now, unknown to me, all these wicker baskets had been placed there for the local walking day. In those days in Lancashire the parishioners had their baskets decorated at church before embarking on a stroll around the locality. I told Mum I'd found the basket as a present for her, but she wouldn't have it. She marched me back with it and drilled into me the lesson that you don't just go wandering about picking up other people's stuff. It was a proper telling-off and it did the trick.

Mother and Father were both firm with me — it was very much a case of spare the rod and spoil the child in those days. Children were seen and not heard. It did me no harm, so I'd happily bring my son up in a similar fashion. The end product, as I'm sure you'd agree, is well worth it.

Now, one absolutely amazing anecdote about my early years is oft recalled by my mother. It revolves round a family trip to the seaside, of which there were many in my youth. On this particular occasion our jaunt was to Morecambe. Now on the way to the town, which has in the past been cruelly dubbed the last resort, Father stopped the car for a quick session with a clairvoyant.

The soothsayer in question was a gipsy, a true Romany with a traditional horse-drawn caravan, who was based not too far from the then thriving port of Heysham. She wore an old shawl over her shoulders and her piercing brown eyes stared out from her leathery tanned face. The wrinkles, like the rings through a tree trunk, hinted at great age. This lady was no sapling and was probably well over the age of eighty. Her appearance simply added to the mystical nature of the visit.

First Frank had his palm read or his crystal balls looked at. Then he insisted Phyllis have a bit of the same. And that is when, believe me, it happened. This wizened walnut of a woman made the most remarkable of predictions — that their son, a certain Kenneth William Morley, would be rich and renowned.

Now this clairvoyant had them both chuckling when she mentioned their chubby child. In the future she foresaw fame and fortune for this little creature far in excess of their wildest dreams. They laughed. We all did. Down the years when I was told of the story I, like them, treated it as a great hoot, never imagining it would ever come true.

But if she's looking down now she'll notice we are no longer laughing. Her revelation appears to have been bang on — otherwise you wouldn't be reading this book and I wouldn't have written it. Yet the path to fame and fortune wasn't anywhere near as smooth as a baby's bottom, so read on to discover the hiccups and hilarity I've encountered along the way.

3

Chorley Childhood

All animals are equal, but some animals are more equal than others. It is a line borrowed from George Orwell's classic book *Animal Farm*. But for me it sums up the primitive society found in playgrounds throughout Britain. My first school was in Leyland, but after a very brief spell the family moved back to Chorley. It was in my home town that I started school proper at St Peter's Church of England Primary ... and boy, were we animals by the time we left it.

I had been dying to get to school and meet new pals. I took to it like a duck to water, but Mother remembers crying when I went through the gates. In fact, I was laughing and crying at the same time, depending who I was looking at.

It was there in the red-brick building at St Peter's that I met a kindred spirit, mop-haired, fresh-faced Peter Smith. Pete and I became best pals — a friendship that to date has spanned forty-five years. We are still buddies today. He now acts as my chauffeur, confidant and minder on the scores of personal appearances I undertake each year.

But in the playground, as in life itself, the name of the game was survival. And both Pete and I were survivors. Schoolboys have to learn quickly who to approach and who to avoid. At the

27

end of your first day at school you can form a friendship that will stay with you for life — we're the living proof of that.

The slugs in the schoolyard quickly fall prey to the predators that lurk listlessly during every lunch-break simply waiting to pounce. Yes, the school bully — every playground has one. St Peter's had several such specimens. Little hard lads in a tough little world. We were all potential victims, but the slugs were the ones who really suffered.

The slugs were simply too thick, or too slow, to avoid the venom of the bullies. They needed only do some minor wrong to find themselves beaten mercilessly. The chant would go up: 'Fight, fight, fight.' And the unwilling gladiator would be thrown into the lion's den. In a matter of minutes the slaughter would be complete as the ill-matched contestants slugged it out.

Then the best bullies of all stepped in: the schoolmasters who'd let the fight proceed with interest until one party fell to the floor. Then both bloodied warriors would be hauled up before the rest of the school for six of the best. In Lancashire they caned people on the hands; caning boys on the bottom was considered rather risqué.

But oh the joy of watching others being punished, especially the school bully — the pleasure from their pain was so sweet. There was nothing more rewarding for small boys than to hear the howls of a bawling bully. One set of bullies beating another bunch ... yippee!

The other great pleasure at school was sex, or rather talking about it. It was a taboo subject, so one had to glean a bit here and a bit there. Sex was one of the big no-nos, particularly for little boys who might want to practise techniques for later in life. I'll get round to boyhood sexual peccadilloes in a short while. Before that I will describe the teachers in my place of early learning.

First there was Fanny Ford; titter ye not, that was her real name. As broad as she was tall, Miss Ford was a first-rate battleaxe. Her instrument of pleasure was a full piano-stool leg, which she used on a regular basis to beat the bad boys. With her horn-rimmed spectacles, white moustache and tied-back

Top left: Sue my wife, my life – she means the world to me.

Top right: Wedding belle. It took twelve years before we tied the knot.

Above: Happy family – I'm leaving the *Street* to change tracks, so I can play with Roger, Sue and grandma Vera.

Top left: The famous Reggie-Specs appeal.

Top right: Fair enough? My fairy prank landed myself and Kevin Kennedy in lumber with the *Street's* producers.

Above: The Presley gates – every time we go through them, Pete says 'Home again, home again, jiggity jig'. I'll throttle him soon.

Top: Napoleon Grown-apart: I posed with another stallion for this snap in County Tipperary after announcing my *Street* departure.

Above: Sex on legs, and Sam Fox isn't far behind either.

Top left: Tribute to the King. A dream comes true as Pete and I visit Memphis. He snapped me outside the famous Sun Studios.

Top right: Christmas crackers – more festive season fun with Kev Kennedy.

Above: Who's that clown with a cap and gown? You've guessed it … Ken Morley, BA, before I graduated as an FB – for those who don't know, that means Fat Bastard!

Top: Hang on, Reg – Kevin keeps a tight hold as I plan to quit in 1994.

Above left: Dead lucky. After this car crash I could have been plain dead.

Above right: My trusty Cadillac Fleetwood after my first and last flying lesson in it off the M61 motorway.

Top: On the road. We take a break far from the madding crowd, but I've covered 190,000 miles in just four years.

Above: Bettagags, loads of laughs and piles of pranks with Kevin Kennedy and Sarah Lancashire. My pals from the supermarket.

Wedding hell – it was Randy Reg's finest hour, but preparing for his screen marriage in January 1994 almost killed me. I was a broken man after spending my Christmas break learning lines virtually non-stop.

Big Breakfast show buddies – I shook hands with daredevil Eddie Kidd. I'd heard he had made some spectacular jumps. Apparently he did his on a motorbike, but most of mine were in the backs of cars.

hair she instilled terror into everybody. Some said she bore a remarkable resemblance to Mao Tse-Tung.

But to her eternal credit, she was the woman who marked me out at an early age when she noticed I was short-sighted. I remember her words as if it was yesterday. 'You, Kenneth Morley, will have to wear glasses and I hope you don't make a spectacle of yourself,' she declared. Sniggers burst out all round me — there is something in the very mention of spectacles that schoolboys find incredibly funny. The National Health Service wire frames were a job lot and they were filled with two-inch-thick glass lenses, or so it seemed. But I immediately stood out in a crowd. I was often mistaken for a Japanese sniper and there weren't many of them in Chorley.

Yet despite the specs, my mind remained nimble enough to help me avoid the bullies. In later years I discovered that one of the playground bruisers had gone on to be the boss of a wallpaper factory. I saw another one of the very tough lads by accident only a few months ago. I was in a building-supplies store in Chorley when I bumped into him. He had turned into a perfectly reasonable human being, although back then he was far from it.

He told me he had been on holiday to Cyprus and on the way back on the plane he had felt a pain in his chest. He got home and found out it was heart trouble and he needed by-pass surgery. Neither of us could believe it. He said: 'I've never been over eleven stone in my life, but look at me now; fifty-three and knackered. Next time I see you, I'll have had it done.' I was astounded that this bloke was the bully we were terrified of at school. Everybody knows them: the Basher Briggs characters, nutters at school, but nice as pie in later life. Now try telling that to a kid who's just been dangled upside-down by one of them.

When they knocked you to the floor in our playground you really knew about it, because it was full of ground-up cinders to stop the mud getting into school. If you were unlucky enough to stumble, it cut right through you. You were immediately slashed to the bone with big purple and red marks all over your body.

In 1953, when I was ten, money was still very tight all over the country. St Peter's was no different — the school was that hard-up that it never even had a telephone. None of the teachers, including the headmaster, spats-wearing Reginald Marsden, had cars. They all queued for the bus with us after school.

Our other prime tormentor on the staff at St Peter's was Mr George Rochford. He was a relatively young man who had served in the Royal Navy during the War. In an attempt to get us to eat the school dinners, he regaled us with stories of his time in India and how he regularly ate meals there while starving children and old folk looked on. He went on about scoffing chicken and potato dinners while ignoring the natives. He told of throwing them a few scraps and the way they would all fight over them in the gutter. We weren't really impressed by this barbarism, because it wasn't too far removed from what we were experiencing ourselves.

But his stories coincided with my father's observations on the Great British Empire. My father was a true Brit and earnestly told me: 'The wogs begin at Calais, lad, and don't you forget it.'

Other gems in his collection of one-liners, summing up Britain's role in history, included: 'We were the nation that taught the world how to behave proper'; 'When th' British went to India they were chucking their wives on to th' fire and stuffing theirselves with coconuts or even worse, eating each other. But we changed all that.' Mr Rochford's tales certainly put that into perspective; once we took over, it appeared they had nothing to eat at all.

He left our school to go and live in South Africa, where he said there was a higher standard of living. Of course, his *Boy's Own* stories never mentioned the oppression of the blacks out there. It was only years later that we realized what he meant by a better place when we saw on telly the squalor the blacks had to endure while the whites lived in luxury. He must have found being an oppressor came naturally. Pete and I rubbed our hands with glee when the apartheid system was abolished, not just with delight at the emergence of a fairer order, but with the thought that old Rochford might at last have to wake up to the fact that we are all equal. Not just in the playground, but in life itself.

My father might sound like an early version of Alf Garnett and in a way he was, but the problem was that there was no element of truth in history back then. His reading during my early years was confined to cowboy books. He loved a good Western and as a kid it was a great treat to be taken down to the Odeon in Chorley to watch the latest rerun of a Hopalong Cassidy or Alan Ladd movie at the flicks. These days the cinema building is a Gala Bingo Hall — what would Dad say if I had told him then that I'd be paid thousands of pounds in later life just to turn up and sign autographs on a bingo hall's first night. He'd probably say, 'Don't be stupid, that's not a proper job.' I don't suppose it is, but it pays well. And as Dad used to say: 'There are only two kinds of fool, lad, the paid and the unpaid.'

Chorley's other picture palace in that era was the Royal, commonly known as the Fleapit. The nickname was given as a result of the fleas in the seats. You often left that place itching all over. The Pathé news bulletins were full of fascinating world events, but it was only later that news programmes started to get answers to difficult questions.

For example, just a decade earlier there was no attempt to tell the working man why the War was going on, or before that, what had been happening in Russia. Royalty were gods — the fact the workers had risen up and shot a stack of them was pretty much unspeakable over here.

I was about at the end of an era. The end of the Empire. We were told that we were part of a British way of life and we ran two-thirds of the world. It was a solid feeling, being British — there was this worldwide Commonwealth, a family of little friends and helpers. The rest of the world was squalid, vile and filthy. People outside the Empire didn't have anything like what we had. But I kept thinking about Gran's house with its outside bog and how very uncivilized that was. I started to question things, along with others of my generation, but before we came along there seemed more of an acceptance of one's lot in life.

In those days religion played a much bigger part in local life. In Lancashire, we had the largest Catholic population in England. I was brought up a Protestant believing in the work ethic. We called the Catholics rednecks — a term coined during the Jacobite rebellions. The county's Catholics backed the Georges and didn't support the Stuarts, like Catholics elsewhere had. To distinguish themselves they wore red scarves round their necks, hence the name. In America, the description redneck means a big, fat, burly worker — in Lancashire it is different: it just means a big, fat, burly Catholic. Just as disparaging.

In those days marriage across the religious divide was considered bad news. People had the idea that because of the Catholics' religious beliefs on contraception, they were at it like rabbits. Having all these children made them a burden on society — it was quite a bigoted view. Needless to say, both my father and I married Catholics. All this talk of them going at it like rabbits obviously had some effect on us — let's face it, they had to be the best between the sheets. Both Dad and I could testify to that. The Morleys were never hindered by tradition.

But what the local minister or clerics said was important. Before TV the vicars, doctors and politicians held a lot of sway. These were the people who ran the society. The ones who decided which houses could be built and where. They lived in big houses and everybody knew the order of things. In those early years I was happy to stay in my place. But I always felt slightly out of order. I was aggravated and embarrassed by the situation I found myself in. I found the reality of working-class life disappointing and dull, not to mention aggressive and often vulgar. I also hated the unwillingness of men like my father to question things.

During the war this mentality prevailed. Working men never questioned why they were being sent overseas to defeat the enemy — they just did it. During the Great War, the Accrington Pals and all the rest of the volunteer forces never questioned what they were doing. They all thought they were going on some turkey shoot. They didn't realize the Germans had a highly mechanized army and were just as advanced as us, if not more so. If they'd been told that, they mightn't have gone so readily. Nobody wants to eat steel. As it is, they did go and all those volunteer forces were completely annihilated. But people were aware of being in a certain order and it wasn't the place of the working man to ask questions.

Things hadn't changed much even after the Second World War. In them days the national anthem was played on every trip to the cinema or theatre and everybody stood up. I was once thrown out of the flicks in Chorley for eating an ice cream during 'God Save the Queen'. It was crazy: the usherette had just served it to me. But the next minute, the national anthem came on and I'm being booted out for having the audacity to eat the ice cream that was melting in my hands. God help you if you were caught chewing your nuts.

It was much later in life that I saw the brilliant comedian Ken Dodd play a superb joke on the audience in Blackpool. The orchestra began to play the national anthem, but after three or four seconds it changed to a different tune and we were all left standing there looking at each other. The nutcase from Knotty Ash and his Diddy Men made us realize that we were all brainwashed into standing to attention at the first hint of that tune.

But at the age of seven or eight, as I mentioned earlier, I was to learn about standing to attention in a whole new way. As was traditional, an older boy explained to me the delights of Mrs Palm and her five lovely daughters. Yes, I was on a voyage of discovery. After years in a boyhood wilderness I was at last finding out all about being randy. My adventures at this stage in my life were to stand me in good stead for later periods. The punishing training schedule I thrashed myself with then helped form an integral part of the red-blooded Beast of Bettabuys.

Yet our early yearnings were very much forbidden fruit. Sex was pleasure and working-class folk couldn't really afford to be enjoying themselves. Pleasurable experiences were often expensive and pennies were short. The price of pre-marital sex was the risk of an unwanted baby, and bringing up nippers cost money. If young people went about copulating and produced a kid, then they would be in dire straits. Girls, in particular, were not permitted to have sex for pleasure, because of the chance of being abandoned with a bairn. It was a moral dilemma. But basically if you were having sex before marriage you were a dirty animal and that was that.

As a result of this, when questioning kids started asking where they came from, parents responded with blank looks. They couldn't risk telling youngsters about sex. We were simply told not to ask questions like that. There was an absolute refusal to discuss any sort of biological functions. The closest they got was telling you which paper to wipe your bottom with. They didn't know how to approach a conversation about sex, because no adult had ever addressed the matter with them.

Kids like me were told that sex was dirty and purely an animal thing. What we should have been told was that sex was perfectly OK if precautions were taken. This shroud of secrecy led to lots of animated playground conversations about what you were allowed to do.

The older boy who informed me of the method of wrist and hand movement that could lead to hours of fun was the equivalent of a modern-day sex-education lesson. And as soon as I tried it I was instantly hooked. Forbidden fruit tastes so sweet, as Adam discovered in the Garden of Eden. Back at St Peter's word soon spread. In no time there were rows and rows of little boys in shorts supposedly doing English, but all sitting there with glazed looks on their faces as they massaged themselves furiously beneath the desks. The girls soon gathered what was going on — they'd say, 'If you don't stop what you're doing we will go and tell the teacher.' Some were too far gone to stop. But thankfully teacher never made them walk to the front of the class — the protrusion in their shorts would surely give the game away.

In the early 1950s you just had to cast an eye round the room and you'd find at least one bored classmate at it in the corner. It was safe sex — especially safe in those early days when there were no sticky side-effects. It was a few years later that my sweaty grip secured a deposit. I recall being called in for tea shortly afterwards. I was in a daze. It had been good, but never *that* good before. My dinner remained untouched on the plate. Mother and Father thought I looked flushed. How right they were. Their little lad had just experienced his first climax. What a mind-blower! So when schoolboys suddenly go off their tea, Mums and Dads, now you know one of the reasons why. They've been giving themselves a quick hand shandy and done their heads in.

My ability with my right hand earned me a new nickname: Bubble — or more precisely, Spunk Bubble. The moniker remained with me for years. I remember, on one trip to the zoo, watching a chimpanzee play with himself. There was a crowd of about sixty pressed up against the wire. Mums were saying 'Don't look' or shouting 'Come away' but the monkey's performance was gripping. At the end of the day we all do it — only some do it more than others. As you've probably guessed from the nickname, I did it more than most. After school there would be huddles of little boys behind Chorley's gasworks practising for all they were worth. It was a case of synchronized hand shandies before going home for tea.

And right through those formative years the number-one fantasy figure at St Peter's was Miss Ishmail, a young teacher of Arab extraction. She was gorgeous, yet she had the power to punish. Later in life, at Granada TV, I was to meet more powerful women who also felt it was better to give than to receive, but we'll come to that in due course.

For the time being let's stick to Miss Ishmail — we'd have given our right hands to do just that at the time. She had our attention for every second in class. She would sit in front of us, smoking Craven As. All the boys in the class found this amazingly erotic and there was much fumbling about under the desks. She'd be teaching us English or Maths, blissfully unaware of the emotional turmoil she was causing, although on occasions she would say: 'You boy, what are you doing there?' As you straightened your garment and took your hands from your trouser pocket, she would raise a piece of paper to her face. She was either hiding her embarrassment, or doing her best not to wet herself.

Now that would have been immensely erotic. I do recall as a small boy in Chorley joining a crowd of other lads in the cinema to watch a celebrated local pianist break some record or other for non-stop playing. The woman must have been thrilled to have such a large audience of boys in attendance for her record-breaking attempt. But what she didn't know was that we were all there waiting for them to bring the bucket, so she could have a wee. She'd play through as this flood of water gushed into the bucket placed beneath her commode. We clapped heartily after each performance. She even played a variation of Handel's *Water Music*!

The 1950s was a period when piano playing was very much in vogue. Winifred Atwell was the star performer and I remember family trips to Blackpool and Preston to see her play. In 1954 she topped the charts with 'Let's Have Another Party' and in 1956 she reached number one again with 'Poor People of Paris'. Us Northern folk, being somewhat isolated, had never seen a black person until the mid-1950s. I remember standing and gaping with my parents as one of the first black families arrived in Chorley. They were dressed in vivid blues and reds and pinks, and that was just the fellas. Winifred Atwell had led the way for West Indians. After her success here, lots of others followed.

Not a lot of people know this, but in 1954 she also produced a single that got in the record books for having the longest title ever to hit the charts. Her track, with seventy letters in the name, held its place in pop history for twenty-three years. But *Rachmaninov's Eighteenth Variation on a Theme by Paganini (The Story of Three Loves)* was replaced as the longest title in 1977 when the Carpenters reached number nine with *Calling Occupants of Interplanetary Craft (The Recognized Anthem of World Contact Day)*. A staggering seventy-three letters in that one. Yet one of Reg's old favourites would have to be The Freshies' 1981 hit *I'm in Love with the Girl on a Certain Manchester Megastore Checkout Desk*. Only sixty letters — yet it brings a whole new meaning to the phrase 'supermarket music'.

But I digress. In the 1950s the rage in theatres were

vaudeville acts. Serious stage plays were posh and not really watched by working-class folk. Jimmy Jewel and Ben Warris were the superstars of the day — they were really big just pre-TV. We would go at weekends to Blackpool or Preston to catch a show. Charlie Caroli was the top clown at Blackpool Tower and his amazing talent was later to brighten up children's TV. Another major celebrity at the time was Max Miller, but he was based in the South and we never got to see him.

Winifred Atwell ended up going to Australia for a gig and liked it so much she decided to stay in Sydney. She had originally come from the West Indies and had really made it big over here. But though Britain was losing one great talent, another was being developed in the back room of our semi-detached house at 67 Park Road, Chorley. Mother and Father persuaded Grandad Israel to splash out on a grand piano, which took up the whole back room. They thought I'd turn into Liberace by moonlight, but learning to play the piano is no overnight occupation. I struggled through basic formulations and finger movements. It is the equivalent of torture as they put you through your paces.

My parents suffered it for years, but one day when I was out they got rid of it. They gave the grand piano away. The poor couple's eardrums had obviously had more than they could take. I only noticed it had gone when I stepped into the back room and tried to lean on it.

I could be a real prat at times like that and regularly came down to earth with a bump. I'll never forget Mum buying a new two-wheeled bicycle for me. It was upon that machine that I first displayed all the hallmarks of a master prat. I was given this sparkling cycle and warned not to take it up Botany Brow, a local hill, until I had mastered it. But I knew better.

Immediately I set off towards the brow. It was on the way down that I did my impression of a slalom skier without the skis. I was a forerunner of that Great British failure Eddie 'The Eagle' Edwards. Just like him, I was travelling at full speed when I took off ... only I went straight over the handlebars. Head first, I skidded along the floor. The bruising was impressive, the blood was everywhere, but I don't remember much more. I was concussed and unconscious for about a day. Have you ever tried butting cobblestones? Don't bother, just take it from me, it isn't pleasant. That was the first and last time I got on that bike.

My earlier bikes had all been three-wheelers and I was most comfortable on them. Mum bought me a real beauty of a bicycle one day in Blackpool. She felt sorry for me being a child in the war years when there were no toys, let alone money, about. We were driving past this wagon, which was unloading these new bikes, when Mum decided to get me one as a surprise present. I was ecstatic. It was a state-of-the-art dream machine and it had cost her a fortune. But it was a great buy and it lasted me for years. After my accident I went back to it despite the laughter from the locals.

Total prat number two involved the school bus. Us boys used to jump off the open back of the bus and run along the pavement. The vehicles were just like the ones made famous in the hit TV comedy *On the Buses* and they all carried conductors and inspectors, just like Blakey off the telly. This particular afternoon, following a nonchalant farewell to the brothers in shorts, I disembarked at the usual full pelt, but failed to notice the lamp post by the kerb. I hit it at top speed — it was like running into a brick wall. With hindsight it could have killed me, but my blubber saved my life.

Prat number three was when I rebuilt a motorbike engine. Dad pointed out: 'No more than thirty m.p.h. for the first 200 miles, or you'll seize the engine.' I replied: 'Dad, don't tell me how to ride a motorbike, all right!' Within half a mile, yours truly was doing another Eddie the Eagle right over the handlebars again, as the engine seized solid.

I often ignored parental advice. I regularly went tree climbing with a girl called Elizabeth Hampson against their orders. The first time I climbed the tree I got told off and instructed not to do it again. The second time I did it I got a further furious warning, but the third time I did it, during a game of Cowboys and Indians, Dad informed me he was leaving me there. I started to whinge, but he wouldn't have it.

Realizing my crying was doing me no good, I decided to make my own way down — you've guessed it: head first. I slipped on the descent and chipped my tooth in the fall. The blood was everywhere and the tooth has been with me ever since. Needless to say, I never went tree climbing with Elizabeth again. Mother tells me she went on to marry a mountaineer.

At this period we lived at a place called Higher Tongs, near Chorley, and my pal Pete Smith lived about a mile-and-a-half away across the fields at 2 Carlton Road, off Botany Brow, on the Blackburn Road out of Chorley. It was a pleasant stroll through the countryside over a rickety footbridge across the canal and up to his home. These days those fields have a housing estate on them and the M61 cuts another swathe through what was once lush meadows.

When we were children we were aware of the great changes taking place in society. One minute nobody had cars, nobody had television and nobody had telephones. They were all real luxuries. Then, in the space of a few short years, cars started to appear with greater frequency on the roads. The period of greatest change was in my early teens.

By the time I reached fifteen everyone had a Ford Anglia, everyone had access to television and people were getting telephones, though in those days, if you got in touch with the Post Office they said they could get you a telephone line in eighteen months. Sometimes I think we've reverted to that system with some of the privatized utilities. Has anyone tried ringing them recently? I hope Mozart and Handel's descendants get royalties every time we join the queue.

Even with all the changes in the world it was still a phenomenal leap for a working-class lad even to consider being anything other than what his dad was, or a train driver, or an electrician. You got told at an early age what your opportunities were. Any suggestion at my school that you should go on to grammar school was greeted by wails of mirth and derision. Somebody would have given you a kick in the nuts for being a prat if you as much as mentioned it.

Any artistic leanings were regarded as the first sign of puffery and as such were discouraged. We had to trot out the well-trodden formulas when asked what we wanted to do after school. It was OK to be a mechanic or somebody who worked on the roads. You were allowed to be sharp and crafty and, of course, hard with a capital H. There was great kudos in any job with a violent streak in it. Hammering things, hitting things, breaking things, or cutting things up were all acceptable work pursuits. As was working in a factory making machines, like my dad.

Mother recalls how from an early age I was good at school. She recounts her pride as, every time she approached the building to collect me, she could hear my voice telling stories to the class. I was a natural storyteller. My mind was packed with vivid descriptions and I regularly took my classmates for a stroll along Imagination Street ... the place where I lived out my fantasies.

Forty years later, who'd have believed I'd be living them out for real as an actor in Britain's number-one soap, walking on the cobbles of *Coronation Street*; back then we didn't even have television. The first episode of *Coronation Street*, on 9 December 1960, was still a decade away.

However, for us television was just round the corner. We were one of the first families in town to get the modern contraption and Mother got it just in time to watch the event of the year in 1953: Queen Elizabeth II's coronation.

There's that word again — in fact before the soap was given the name we all know and love a couple of others had been in the running, *Jubilee Street* and *Florizel Street*. The show's creator, Tony Warren, dreamed up *Florizel Street*, but they decided in the end that it sounded too much like a leading detergent of the time. And *Jubilee Street* was pipped at the post as the show's title. The first episode was broadcast live to the nation — as all television was in those days. No one had predicted the sensational impact it was to have on viewers.

But in the beginning there was just BBC 1. When independent TV started it was like the second coming of Christ to see adverts on television. The Brooke Bond advert was the first I ever saw on TV. There was a little man in a little lorry laden down with tea and it was dull as dishwater. Yet I was engrossed. Until that moment I'd only ever seen adverts on billboards or in the cinema. Little did I know that one day yours truly would be paid loadsamoney to appear in them.

As an early TV viewer I was a little confused. I remember sitting down in front of the big wooden box and talking to the characters on it. We were that naïve about the new invention that many of us thought, because you could see and hear them, then it followed that they could see and hear you. I thought it was a visual telephone. Nowadays if you go round talking to your television set you're only a step away from the madhouse or the Royal Family. Let's face it, Prince Charles is one of the few people who can get away with talking to plants without being put in a straitjacket. Mind you, I've talked to a few vegetables in my time.

Despite my early conversations with the telly I was still considered quite a bright child. Mother wanted me to go to grammar school and so I was entered for the eleven-plus. The bus to school was late on the morning of the test. I had to dash down and only just managed to get in to the exam on time. Mum reckons me being flustered was the reason I fluffed it. I just missed out on a grammar school place and Mother made representations to the education authority on my behalf. She was told if anyone failed to take up their seat I'd be first in. Needless to say, nobody pulled out.

But Mother was determined I should get a better education than that at the secondary school, so she sent me off for private tuition. I left my pals behind in Chorley and went to school in Preston. Basically, it was a terraced house run by an old gentleman. He used to give us six of the best for failing our French translation. A friend of mine once received eighteen strokes at one go and shortly afterwards joined the Royal Navy. As the matelot used to say: 'Up her transom, me handsome. We wants no babbies here!'

During this phase of my early/mid-teens my parents contemplated emigrating to Australia. I told Pete we were on our way to the other side of the globe. It was upsetting, but it was set to happen and there was nothing I could do about it. Then at the last minute they changed their minds and my uncles and aunts went on their own. It was strange how folk who had never left their home town could contemplate travelling 11,500 miles to a country previously inhabited by convicts and kangaroos. Must have been the ten-pound ticket that tempted them. For the time being, the Morleys stopped where they were.

The most amazing change during this time, for me, was the emergence of a new kind of music. Rock 'n' roll was coming our way. And in about November 1956 we saw Elvis perform on newsreel at the cinema. The phrase 'rock 'n' roll' had been coined earlier that year by Alan Freed. But seeing Elvis simply blew our brains. His first single, *Heartbreak Hotel*, reached Number Two in the charts, quickly followed by *Blue Suede Shoes* which walked into the Number Nine slot. We'd catch the music late at night under the bedcovers listening on the wireless to AFN (American Forces Network) and Radio Luxembourg.

At about the same time, or shortly before, I'd seen the film *Rock Around the Clock*. Banned by local watch committees throughout the country, the burghers of Chorley let it slip through. When it was screened at Chorley Empire the whole cinema audience was twitching in anticipation. As the title number, Bill Haley's *Rock Around the Clock*, began, the entire cinema started rocking and rolling. The track had made Number Seventeen in 1955. Kenny had found Elvis and rock 'n' roll. I love it even in the 1990s.

In the 1950s the music shows were live and included the *Six-Five Special* and Jack Good's *Oh Boy!* They introduced home-grown stars like Cliff Richard, now Sir Cliff, and Marty Wilde. But Tommy Steele, Billy Fury, Gene Vincent and Eddie Cochran were also just exploding on the scene.

It was an incredibly exciting time. In 1955 James Dean died when his Porsche crashed off the road in Salinas, California, but his films weren't released until after his death. They really had an impact on the younger generation. When Pete and I saw him in *East of Eden* we were knocked out. To this day, Pete reckons Dean's performance in the film could have lit the spark of ambition that led me into acting. I was mightily impressed, but that wasn't the catalyst. His other classic movie was *Rebel without a Cause* — everyone worshipped Dean along with Presley.

With all this going on in the world I didn't want to get left behind, so at fifteen I got out of school to get a proper job. Mother had wanted me to stay on at school, but at that time she was ill in Sharoe Green Hospital in Preston. I quit school while I could and started my apprenticeship. And there begins another episode on the long road to creating Reggie.

4

Hard Labour

Overnight I made the spectacular jump from schoolboy to apprentice mechanic, picking up the princely sum of £4 a week. It sounds a pittance and believe me it was. But before I even collected my first wage packet I was put through a traditional initiation ceremony. As in many ancient rites, the ritual at Hill's Bakery involved the forcible removal of the sacrificial lamb's trousers. Then the modern touch came in as several of my elder workmates pinned me down, so another chap could paint my testicles with Bluecol — an anti-freeze.

With my nuts coloured blue, two sanding discs were attached to my back to resemble wings and a halo of welding wire was put round my head. I was done up like a fairy. I was then subjected to the really embarrassing bit — as if all that they had done already wasn't bad enough for a pubescent boy entering a man's world.

I was strapped to a wheelbarrow and taken on a tour of my new workplace — the local bread factory, Hill's, which was sited just half a mile from my current home. Everybody in the place got to see me. I was a little red-faced by the end of it, to say the least, but years later this experience was to come in handy when I was asked to play the part of a fairy on the stage.

But at the time I wasn't looking towards a future treading the boards; I just wanted the earth to open up and swallow me. Pals have similar tales to tell, because apprentices everywhere were considered the lowest form of life and probably still are to this day. They are often put through some bizarre ordeal or other just for the amusement of their older workmates. How many young lads have been sent along to the stores for a glass hammer, a tin of tartan paint, or even that old favourite, a long weight.

The naïve apprentice approaches the storeman and says: 'I've been sent for a long weight.' The storeman, in on the game, says: 'OK, stand there.' The lad waits and waits, unaware he's sprouting mule ears. After quite some considerable time he plucks up the courage to disturb the storeman again. 'Can I have it?' And then the older chap lets him in on the joke, saying: 'You've had a long wait there son — now bloody get off and do some work.' He knows he's been jackassed and returns to his section, much to the amusement of his workmates who've been timing his absence.

Young Kenny was too smart to fall for the long weight, but I'd already endured a worse humiliation. It was a cruel world and I was finding that out fast. Every day at work my overalls would get covered in muck and oil as I tinkered about with repairs to the bread delivery vans.

The people who owned the factory were bakers born and bred. Three generations of Hills had made crusty cobs on the outskirts of Chorley. When I was there the place had been passed on to the last baker's lads. The two brothers were typical owner's sons. They were part of the *nouveaux riches* of Chorley and regarded the workers with a mixture of condescension and loathing.

You were never addressed directly by them. You were always spoken to through an intermediary, such as the foreman. These blokes would come into the garage, where the trucks were serviced, and ask: 'What is he doing over there?' The foreman would say: 'I'll just ask him, sir.' And then he'd shout: 'What are you doing, Morley?' There was no need to shout; I'd heard this plonker ask him in the first place.

But I'd play the game and shout back: 'I'm just changing a wheel.' And then the foreman would turn to the chap next to him and say: 'He is just changing a wheel, Mr Hill.' It was a hilarious performance and I don't know how the foreman kept a straight face. It was probably the first time I had recognized a Holdsworth. The pompous, extremely supercilious approach to employees was prevalent then and remains so in many factories today.

The brothers swanned round in Jaguar cars, or Aston Martins or Alfa Romeos. They had more money than sense, as the saying goes. The foreman, who was below the transport manager, but above the chargehand, four workmen and me, was also prone to being a prat. He got the first Peugeot car imported into Chorley in 1958. It was red, which made a change from the normal drab colours of motors then, and was left-hand drive. It was considered very racy and close to the edge. He was a bit of an exhibitionist, but the Hill brothers were simply born into being swish.

Yet one thing all manufacturers should remember is they can push their luck too far with employees. And when they do that there is nothing they can do to stop the disgruntled member of staff shoving the proverbial spanner in the works. At the bakery, workers took swift retribution when sorely provoked. Some of the older lads — don't worry, boys, I'm not naming names — would add a little spice of their own to the mix rather than visiting the loo.

A small indentation would then be made in the loaf tin, so the special product could be retrieved later from the oven. When the loaf was still warm it would be wrapped and later presented to the offending official to take home as a treat for the missus. They would then all wait with baited breath for the following day.

Then, in a casual manner, one of the lads would ask: 'How was your crusty loaf, Mr Atkinson?' The reply came back: 'Very tasty, lad, a bit of extra malt in there, was there?'

Keeping a straight face, he'd reply: 'Aye, you could say that.' Then he'd be put back in his place: 'Well that's enough chat now, get back and get some work done.'

As he walked away, the shoulders would be rising and falling as he tried to control his mirth. The arrogant bloater had had half a pint of something special on his table last night — a victory for the workers. When he relayed the result to the rest of the lads the whoops of delight couldn't be hidden. The boss would bound over, Holdsworth-style, bleating: 'What's so funny?' More unrestrained laughter. He'd bark: 'Pull yourselves together and get back to work.' He might have guessed the gag was on him, but nobody ever told him. To this day, when some boss gives a prat performance Pete and I still use the term: 'Well, he's gone and pissed in the mix.'

Another phenomenon during my time at Hill's was the archetypal lovely who worked on the clerical side. There were a couple of very stunning girls, who were above and beyond the dreams of your average worker. As these girls passed by, with their seamed stockings and tight skirts, all the lads would leer. Then they'd start to wolf-whistle and come out with the suggestive comments.

The girl would stride purposefully past and wiggle confidently up the steps to the boss's office. She had been summoned to take down some letter or other. But we all imagined she was about to take down lots more. Always, as the door closed behind them, there would be an avalanche of vulgar and vile suggestions as to what they might be getting up to. 'I bet he's giving her one, the old bugger,' someone would say.

These classy ladies would never give us lads on the shopfloor the time of day. Looking back, I can't blame them really, but at the time it just seemed so unfair. We were working in a rough, ugly world and the only bits of true beauty about just passed us by. On one of the occasions when one of the workers approached one of these goddesses he was put in his place in no uncertain terms. She said: 'I may not have seen your willie, luv, but I type out your wage slip and that's not big enough to satisfy me.'

When I heard that story I decided it was time to leave Hill's. It was no place to work if you wanted to pull gorgeous women. The wages wouldn't pay for pleasure. And I desperately wanted to pleasure gorgeous women. My grandfather had worked down the pit at nearby Coppull and from his stories I knew mining wasn't the business to be in either, if you wanted to attract glamorous girls. I was very much into stylish, mature women.

One of the fantasy females in my youth was Sylvia Peters, an early BBC announcer. She would come on TV wearing an evening gown and high heels — not a sight you ever got in Chorley. She was such a refreshing change and I was infatuated. In her posh Beeb voice she'd say: 'Hello children everywhere. What shall we do today? Well today we will look at flags of all nations and also how they make sausages.' Meanwhile, back home, I'm sat on the settee with my own sausage standing proud like a flagpole. It is amazing what boys like on television.

I'd spent a deal of time improving my techniques for chatting up girls, but I realized some props could come in handy, so in the late 1950s I had a light blue suit with silver thread in it made by a local tailor in Chorley. You couldn't just go into the shops and buy the latest fashions then like you can today. Drape jackets, drainpipe trousers that tapered to fourteen inches round the ankle, quiffs and crêpe-soled suede shoes, nicknamed 'brothel creepers', were the fashion.

But Mother was horrified by my new suit. When Peter called for me, wearing the fashions of the time, she saw him as a corrupting influence. Having lost his father during the war, he lived with his grandparents in Chorley and they were a bit less strict with him than my mother was with me. He's bald and fat today, but back in the 1950s he was thin as a whippet with an ultra-trendy quiff of thick black hair. He really looked the part, a real heart-throb, but his appearance appalled my parents.

Shortly afterwards, he went to live with his mum in Rotherham, South Yorkshire, and my mother was delighted that we were separated by sixty miles. To avoid family rows I ended up giving my suit to my cousin James, who was delighted with it. In those days lads wore the full teddy-boy regalia and often carried the obligatory cut-throat razor in their pockets.

People were terrified of teddy-boys. The name might make

them sound cuddly, but they had a fearsome reputation for fighting and trouble. I'll never forget my encounter with a gang of them when I was an apprentice at Hill's. I was walking down through Chorley one weekend when a group of five teds went by on the other side of the road. They were fully tooled up with the velvet Edwardian suit and shoes. Passing by, I couldn't resist staring ... what a mistake!

In next to no time I was looking at them from much closer quarters. 'Hey you, Specky — just stay right there pal,' a chap in a turquoise jacket shouted. He sauntered across the road towards me. This guy was very intimidating. He was about eighteen or nineteen, with the big sloppy, greasy fringe and the duck's arse haircut at the back. The crêpe-soled shoes put another couple of inches on him and he towered over me.

Eyeball to eyeball, as he pushed his face down to mine, he asked: 'What do you think you're looking at pal?' Gulping and trying not to show fear, I replied: 'Nothing.' He said: 'No, you weren't looking at anything?' I said, 'No.' 'Right,' he said. 'Well the next time you're looking at nothing, you will end up looking at something. Right?'

Then he reached inside the pocket of his jacket. I thought, 'Here comes the knife ...' but he pulled out a comb. He stood there looking at me and combing his hair. It was heart-stopping. Then, jabbing the comb at me, he said: 'Just fucking watch it, right?' I got off lightly. I really thought my time had come. His pals might as well have been the Four Horsemen of the Apocalypse.

I've never forgotten just how menacing he was with that comb. Years later, on *Coronation Street*, Holdsworth would on occasion handle his own comb in a similar fashion. Sometimes, just before he combed his wig, I'd flash back to that moment near Chorley market. It helped add a little menace to my performance. Because, as everybody knows, the world of work is full of Holdsworths with their combs and knives in the back.

My next employment was with Radio Relay as an apprentice TV engineer. Pete also got a job with DER Rentals and remained with them for almost thirty years, but I was destined to go on to different things much earlier.

Murphy, the boss at Radio Relay, had a real touch of the Reg Holdsworths about him — he wanted to play everything by the book. In those days we had to do repossession work — getting tellies back when people failed to meet the rental payments. The older hands found the best time to do it was about 4 p.m. when the kids got home from school, but before the parents got in from work. So you'd knock and say to the kids, 'We've come to look at the telly.' Then you'd go in, unplug it and whisk it out. The little ones would be crying as we left, because we regularly had to switch off their kiddies' TV. It was awful, because nobody likes to see innocents suffering, but the bills hadn't been paid, so the TVs had to be retrieved. Sometimes, if you were a bit slow, the parents would come in and you would have to explain things sharpish. Things like: 'We'll be back in ten minutes, luv.' Lies, all lies.

Many times people would wallpaper over the aerial cable, which ran from the window, along the skirting board, up and over the fireplace and down the wall to the telly. Sometimes, if in the mood, we'd simply yank it sharply clear, leaving a giant rip all through the wallpaper. Touché! But nobody likes losing their telly, so we often had to rev the car up and clear out pronto, with angry former telly-owners waving their fists and shouting obscenities after us.

Because of the problems with people not paying the rental, the company used to have a chap call at homes to collect the cash. Hardly anybody would bother walking into the office to pay the rental. Now this older bloke still lives in Chorley and must be in his eighties. He'd worked it out that during his career he'd walked the equivalent of a trip to the moon and back on his rounds. That's a staggering 239,900 miles, and he'd covered the distance mainly round the streets of Chorley.

As trainees we used to hoot at some of the stories he'd tell. I recall him once telling me how a woman answered the door in a dressing gown and when he asked for her rental she opened the robe to reveal her naked body, saying: 'Take it out of this.' We excitedly asked if he'd taken her up on the offer, but he said: 'Even if she had her own teeth, I wouldn't have. You must remember, lads, you've got to do the job first.' After this story I was living in hope of a similar offer — only not from some old hag. Needless to say, it never materialized.

He also told us about the times he'd knock on a door and somebody on the other side would shout: 'Who is it?' On more than one occasion, when he revealed his identity, an upstairs window had opened and a jug of the golden rain had been poured on his head. That is obviously why you sometimes see rent collectors walking around with their umbrellas up even when it isn't raining. From what he said and what I witnessed, I knew working for Radio Relay wasn't going to make me popular with the girls.

But that story reminds me of the hilarious 'Who is it?' parrot gag from *The Comedians* TV show. It goes like this: a gasman calls at a house and when he knocks on the door a parrot asks: 'Who is it?' The caller replies: 'It's the gasman. I've come to mend your pipes.' But the bird says again: 'Who is it?' The man gives his reply again. Anyway, this goes on for some time, with the gasman replying louder and louder: 'It's the gasman. I've come to mend your pipes.' He gets so worked up shouting this reply — to the repeated question: 'Who is it?' — that he keels over and has a heart attack. When the chap who lives in the house gets home hours later, he trips over the body on the doorstep and screams: 'Who is it?' The parrot replies: 'It's the gasman. I've come to mend your pipes.'

This classic gag was made famous by comic Duggie Brown, who, coincidentally, is the brother of Lynne Perrie. In *Coronation Street* I played many side-splitting scenes opposite Lynne, a comedienne in her own right who starred in the soap for over twenty years as Poison Ivy Tilsley. There'll be more about her wickedly funny ways later.

My own sense of humour was inherited from my father, who was a very funny bloke, sometimes unwittingly so. I may have painted a black picture of him, but that would be unfair. At work he was regarded as a great joker and prankster. I discovered this as a teenager when he took me out for my first pint. It is always a bit weird when you go out with your parents and the humour starts. My first pint of bitter with Dad was at Horwich Labour Club, near Bolton.

Dad introduced me to his pals and proudly announced I was going into teaching. They said: 'That's funny, he looks a useless bastard. He's got some brains, hey Frank? That's unusual for your family. Are you sure he's your son?' Quick as a flash, Dad's riposte was: 'What he's got you don't need to see. This lad only needs two muscles. One between his ears and the other between his knees. You lads can have the rest.'

All your life you played by a certain set of rules with your parents and then, all of a sudden, you are in a different situation. Living with somebody, you know them on one level, but go into their place of work and you see an entirely different side.

As a youngster I was very frustrated. The only links we had with the outside world early on had been the radio and the tabloid newspapers my dad bought. From the age of ten I started to become acutely aware that there must be something better than this. We lived in Harpers Lane, Chorley, in a shop next door to Brigg's Laundry. Then, later, we moved to a semi-detached in Preston Road, Whittle-le-Woods. It was there that I started to notice big differences.

On the other side of the road were the big houses — the people who ran the show lived there. I had friends in the big houses, but you were never allowed to go inside. There was this awful class thing: 'He's one of them, we can't trust him in our home.' I used to have to wait outside no matter what the weather was like. That bunch of moronic middle-class businessmen really got up my nose — I now know they were Holdsworths. They owned the shops, they owned the factories and they behaved as if they owned the people too. It was a case of 'Might is right' and, 'Don't speak to me, I have more brass than thee.'

It engendered a great feeling of inferiority in me. You were conditioned into being second-rate. But I embarked on a quest for knowledge and this led to violent rows with my father. He used to take his belt off to me, because what else can a working man do when he's faced with a child, or youth, who is getting too sharp by half?

I used to ask him why he voted Labour. He just said he did

and that was that. It was the done thing, but I wanted him to think about it. I suppose deep down I wanted him to be an achiever. When I was younger I didn't realize he was contented, he was happy. In fact, he used to say: 'Contentment is worth the world.' I used to think, 'You daft old sod.' I was the one who wanted more. I wasn't content with my lot. That was why I couldn't settle in the manual jobs I landed. I kept thinking there had to be more to life than this.

I remember one blazing row with Father during those difficult teenage years. He was only 5ft 4ins tall and weighed over fourteen stone, but he chased me down the road with his leather belt. His frame wasn't suited to athletics, a bit like mine now, so I got away. But I'll never forget him yelling after me: 'You'll have to come back and I'll be here when you do.' I was always questioning him. I'd say hurtful things like: 'Why haven't you made more of your life?' He'd reply: 'Because I spent six years of my life fighting Adolf Hitler.' I'd fire back: 'I thought you never left Leyland.' And he'd get his belt out again.

A lot of bright working-class lads will have had rows just like this with their fathers. I was always aware that, try as he might, he could probably never keep my mother in the fashion that her father had. Her dad had hit hard times and had been made bankrupt, but he bounced back from that. Mother's family were very proud. They always kept spare cups in case a tramp called on the scrounge. In those days, gentlemen of the road would be just that and would call at houses and politely ask for a cuppa or whatever charity you could give them.

During the 1920s, my mother's parents got divorced. I only met my grandmother once and because there was such great shame in divorce she wasn't able to tell me who she was. I only found out later. Mother took me on a journey to Barnsley when I was about nine. It was a real expedition. Journeying by bus to Manchester, across the city to catch another bus from Manchester to Sheffield and then another bus from there to Barnsley. It seems like light-years away now, but we took flasks of tea and sandwiches just for the trip. We were on our way at 7 a.m. and didn't reach our destination until about noon.

The whole purpose of this mega-journey was to visit an old woman I didn't know. There was something about her that was very odd and she was very ill. I said to her: 'If you are very ill I'll give you one of my grandad's lollipops and that will make you better.'

Tears suddenly appeared in her eyes and she asked Mother: 'Please can I tell him who I am?' Out of my earshot Mother said: 'No, don't do it. He doesn't know that you are my mother and he doesn't know that you ran off and left me.' There she was on her deathbed, looking at her own grandson, yet because of the stigma of divorce she could not tell me. She had breast cancer and it killed her before she was fifty, so she wasn't even really that old. It broke my heart when I found out much later who she was. After all, every boy needs a granny.

We had to make the same massive journey back home. At the time I thought, 'All that to see an old woman I don't even know.' I hated visits to relatives over in Accrington. It took a couple of hours to traipse eighteen miles. Buses and trams and buses, and always in that never-ending Lancashire rain. And when you got there, there never seemed to be much going on: no music, no politics, no culture and no fun. Talk about birth, copulation and death!

It seemed so demeaning going all that way to see someone you didn't know. All the women on my mother's side appeared a bit unstable. Nervous breakdowns seemed to run in the family. My life for years featured women who were rather peculiar, to put it mildly. They either ended up in the funny factory or were throwing themselves downstairs.

There was one woman who never left her house for three-and-a-half years. She was absolutely terrified of meeting anyone, completely agoraphobic. They all seemed to have problems with blokes and all of them had worked in the Lancashire mills. They were just like the characters the late great Les Dawson and Roy Barraclough brought to life in their famous gurning sketches. It was a very astute observation, because thousands of women in Lancashire were deafened by the noise from Kay's flying shuttle, the machine at the mill that changed the weave at each end. The machines made a noise like a plane taking off and these women sat without earmuffs just feet away. They learnt to lipread so they could communicate at work. And when the job had made them deaf, as it inevitably did, the lipreading came in very handy.

Industrial injuries were a fact of life. My uncle once said that there were 40,000 injuries and deaths a year in the mining industry and nobody gave a damn. But when nuclear power came along and threatened Joe Public there was plenty of shouting going on. How true!

These marathon jaunts were always to see relatives on my mum's side, because my father actively disliked all his family and rarely visited them. During the period not long after I started working, I did go across the Pennines on my own to visit my old school pal Pete Smith in Rotherham. His house wasn't far from the steelworks, and every three seconds this giant steamhammer went 'BANG, BANG, BANG!' The noise was incessant as this five-ton monster pounded steel girders into shape both night and day. The whole area was covered with this devilish fiery glow. I said to Pete: 'How do you sleep with that noise going on?' He asked: 'What noise?' He'd got that used to it that he didn't even notice the racket.

Trips to Rotherham were like holidays to me. When I was a child we couldn't really afford holidays. I only remember going on holiday twice in my life. Blackpool was the destination both times.

The Golden Mile, the magnificent tower in the middle of the resort, and the ponies and traps on the promenade were all a world away from the daily grind in Chorley — just twenty miles down the road. We stayed in a guest house on a road off the prom. We were that skint that Mother used to buy all her own food and the landlady would cook it for us.

People never went to Spain or Barbados, because foreign holidays were virtually unheard of. In those days, Cornwall was the most exotic place anyone got to. I remember sitting enthralled when my dad told me he'd been to Penzance and that there were palm trees there. As soon as I left school at fifteen the first thing I did, when I could afford it, was go to Cornwall. I couldn't believe it when I saw they had the same colour grass as us!

I was loaned a Volkswagen caravanette for the trip and took Mum and Dad. It was a real long haul. No motorways then, just A and B roads. Mum made sure we got fully comprehensive insurance for the journey and that proved a godsend. For as I was pulling out of a parking spot I clipped another car's bumper. We got out to approach the houses with long gardens nearby, but a chap came out of one and looked at the damage. He told us not to worry about it — it was nowt. But the week after we got back, the police turned up and accused us of failing to report an accident. Mum explained what had happened. The police left us with the bill. The other driver was trying it on. We told our insurance company and everything got sorted out satisfactorily.

It was the second hiccup of the holiday. The first came early on, when we stopped off in Somerset on the way down. We were in Minehead when Dad and I took a motorized rowing boat out into the harbour. We saw a buoy with the ambiguous warning: 'Don't cross this side of the buoy.' I reckoned it meant don't go any further out of the harbour, but Dad believed it meant pass the buoy on the other side. We chugged on for a short distance.

Meanwhile, Mother saw a crowd waving and shouting on the harbour wall. She wondered what they were up to and walked a bit closer. It was then that a chap came running up to her and said: 'Are you with those two over there?' Pointing to our boat in the distance, Mother replied: 'Yes, it's my husband and son.' The fellow said to her: 'They've gone too far. If we can't get them back soon the current will have them. You'll be a widow without a son.' A very comforting comment, don't you think? Mother was horrified. She ran down the harbour wall shouting after us.

We were heading round the bay by this stage, oblivious to the drama on the shore. We saw them all waving and wondered what was going on. Then this chap came up to us in a motor boat and told us how close we'd come to getting lost at sea. We were apparently very lucky, because there had been fatalities on that stretch of water. The nervous tension my mother suffered that afternoon virtually ruined the rest of the holiday for her.

We had the clumsy chap who told her she could soon be a widow to thank for that. Soon after, we discovered the locals were charged one price for goods and tourists another. You've no doubt guessed who was paying through the nose ... yes, us.

The next time I went to Cornwall was years later, when I drove over on a moped to meet up with Pete and his then wife, Monica. I had bought this new moped in Preston, ridden it to the railway station and put it on the train. When I got off at Euston, a light rain was falling, so I slipped on the old rubber protectives, the faithful wellies, and as a temporary measure, a World War Two Nazi helmet, which I'd borrowed from a play. Unfortunately, as I crossed London Bridge the moped died on me. So, switching to pedal power I rapidly reached 15 m.p.h. passing straight through a set of red traffic lights in an attempt to get it going again. Guess who was watching? Yep, 'Evening all.' It was Dixon of Dock Green. Quick as a flash he clocked the Nazi helmet, the white sweating face, the bulging eyes, and invited me to accompany him to the nick. After half-an-hour I asked him if I could leave the moped chained to the station railings. He replied: 'No don't do that — you can't trust anyone round here. It'll be gone by morning.'

But for now, back to our teenage years. Just as Pete's career in Radio Relay was about to blossom, mine was being nipped in the bud. I had a very lucky escape when the company's new Morris 1000 van was crushed just twenty seconds after I jumped out of it to deliver a telly. I opened the back, lifted out the box and walked across the road. As I got to the other side there was an almighty crash and I spun round to see a twenty-five-ton truck rammed right into the back of the van, where I'd been standing just moments before. I wouldn't have stood a chance. In another thirty seconds I'd have been back in the driver's seat and if I'd been there at the time of impact I'd have been decapitated. It was the end of the van.

It wasn't my fault, but I had a typical boss, who had little sympathy and even tried to blame me for it by implying I shouldn't have parked there. However, that wasn't my downfall. The problem was I had a heart — and as Holdsworth would tell you, having a heart and being successful in business isn't a natural mix. It was Christmas Eve when I called on an old-age pensioner's home. The poor old dear's rented telly had gone on the blink, but it couldn't be mended until after the festive period. Her problem was that she was only paying a low rental for a small reconditioned set and wasn't entitled to a new replacement. Well, when I explained this meant no telly for Christmas, the old dear broke down in tears. 'Please, luv,' she said, 'I'm on me own. I've nobody and now I've no telly at Christmas!' What could I do? I decided to help her out, and drove back to the shop to pick up a demonstration telly. The shop would be closed and nobody would be watching all the TVs in it over Christmas.

But somebody *was* watching the tellies — Murphy, the boss, had noticed one was missing. So on the Tuesday morning after the holiday I got marched into the office. I explained the situation. How there were no spare tellies in the workshop and I'd given her the demo. He shook his head Reggie-style. He gave me the lecture ... swiftly followed by the sack.

Mind you, the formula has always been the same. 'I, Holdsworth, am the boss! I will come to work last and I will leave the earliest. You, on the other hand, are a mindless grub and I will work you to death for the smallest amount possible. Yes?' Answer from the worker: 'No, and get stuffed.' Holdsworth: 'You are sacked and let that be a lesson to you.'

Another notch on the Reg Holdsworth make-up, carved into my memory. How to behave like a complete prat and play it by the book. The old woman had nothing — they were concerned that I'd given her a nearly new TV. I'd worked there for three years, the last eighteen months on the road as a service engineer. But there I was, fired just after Christmas.

There followed the worst winter of my life to date. I was eighteen, I had no job, no education, no money, no nothing at all. All because I'd helped an old lady out. I was unemployed for months. I trudged round Lancashire looking for work. It was freezing and I had holes in the soles of my shoes. I thumped on factory doors in Blackburn, Preston, Darwen and Chorley in my search for work. I was part of an ever-lengthening dole queue.

When you are out of work you see the condescending smile of those responsible for turning job-hunters away and you hate it. It is like another nail in your coffin every time you hear them say: 'Sorry, there is nothing at the moment.'

Temperatures were about zero and I had nothing to do and no money to do it with. It was a period of awful despair — the most miserable winter and spring imaginable. I sympathize completely with anyone who has the misfortune to have to sign on at the Department of Social Security today. You can become that desperate that you even contemplate doing a bit of thieving to make ends meet. I never did and don't condone crime, but when you are on your uppers life is hard. As my father pointed out: 'If all the thieves were to leave England the place would be a desert in a fortnight.'

To escape from the poverty trap I found myself in, I decided to take a step in another direction. I began to realize that knowledge is power and decided, belatedly, to get myself an education.

5

Legover Land

The Swinging Sixties heralded the second most important invention known to man after the wheel ... the contraceptive pill. The availability of the pill gave women the freedom to enjoy sex for the first time in history. It was a momentous creation. If you didn't get your leg over in the 1960s — you didn't have legs.

After the pill was launched there was an intermediate period when they didn't know if it was harmful to women. So it was swallowed by the bucket-load by a whole generation, which basically allowed them to roger themselves rigid. There was no worry of a pregnancy with it and at that point, of course, there was no AIDS. It was non-stop sex for the lucky lads and lasses around at the time.

I started the decade as I meant to go on. I lost my virginity in the back of an Austin 7. I was sweet seventeen and so was she, a voluptuous young thing with curves in all the right places. I was ecstatic after it happened on the back seat. The car was purchased as my number-one prop to help me pull girls. It worked wonders. Within a week I was dating.

It was right at the beginning of the decade when I discovered there was no Father Christmas, but there was fanny, as we called it. Fanny beat Santa hands down — it was available all year, was less hairy and much more fun.

But before getting down to the business you needed some johnnies, which translated into modern parlance means condoms. It was when you got fanny and johnnies together that the party started. Initially you had to ask an older boy to approach the ubiquitous barber, who after a trim would say: 'Anything for the weekend, sir?' Some of the older lads ran the risk of having their heads shaved bald if they'd have gone to the barbers every time we asked them, so instead a roaring trade in second-hand condoms started. The older boys would use them, wash them out and offer them for sale to younger lads. As part of the sales pitch the used condom would be popped in the mouth and inflated as proof it was perforation-free. 'No holes in this one. Only used twice. When you get up, it won't let you down,' they'd say.

But as time passed it became apparent that if you had the balls to chat up girls, you also had the balls to chat up the barber. Then you too could go into business selling part-worn johnnies. But the first time a rubber was required was after I forked out on the Austin, which I acquired for the sum of £10. It was money well spent.

I chatted this nubile creature up and fixed a date. Pete was invited along on a blind date with another girl. The other girl was a couple of years younger, a lass called Monica Porter. As we drove down the street to meet them on the designated corner, we were talking about rutting. We spotted them in the distance and the conversation changed slightly. Pete said: 'I'll have the blonde if she isn't too tall.' I replied: 'Aye, right enough.' Unbeknown to us, the ladies had heard our manly chat, because our voices carried above the noise of the engine as we pulled up.

But it didn't put them off. Pete and Monica, who was a trainee nurse at the tuberculosis sanatorium, hit it off straight away. Six years later the pair of them were wed. And they're still together — thirty years as man and wife next year and all from that blind date. She was a grand lass, but I had no complaints about my own curvaceous goddess. It was a night to savour. The right hand was taking early retirement. It was time to stop abusing oneself and start abusing others.

I obviously remember my first love's name, but she is still around in the town. I often see her, but in all honesty she does look, if you'll forgive the expression, shagged out. I take some solace in the fact that at least I did my bit to help her get that way. She probably tuned into *Coronation Street* when I was on and said the same about me.

Yet in those days she was a regular fixture in the front and back of the Austin. In fact, you name the position and we managed it in that old car. We enjoyed six rampant months together. But after we split I sold the car as a mark of respect. It would never be the same without her lithe form adorning the upholstery.

Austin 7s are great little cars. They go round corners as if on tram tracks. This was very helpful for me, having already displayed the ability to fall off anything that wasn't fixed to the ground. My Austin 7 had hardly anything on the clock, but the man from the garage said it was remarkable inasmuch as the springs on the seats were similar to those you'd find on a car that had done 90,000 miles. He was also perplexed at marks on the ceiling and, scratching his head, said: 'It's as if someone has walked on the inside of your roof wearing stiletto heels.' He was pretty close, but I refrained from telling him about the action the inside of that car had seen.

I'll never forget driving out one night for a spot of rumpy-pumpy. I unrolled the sheath in semi-darkness and fitted it like an expert, with the deftness of a marine greasing his gun. But we'd parked on the edge of a freshly ploughed field and a gust of wind grabbed Pete's condom. The rubber shot across the field and Pete shot after it. By the time he caught up with it, it was covered in mud along with his pants, which by this stage were round his ankles. He was then left with the dilemma as to whether to ride bareback or not. That moral decision was one only he could make.

Still at the start of the 1960s, the legacy of not talking about sex remained. And condoms were not as freely available as they are today. Back then, as I've already pointed out, you could get them from the barber or a chemist. It is only with the emergence of AIDS that condoms have started popping up everywhere. Nowadays they're even on sale in the local garage. You can go in there and a winsome young lass will serve you with all the finesse of a madam. A few years ago they were considered bad taste. Now you can get them to suit all tastes — from liquorice to cheese and onion, from vinegar to vindaloo. You can get them small, medium, large, heavy-duty, extra-sensitive, ribbed, and in every colour imaginable. Black, green, yellow, white and red — you name it, they've got it down on the forecourt.

And attitudes to sex in general have changed, probably largely because of the sexual liberation of the 1960s. These days in the back pages of downmarket tabloids there are adverts for sex aids and seedy 0891 sex lines. If in the 1950s you'd said that would happen, nobody would have believed you. It is a bit like opening up the Bible and finding an advert at the back saying: 'If you fancy a good rumple ring Jeremiah 0891 ... for a full service.'

It all makes our early fumblings and gropings seem rather feeble. But we did get down to some serious rumpy-pumpy in the 1960s. One of the most memorable occasions early on was when I was driving along as one of my pals was rogering a gorgeous girl on the back seat. Then as we approached the cemetery she pushed him off and the clinch finished. She was a good Catholic girl who refused to roger as we drove past the graveyard. Such devotion. But as soon as we'd gone past they got down to it again. It was hilarious.

As I've already outlined, my pulling power and everything else was severely curtailed when I lost my job at Radio Relay at the end of 1962. Those grey days that followed were rarely highlighted by exploits in the back of a car — I couldn't afford to run one. But I did spend hours upon end assembling a motorbike from a pile of scrap. Dad helped me get the machine together, but when Mother saw it complete she went spare. She was very possessive and protective, with me being her only child. She refused point-blank to allow me to ride it. She told me afterwards it was because she feared I'd fall off and get killed. She had a point, inasmuch as I didn't have a very good record with two-wheeled transport.

Anyway, cars are better for getting girls. And I was soon going to get a lot of them as I'd decided to go back to school. In September 1963 my spell as a dole-ite ended and I started at Alston Hall College of Further Education on the other side of Preston. I now had an Austin 35 in which I would cruise Chorley. When the night fell, that's when I began my labour of love, buzzing round the town. I was, you must understand, a nubile, blond-headed, blue-eyed sex machine in those days. I still see lots of the girls I was humping back then walking round the town. Only nowadays they're no longer pushing prams — just their husbands in wheelchairs.

I'll never forget the day John F. Kennedy was assassinated. It was 22 November 1963. It was an event that set everybody rocking back on their heels. It is difficult to imagine now what absolutely shattering news it was. People were crying on the streets of Chorley, Lancashire. Everybody thought the Russians had done it after the Cuban missile crisis when the USSR sent ships to the island. The missiles on board could have reached New York. People feared that another world war, but this time a nuclear one, could be round the corner. There was a great sense of relief when Lee Harvey Oswald was caught, but with the benefit of hindsight I'm sure he was just a patsy. To this day, who shot J.F.K. remains one of the big mysteries of our time.

I had 'O'-level examinations with the Joint Matriculation Board on the day of this earth-shattering news. The Board had two sittings a year — the next lot were the following summer. By then I was ready to leave Alston Hall with a collection of six 'O'-levels and two 'A'-levels under my belt.

Back home in Chorley my teenage tastes had expanded, thanks to meeting a chap called John Hughes. He was very Bohemian and he had some great parties round at his house. Before I met John I thought Tchaikovsky was a Polish window cleaner. But he was into all sorts of things and in no time at all I was listening to Beethoven, Bach, and Mozart, and finding them all fascinating. I still adore classical music.

John was the son of a local hairdresser and lives in Chorley to this day. He is a driving instructor nowadays, but in our youth he was the nearest thing Chorley had to a movie producer. He was into photography and had a 16mm cine camera and projector. He would use the camera to make his own avant-garde films. And he gave me my first taste of the role of director when I took Pete and Monica up to the nearby moors at Rivington to make a home movie. John also fired my interest in the theatre with his knowledge of the Shakespeare classics. He was into Laurence Olivier and would hire films such as *Henry V*, *Hamlet* and more modern classics like *The Guns of Navarone*.

Towards the end of the 1950s several rock heroes were killed in car crashes, which added to the excitement of the time. There was a point where everybody wanted to be killed in a Porsche like James Dean. Unfortunately we only had Austins and Ford Populars, so we had to carry on living. It was a cruel world, but looking back I'm glad I didn't have a Porsche.

What I did have was a fifteen-hundredweight Morris van. I had kitted it out like a four-wheeled boudoir. I fitted a carpet in the back, curtains on the windows, a mattress, and it even had a couple of wine bottles attached to the inside by the wheel arch. I regularly worked myself into a sexual frenzy with a willing partner in the back of that van. The goings on were quite violent at times. It was during one such energetic session that we literally broke the back of the van ... the chassis snapped. In those days one didn't discuss with one's parents what was going on. Mother will probably be horrified by my antics, but I'm not ashamed that they happened. It's all part of my life.

Having a car was so important in giving me freedom from home and the watchful eyes of Mum and Dad. The car is the driver's territory and gives you a degree of independence. In my case they were always rumpy-pumpy mobiles.

After finishing at Alston Hall in 1964 I applied for a three-year army commission. I was summoned to Chester for a medical. It was held at a rehabilitation centre, which was swarming with all these blokes who'd had accidents. There were lots of chaps hobbling about with legs and arms in plaster and other soldiers being pushed round in wheelchairs. It was an instant put-off. The first question the Colonel Blimp-type asked me was: 'Have you ever had VD?' I thought: 'Kenneth, you don't really want to be here.' The chap then gave me a form and said: 'I'll leave you to fill this in.' When he'd gone I just got up, and as the tabloid reporters say, I made my excuses and left.

Nobody with an ounce of brain would have hung about, having seen all those injured men. I thought, 'If this is peacetime, what is it going to be like if there's ever a war?' If they could manage to do all that damage just pretending to fight each other what would they end up like if they did it for real? I was reminded of Wellington's comment on some troops sent to him in Spain in 1809: 'I don't know what effect these men will have upon the enemy, but, by God, they terrify me.'

I went home and was greeted by a telephone call from a Captain Smith at the Ministry of Defence in Whitehall. He'd obviously eaten half a hundredweight of plums before the call and asked: 'Did yoo hev a problim?' I explained the situation and he tried to reassure me that all the casualties were from a recent parachute drop. My feet, however, were firmly on the ground and that was how they were going to stay. I wasn't going to change my mind for him or anyone else.

Instead, I set my sights on a different career and landed a job as a probationary teacher at Croston, just a few miles from Chorley. It was a peculiar school and the pay was just £9.50 a week. With it being a small village, they had in essence been rogering each other for hundreds of years. You had two or three kids who were the products of the same father. Even in the 1960s, in-breeding was prevalent. It is probably still like that in isolated villages up and down the land. The average person remains where his or her parents lived.

I recall asking one youngster who his father was. It turned out the same chap had fathered three of the class. The parents all went to school together and knew each other from day one. They worked together, lived together and slept together. And when a marriage broke down they simply ended up marrying one of their old school pals, in effect wife-swapping. The only thing that was missing was the guard's whistle — all change.

The lads were all quite burly, sons of farmers or farm labourers. I remember one boy coming in to class nursing a slight wound. I asked what had happened. The lad said: 'We were doing apples when the gamekeeper saw us and gave us the barrels, sir.' Apparently it was standard practice for the gamekeeper to let scrumpers have both barrels of his twelve- bore. It was run-of-the-mill to them, but I couldn't stop laughing.

I had done kung fu and karate at primary level and because I was the youngest teacher I was assigned games lessons. I decided to pass on some of my martial-arts skills to the class. I announced: 'Right boys, I'll show you some of the basic moves. Now the first boy come forward.' Well this lolloping oaf came to the front, grabbed me by the lapels and kneed me in the nuts. I fell to the floor in great distress. My first and last martial-arts class had just finished. 'You carry on boys, I'll be back in a minute,' I squeaked as I staggered off.

The next sport I took up in the physical-education class was basketball and during that I ended up breaking my leg. I obviously wasn't cut out to be a PE teacher. And by this stage my thirst for knowledge was driving me on to teacher-training college.

But that sporting injury turned into a real lucky break. I'd done my leg in when I spotted this really stunning woman in Chorley with red hair. She worked in a gown shop and I found out that she didn't have a boyfriend. I went past the next day in my Saab 94 and offered this flame-haired vixen a lift. I had these crutches on the back seat, but I didn't let that put me off. Although, when she got in and saw the crutches, she thought I was a permanent cripple, I explained it was just a temporary thing.

A very pleasant interlude was to follow as I fell madly in love. Inside a few days I got the cast off and the proverbial legover, proving yet again that there is no situation that can't be overcome. She had a marvellous alabaster skin and fabulous fire-red hair.

I recall one night I was giving her one of my wonderful intimate performances down a country lane. Before we reached a crescendo, the full moon came out from behind a cloud and shone on what appeared to be an enchanting field nearby. I pointed over and suggested we move the car to this glorious grassy moonlit spot. She agreed and on that note I spun the car through a nearby gate.

On that field I gave one of my finest exhibitions. The music was on the car radio so we could roger to the rhythm. Having completed the evening's entertainment I got back in the driving seat and off we went home.

The next morning I couldn't resist a nostalgic drive past the field, but when I got there a group of men in smart pullovers, carrying golfing bags, were standing on the very spot, shaking their heads in animated and furious conversation. I didn't know it at the time, but we'd been fornicating on one of the foremost putting greens in Lancashire. They were scratching their heads at the pair of tyre tracks going right across and round this once pristine green. It was a picture — artwork by Pirelli. Even Picasso with a shovel couldn't have made a bigger mess of it.

I know the gents down at the golf club probably still haven't forgiven me. And there must have been a witch hunt for the vandal at the time. But I can only hope they'll sympathize with me. After all, surely a golfer can appreciate the beauty of a hole in one. If I'd realized it was the golf course I'd never have driven on it — at least not that way.

It was around this era that I and my friends were becoming aware that women could be stimulated by things other than sex — inanimate objects. With this in mind I purchased a set of nobbly-headed screwdrivers from Woolworths. They had the benefit that if anything went wrong with the car you could carry out repairs at the same time. Sadly, I never got to try my new tool-kit out on the love of my life, because she dumped me even before I'd shown her the screwdrivers.

I was broken-hearted. But Mother tried to console me. 'Don't worry about it, you daft fool,' she said, 'she's been having it away with the local policeman.' I said: 'I know, Mother, I've just been having a drink with him.' I suppose a truncheon beats a screwdriver hands down, but it still hurt like hell. She later went off and married somebody else. They had kids and lived happily ever after.

Meanwhile, I was about to arrive at heaven on earth. It was 1965 and I was applying all over to go to teacher-training college. But everywhere I wanted turned me down. I was starting to get despondent when out of the blue an envelope landed on the doormat offering me a place at Northumberland College. My immediate thought was: 'Where?' It wasn't a place I'd ever heard of before. Not surprisingly, because it turned out that it was a girls' college opening itself up to blokes for the first time. Young Kenneth had landed on his feet again.

I flew up from Blackpool to Newcastle. The ticket was £2.20 one way and £4 something for the return. When I arrived at the college I suddenly found myself deposited into a living fantasy. There were 850 women and just 87 young men. It was a dream situation and we were not to be disappointed.

It was midway between a nunnery and a harem. It was only a matter of days before you bedded your first piece of crumpet. It was the eunuchs' dream come true, and we had balls. Brilliant would be an understatement. I never heard talk of male contraception for the whole three years I was there. They were halcyon days. It was an enlightened atmosphere. It was the beginning of flower power. There were parties nearly every night.

After classes, the lads were running across the lawn from lady to lady, criss-crossing past each other and often comparing notes. The girls were insatiable, but we did our best. We had to screw them in shifts just to keep them happy. We were like the Spartans. To service all the girls we had to be athletes. The Spartans' motto was 'Come back victorious or dead upon your shield'; ours was closer to come back dead upon your bed.

Three or four female students a night was not unusual, and that is no exaggeration. Randy Reg would have been in his element. I certainly was in mine. We would dash from door to door, disappearing, and then dashing out again and on to the next rendezvous. It was like a serving shed. They locked the rest of the world out at night and pulled up a drawbridge to keep the girls and us in. It was paradise. It gave a whole new meaning to the term extra-curricular activities. We went in boys and came out old men.

Before going to Northumberland I used to go hunting for girls. We called it the hunt for c*** in Chorley. And we would regularly bag young virgin-like creatures and give them a good seeing to, for which they were grateful. But not even in my wildest dreams could I have ever conjured up anywhere like Northumberland.

I met all sorts of women. A particular favourite was a Jewish lady from London. She was extremely well read. Her mother was a doctor and her father was a barrister. She was full of contradictions. For example, she loved a bacon sandwich in the morning, but then she didn't want you to take your trousers down when you were rogering her. She was strangely orthodox in some things, yet wonderfully free in others.

In the second year I fell hopelessly in love again, with another redhead. Her name was Ann and she came from the border town of Berwick-upon-Tweed. It was a real head-over-heels job. I fell harder, much harder, than I'd ever fallen before. She had the most extraordinary long legs and a ready wit. We initially got chatting at a dance and she said to me in her lilting Scottish accent: 'Now I wonder what you would be wanting?' She knew all right. And I got it.

Now there is something about Scottish women that I find extremely attractive. It could be the lilting accent; the sardonic humour; the ready acceptance of a good night out followed by ample nookie; and a love of the bottle, as anybody who has ever been to a Scottish New Year celebration — Hogmanay, as they call it — will tell you. But most likely it is a combination of all of these facets that I find irresistible.

When the Scots decide to let their hair down they will have your kilt and your sporran round your neck and their tongues down your throat in a thrice. The women aren't bad either. The lovely Ann and I had a fabulous time together. She would play Chopin and Beethoven on the piano while I accompanied her on the flute. I love to make love to music.

As well as expanding my sexual knowledge, I also soaked up all the local culture in Northumberland. At that time I came to enjoy the realization of what history meant in terms of coming to an understanding of the background of the county. I always have liked historical details.

Hadrian's Wall was a magnificent structure stretching right across the country from the North Sea at Tynemouth, past Carlisle to the Irish Sea. It is over 100 miles long and runs across rivers, swamps, down dales and over some of the highest hills in the region. It was created by the Romans with enormous ditches on both sides to keep out the Celts. The soldiers who stood guard and fought on the wall came from all over the Roman Empire, from as far afield as what is now Turkey and Syria. They came over here and stayed for twenty years before being pensioned off. You can't imagine what it must have been like for them facing a lot of blue-faced barbarians, whose idea of a good night out was having someone's head off.

There were famous victories for the Scots. The Romans sent one army of 1,200 men north to do battle, but the entire legion disappeared in the swamp lands, near present-day Ponteland, and were never heard of again.

Ponteland, to be precise, was where Northumberland College was based. You'll never believe it, but these days our carnal sin city is part of the Northumberland Constabulary's training school.

Newcastle is close by and that is a stunning city. With it being 300 miles from London, it has its own culture and always will have. Along with other east-coast towns, like Norwich and Hull, Newcastle has its historical links with Vikings and their Scandinavian neighbours across the North Sea. The area has its own distinctive dialect, which even today is often difficult to understand. Many of the words, such as 'doon', are derived from German. They have a deliberate impediment in their speech patterns, which is a legacy of their German forebears.

During my three years at college I was sent out on five-week work placements. One was at Allonby in Cumbria, but the others were at Gateshead and Newcastle. Even back in the 1960s the kids over there were poor and in those days the shipbuilding trade was still on the Tyne. I worked in a primary school in the Dunston area of Gateshead. And I'll never forget asking the headmaster for some equipment, basically books for the kids to write on. He said: 'You'll have to use these, Ken' and handed me a pile of small wallpaper sample books that had been scrounged from a decorating shop. The school couldn't afford books and the kids had to write on the backs of the wallpaper samples.

When we asked the kids where they were going on holiday they explained that they only ever had day trips to places like Seaton or Whitley Bay, just a few miles away. Most of the parents were either unemployed or single parents even then. But I do remember the lads were always playing football. The England soccer star Paul Gascoigne comes from Dunston and probably went to that same primary school.

It was while I was at college that I was invited to my first football match, at Sunderland's famous Roker Park stadium, by a friend of mine, Leslie Hull, now a headmaster in Gateshead. When the local side scored, I was carried down about eight steps and then carried back as everyone surged forward. It was the first time in my life I had ever been in a crowd of 40,000 people. In those days Sunderland were the equal of their Tyneside neighbours Newcastle on the soccer pitch. A win, like the one I saw over Hartlepool, apparently isn't such a frequent occurrence these days. Mind you, there's nothing a lot of money can't cure.

The changes in language and accent can be very exaggerated in the region. The Geordies in Newcastle speak differently from the people in Sunderland. If you go to the small border town of Coldstream on the River Tweed, you'll notice that in a journey of just 200 yards across the river the accent switches very markedly from English to Scottish. In that same area of idyllic countryside one of the bloodiest and most violent battles of all time happened near the village of Flodden.

On a very cold morning in 1513, the entire Scottish army led by James stood waiting on a large hill overlooking Flodden Fields. The English attacked from a disadvantaged point at the bottom of the valley. They had to run uphill as the Scots charged down into them. Carnage ensued and in the space of just thirty-five minutes a staggering 13,000 men lay dead or dying. As you look at the rolling Flodden Fields today, it is hard to imagine the scale of the slaughter. It was the battle that put paid to the Scottish. An entire line of Scottish kings for more than 350 years had died before the age of thirty-five.

The isolated county was at one time strategically vital and the Dukes of Northumberland were like kings. They were left to their own devices. But the Border Reivers, as they were known, were constantly at war with the Scots. The Border Wars were bloody affairs. The Border Reivers were no better than bandits. So Robert Carey, the Constable of Carlisle, was despatched to round up the Stapletons and the Armstrongs, the leading brigands. They were given the option of being hanged or deported to Northern Ireland. The whole bloodthirsty bunch of them were shipped out to Northern Ireland. The thinking at the time was that it would be cheaper to have armed settlers in place, rather than a garrison. They ended up running the place until 1914. It was a classic case of the domino effect — one decision made hundreds of years ago being responsible for murder and mayhem for centuries. But you can't revise history. That action ended up costing thousands of lives and putting our own Government into a hot spot.

Ann and I trampled the fields of history together, but there was a huge shock lurking just round the corner. One day she told me the terrible truth. She said: 'Look, I have something to tell you. I have a boyfriend.' I thought: 'Yep, that's me.' But then she explained she'd been dating an engineering student from Newcastle. She said: 'I'm pretty serious about him. He has asked me to get married and I have agreed. He has a job lined up in America, working in Carolina, and I'm going there.'

I was completely gobsmacked. We were an item and then suddenly she was getting married to somebody else. I found it very hard to handle. It was the night before we finished college in 1968 that she made this amazing confession. I was reeling. I begged her to reconsider, but she insisted: 'I've got to go with him.'

Stupidly I insisted on taking her to the railway station the next day. The whole scene was heartbreaking. As I bade her a fond farewell, I suddenly realized I was completely devastated. I waved her off, then ran into the goods yard sobbing, a completely broken man. I was seriously upset for six months. This emotional trauma brought me to the point of nearly killing myself.

It was just like Ken Barlow's Christmas suicide scene in *Coronation Street*. I got out the bottle of whisky and some aspirins and I was going to top myself. Weeping, I sat in front of the bedroom mirror. I was in the depths of despair. The dream days at college were over, my dream girl was marrying somebody else and it was a nightmare for me. But then I caught a glimpse of myself in the mirror glugging the whisky. I snapped at myself and swore out loud: 'Don't be so fucking stupid, Kenneth.' At the last minute I realized ending my life wasn't the answer.

Weeks after this dreadful suicidal period I went out for a drive and was passing Bolton Palais when I saw a stunning woman. The sight of her helped break the spell. I was smitten again. I just started thinking about all the pleasure I could miss out on. One memorable incident sprang immediately to mind, a time when I truly felt on top of the world. It was the day in a tiny Fiat that I gave one of my most remarkable performances at 1,291ft on Hard Knott Pass in the Lake District, between Skelwith Bridge and Eskdale Green.

The scenery was spectacular. A Rossini overture was caressing us from the speakers as we climbed to the summit of passion. The music went faster and faster, as we did, reaching a crescendo just as our magical moment arrived. I had been in such haste to give the young beauty a full service, and the car was so small, that I had settled for an unconventional position ... me in the front seat, she in the back with her legs akimbo. It was a difficult manoeuvre made more so by the proximity of the gear stick to my rear end. It had a big knob on it, which constantly played with my backside. My only concern was having a flat battery at the end, because we'd kept the music on.

We managed the feat to perfection, but it was only a week later that I realized how lucky we had been. As I drove into the drive in this battered Fiat, I pulled the handbrake on and the seat of the car fell through the floor on to the ground. A corroded crossbeam had snapped. It had been waiting to happen, but I just thanked my lucky stars it hadn't happened on one of the highest and steepest roads in the Lake District. I could see the headline: 'WOMAN CHOKES TO DEATH IN CAR LOVE TRYST'.

These days, with the threat of AIDS, such unadulterated fun is hard to find. In the 1960s a dose of venereal disease was the only thing to avoid. My exploits must have made me a red-hot favourite for the clap clinic. Inevitably, I ended up having an appointment with the VD doctor. I had a dose of non-specified, but thanks to our brothers in arms at the pharmacy it was cleared up in no time. Three cheers for penicillin.

I had an experience at Hartwood Hall, just up the road from our house in Chorley. As children we used to visit this privately-owned grand house and for a penny you were allowed to go and swim in its open-air pool. Pete and I would regularly go along and have a dip in the water, along with the algae and the frogs.

One night there was another slippery animal at hand — a giant python. This snake was the prop of a Liverpudlian stripper called Denise. On a Friday Hartwood Hall, which had now been converted into a nightspot, would feature strippers. The lovely Denise had been the star of the show, so I slithered across for a chat. We had a drink and I cheekily invited myself up to her room to admire her python. She was an older woman and wasn't slow at coming forward. Her pet python was in his case when she started wrestling with a different variety of snake. The beast had two mice in its glass cage, which put me off my stroke somewhat. I asked: 'What are the mice for?' She replied: 'He likes his meat fresh, just like me.'

At that period Chorley had about three stripclubs. It was a real wild town. In the early 1960s, I'd set up a business with my mum and dad to cash in on all this late-night weekend revelry. I bought a fast-food van and opened up Morley's Hamburger stall. It caused quite a stir in the town. Mother worked at Marsden's Pork Butchers on Pall Mall in Chorley for

£4.10 a week, but at the weekend she could earn more dishing out hamburgers. She worked really hard, catching a bus to the butcher's at 6 a.m., going home from there in the afternoon to prepare hundreds of burgers and onions and then going out to sell them until the early hours of the morning. After they'd sold up each night, she and Dad would go round tidying up and collecting all the litter in the street. We used to clear 400 burgers a weekend, and they were the best burgers you'd ever tasted.

There were stories in the local paper, the *Chorley Guardian*, and a lot of fuss about this innovative late-night food stop. Mother used to have her lunch on a Saturday with the Marsdens, and on one occasion early on, the subject of the new hamburger stall came up. Now nobody at Marsden's knew that Mother was involved and she kept quiet as they were slagging it off. When they later found out, they said she was a horrible creature for not letting them know. But after the initial controversy the stall survived and flourished. They would queue for miles after the pubs chucked out in Chorley just to get their lips round one of our burgers or hot dogs.

One summer, Mother rang the council to ask for a pitch at Chorley Carnival. They tried to refuse, but she promised to kick up a big stink when she found out that they had granted a permit to a Manchester firm. She quite rightly got her own pitch. She made up 400 hamburgers that morning and they were sold out in no time. I was home from college at the time and was recruited to help out. The Manchester burger firm hardly sold any and the stallholder came up to our pitch and told us we weren't charging enough. Hamburgers, in these pre-decimalization days, were one and six and the hot dogs were one and three. We were giving people value for money and that's what they wanted. It wasn't our problem if the other chap was going home with all his stock.

To start with, I'd been heavily involved with the hamburger van, but on going away to college I left it in the capable hands of my parents. When I returned with my teaching qualification three years later, both Mum and Dad were very proud. I was the first Morley to achieve any qualifications. In those days, being a teacher was considered quite a good job. At that time, with a new suit and my leather holdall, I was very happy to be a member of the teaching profession. I went to work with a whistle and a song, I kid you not. The kids were great, staff were fun and the money? Well, you can't have everything! But little did I know at this point that my destiny lay elsewhere.

6

More Sex

My first telephone call in search of work after leaving college was to Lancashire Education Authority, which had given me the student grant so I could train as a teacher. The phone was answered and the woman's voice at the other end said: 'Eh, luv, there's no work here. You'll have to go somewhere else.'

I thought: 'Great, they've just paid for me for three years to become a teacher and they don't have a job.' So I left Lancashire for London and landed my first proper teaching job in a primary school on the Holloway Road. The pay was £15.40 a week. It was a rough area and the school was full of Greek and Turkish children. It was like a madhouse. The kids were unruly. It was the old story: father working nights, mother working days. One woman actually said to the headmaster: 'You have him coz I don't want him.'

By the time I took over my class they had been through three teachers in six months. That tally was to increase, because after a month I'd had enough. On my first day I tried to instil a bit of discipline and ended up having a ten-year-old Turkish boy run from the back of the class, jump straight on the top of the desk and say: 'Fuck off specky.'

My father had suffered a heart attack out of the blue and I

wanted to be near him, so one day I just walked out on the job. I just didn't want to know. My dad's heart attack was a warning. He was only in his early fifties, but none of the males on his side had ever lived to a great age. I'm only hoping I take after my mum's side, because they have a fair record of reaching their eighties. But with my dashing good looks and well-muscled physique, I guess I take after my father, so I mightn't have long left. In the 1960s, though, I wasn't thinking about dying — I was eager to live life to the full.

I soon found that if you're looking for love then you can't beat a good teacher. I got a string of jobs in Lancashire as a supply teacher, doing mainly English and History. The children were very nice, in contrast to the kids I had in my care in London. Doing supply work I always found there was an available woman in each school I was sent to. At that time I never went for younger women, but things changed later in life when I met my wife Sue. When I was in my twenties I had a penchant for older women and there were quite a few about, as the divorce rate among teachers was very high at that time. All of them were in need of the expertise that I had to offer. I was working in a new school every term between 1968 and 1970, and virtually every term I found a new lady friend. The turnover of female companions was fantastic.

I had several letters from women thanking me for helping them over the period of desolation following their divorces, and also congratulating me on being such a wonderful and inspirational lover. It was an enchanting time. There were lots of parties, lots of idle chat about culture, trips to Bordeaux in France and to Amsterdam. A lot of history, nature, fine food and drink. Altogether a very enlightening period.

But my first job at a school in Houghton, outside Preston, held a nasty surprise for me ... I never got paid. I'd left it six weeks and still received no wages, so I rang the education authority. The conversation went like this: 'I've just left college and I've not been paid.' 'Where are you working, love?' 'Houghton.' 'Who for, love?' 'You!' 'Oh I see what's happened, we've got no record of you.' Very comforting, I thought to myself. The woman then said: 'Well, you're going to have to wait until next month.' 'But,' I said, 'I don't have any money to live on.' The sympathetic official said: 'Well, that would be a problem of course. We've obviously missed you; you'll still have to wait a couple of weeks.' I couldn't believe it: here I was, working for nothing.

Years later, before the demise of the Inner London Education Authority, there were hundreds if not thousands of teachers who were not being paid. You'd ring up, a chap would answer and give you another phone number, saying that's the number for the 'M's. You'd dial that and find it either permanently engaged or nobody would answer. They say you go into teaching for the love of the job, not the money, but perhaps naïvely, I expected to get paid.

Not having any cash seriously curtailed nights out and in those days Friday nights were very important, because that's when everybody got down to dancing and drinking. By the end of the night you generally had someone to screw. I remember going out with one lady who had just returned home from Nigeria after her marriage to a black chap had collapsed. They had met over here and he was charming, but as soon as he got her to his homeland he turned into a different man. She had been on her own for six months when I stumbled across her.

After one night of intense passion, she asked: 'Do men like you prey on women like me?' What she meant was that I wasn't playing the suitor, just moving straight in as a lover. Lots of people enjoyed so-called casual sex in the 1960s, but I hasten to add there was never anything casual about my performances. You entered into a short relationship with somebody which was fun, got them between the sheets, gave them what they required and moved on to the next.

This I did with great fervour. Often it happened in the back of my trusty Saab, which I used to drive to work. The Saab was a wonderful car. It had front seats that pushed right down and back seats that reclined into the boot, so you could sleep in it. In Chorley, at that time, there was a teacher-training college and lots of lithe ladies from there wanted to get into the profession. I was happy to give them the benefit of my experience in every department.

The first wannabe teacher I bedded from Chorley was a lady of about thirty-two — a good seven years older than myself. She had been married and had kids who went off to stay with her mother at the weekend. So on several occasions I had the pleasure of her in the Saab.

There was another lady I started seeing when I began working in the nearby village of Brindle in the primary school. I was reminded of this interlude not so long ago when a Sunday newspaper probing my past ran an old photograph and a story cleverly headlined: 'HERE'S REG IN THE WHACKS MUSEUM'. The yarn revealed how my former pupils recalled me ruling the roost with a twelve-inch ruler. I don't deny it. And it seemed to do the trick for one of them at least, because the story said he'd gone on to work for Lancashire Constabulary.

This chap, Brian Hunt, apparently recalled me humming the *Death March* and waving the ruler round like a baton. Try doing that these days in a school classroom and you'll have the politically correct lobby baying for your blood. But I don't see that it did any harm. A smack with the ruler might have stung a bit, but it was hardly going to scar anyone for life. Another former pupil, Anne Rea, quoted in the same story, said: 'He was a very funny teacher, prepared to tell jokes and organize games. It was discipline wrapped up in fun.' I thought that was a very good reference. I've kept a copy of it ... just in case I fancy going back into teaching. But somehow I don't think that will happen. Can't even spell 'psychology' any more.

That same story claimed my wages in the 1960s were £150 a week. That was way off the mark — it would probably have been less than a quarter of that. And teachers' pay hasn't improved much down the years. It is a damned difficult job and deserves better rewards. After all, the nation's future is being put in teachers' hands.

After my short and enjoyable spell in Brindle, I came across two other women, one who had been deserted shamefully by her husband abroad. This woman had suffered the trauma of being ditched. Her husband had been a violent man. She needed the gentle touch and at that time I did have very soft hands. Also, as a keen pianist, I was able to offer her the dexterity for which her body yearned. She lived in the village of West Houghton, outside Bolton.

The other lady was in fact still married, but her husband was not satisfying her fully. She turned to me for a little extra-marital ecstasy. I dealt with the situation much as I'd deal with any other extra-curricular activity, putting in lots of time and energy for free.

She was a teacher, and I'd pop round to her place after school. Her husband was a travelling salesman and blissfully unaware. I didn't feel guilty. I was simply helping him out by fulfilling her needs. He was away from home a lot and she was bordering on being a nymphomaniac. Fantastic in bed, I can tell you.

I found myself on a sticky wicket when I met the pair of them once in the middle of Bolton. They were out with their dog, which I'd met many times before. Anyway, this great daft hound started wagging its tail and jumping up. It obviously knew me very well and I thought the game was up. But this didn't register with him. All the time I was patting its head and using my leg to try and get it to go away. If it could have talked it would have said: 'Hiya, Ken, when are you coming round to give the mistress a seeing to?' Thankfully the husband didn't twig, but it confirmed what she'd said about him not paying any attention to her. He was a strapping bloke. If he'd known, yours truly would have had his spectacles wrapped round the back, not the front, of his head.

I was living dangerously, but it certainly spiced up the sex. In my last supply job in the region I had the good fortune to find a beautiful blonde, who had just been divorced. The introduction: 'Hello, my name is Miss X. I've just been divorced,' was music to my ears by this stage. With this lady in particular I really did make sweet music. She was a woman in her mid-thirties, who was stunning with fabulously long legs.

I was working at Smithills High School in Bolton at the time. This tasty morsel invited me round to her place for dinner and served up a dish I'll never forget. Expectation was in the air as I headed off for this early rendezvous. I fancied her like mad. She opened the door and was dressed exquisitely.

She looked good enough to eat there and then. But I waited.

Would-be Casanovas take note, because here comes the Ken Morley master class on how to succeed between the sheets. Part of young Kenneth's charm is his ability to put the opposite sex at ease. A lot of men look at women like a famished man looks at a meal. Take it from me, it is absolutely no good drooling until you've had that first bite. I have always had the natural ability to slip my arm round a woman's waist without terrifying her. If you radiate a warmth and confidence, women can relax with you. If they relax with you, they trust you, then they'll soon want to roger you. It works — believe me!

Enough of that. Now back to the old technique in action in that lovely lady's home. We chatted over a glass of wine. She was nervous at first, but my smooth smile and laid-back style helped her relax. She was enjoying herself and there was a twinkle in her eye when she asked me if I'd like to taste the chicken. 'Of course, I fancy a nibble,' I flirted back.

She popped into the kitchen. When she came back she put her lips to mine, slipping a chunk of succulent cooked chicken straight into my mouth. I was knocked out by it. The meal was magnificent and we both knew what was for dessert.

Since then, I've tried that epicurean trick several times myself. I've just got the one piece of advice though ... never use smoked kippers: there are too many bones. After six juicy months I'd put on a bit of weight and decided to move on.

But I was also about to suffer a terrible personal trauma: the death of my father on 1 April 1970. He'd had a second heart attack after hauling a heavy toolbox along the factory floor. After that, he was living on borrowed time. The doctors had given him some heart pills and said he would have to take them for the rest of his life. I knew immediately it would be six months or something like that. He was very ill, and on the heart specialist's advice had stopped taking some cortisone tablets for the awful arthritis that he suffered from. This day he wasn't feeling well and there was liquid pouring out of the pores in his legs. I knew straight away what it was: liver failure. His liver had packed up and he was going to die.

But he didn't know. He sat in his armchair and showed me

his legs. I told him he'd best call the doctor. He went into hospital and I knew he wasn't coming out. It breaks my heart thinking about it. I cry every time I think about it. I was just twenty-seven when it happened. I'll tell you about my greatest regret later when more grief cast a shadow over me as I starred in *Coronation Street*.

After Dad's death, I tried to console myself by thinking about the happy times we'd had together. Even some of the rows were funny with hindsight. Dad had this ability to make people laugh, as I've mentioned. It's a gift you've either got or you haven't. He could be infuriating. When he was on good form he was enough to upset anyone.

One of his foibles was that he regularly put stuff on the oven hotplate despite being warned not to. This happened fairly frequently, much to the annoyance of Mum, but try as she might she couldn't get the message across that it could cause a fire. He found out the hard way by leaving his treasured new transistor radio on it. He dashed out from the living room when he smelled burning to find his radio transformed into a blob of molten yellow plastic dotted with resistors and melted fuses. He never left anything on the hotplate after that.

Another habit he'd been warned and warned about was bringing car batteries into the house, standing them on the carpet and charging them up. One day he sneaked a large battery into the bedroom upstairs and, as was his way, didn't bother putting a cloth or paper down to keep it off the carpet, which incidentally was brand-new. Well, he left it too long and the battery acid bubbled over on to the carpet. He tried brushing it up with a cloth, which was not the brightest thing to do. It was a couple of weeks later when Mother popped in with the Hoover. She switched it on and half the carpet disappeared. She knew it was battery acid that had burnt it away and went ballistic. Then Dad tried that Holdsworth grin just seconds before being felled to the floor.

He received another whack on the head from Mother for not heeding my advice after the delivery of a brand-new van for the hamburger business. The vehicle had a canvas roof and I told him it needed waxing. But, oh no, Dad knew best and gave it a coat of creosote. It would have been fine if it was a wooden fence, but that night it rained and it simply poured in. Mum was not best pleased to put it mildly, and lashed him with her tongue in front of all and sundry.

He was something of a Mister Magoo figure. On one occasion he undertook to paint the woodwork outside the house. He wasn't cut out to be a decorator. He had more paint on the brickwork than the window frames.

If he ever needed any nails or screws he would pinch them from work. He would walk out of the factory gates with rolls of aluminium down his trousers, or his sleeves. He'd stroll up the street looking like the Tin Man who went up the Yellow Brick Road with Judy Garland. He'd only get the offending items out when he was out of sight of the factory security guards.

But his most comical Mister Magoo impression was when he decided to drive his 200cc Bella Zundapp scooter down to London. Mum and I were travelling down on the bus, but he insisted on covering the marathon 240-mile trip on two wheels. He fell off twice en route and when he finally arrived he had to go to bed for a day and a half, because his legs were that stiff. After a day in the saddle his bottom was pretty sore, too. And the soft sod knew that after the visit was over he faced the same trip back. He cut a swathe through many a crowd when he jumped on that bike covered from head to foot in rubber with his Noddy crash helmet on.

Eight days after Dad's death the Beatles split up, and at the same time I was taking stock of my own life. I was getting restless in teaching. I wanted a change in direction and fancied doing something in the theatre. My only acting up to that point had been at teacher-training college when I and a couple of friends had put on an end-of-final-year revue. It went down very well. It had our contemporaries rolling in the aisles.

In a way my father's death released me to leave the area. Shortly before his death, Mother sold up the family burger business. If Mum hadn't packed up I could have ended up serving burgers with her, because she made the best hamburgers I have ever eaten, bar none. Mother was an absolutely excellent cook, but her decision to sell up freed me to enter the world of footlights and greasepaint.

I bought a copy of *The Stage*, the entertainment industry's weekly newspaper, and saw an advert for a small part in *Romeo and Juliet* with the Northern Theatre Company based in Sheffield, South Yorkshire. They wanted somebody who could play the fife, which is a small shrill flute. I was a flautist, so I fitted the bill. I got the job as a servant to the Capulets. It was a very small part; basically he was the guy who came on right at the beginning of the play. But it gave me a taste for the theatre.

Mel Smith, who later found fame with Griff Rhys Jones, was the assistant director of Sheffield's Crucible Theatre. It was in Sheffield over after-show drinks that I became friendly with two other guys who were to play important roles in my future life. One was a writer called Andy Smith and the other was actor Howard 'Lew' Lewis, who later achieved television fame as Elmo in *Brush Strokes* and Friar Tuck in the kids' TV programme *Maid Marian and Her Merry Men*. The acting experience stood me in good stead for my next career move, later in 1970.

I attempted to combine my profession as a teacher with my thespian leaning and applied for a job in Edinburgh in the relatively new field of drama. I got the teaching post at the Craigmount School, which housed the James Bridie Memorial Theatre. Bridie was one of the city's most famous sons and had been a playwright in the 1930s.

With confirmation that I had secured the job I drove up to look for a flat. I picked up a copy of the *Edinburgh Evening News* to look for accommodation. One advert in particular caught my eye: 'Wanted: someone to share a flat with four women'. I was about to land on my feet again. The girls were surprised when I showed up. They said: 'We hadn't expected a man.' But the Morley magic cast a spell over them and they let me have the room. I couldn't believe my luck. I knew I was going to enjoy Edinburgh.

It was that very night that they discovered it was handy to have a man about the house. One of the girls' bedroom lights blew and she asked me if I'd come and hold the chair for her. As she twiddled the light bulb, her incredibly long legs were just an inch from my face. I was in love again, but I didn't know just how hooked I was going to get on this beautiful blonde.

We went out for a drink and there was a definite chemistry. She worked in personnel for a large company and was a yoga expert. I soon discovered she could wrap her legs round all the right places. After that first drink we became an item and enjoyed a remarkable eighteen months together.

For the first time in my life I started thinking about marriage. We were very, very close. I was but a humble teacher and she came from a wealthy middle-class family who owned this big farm up near Aberdeen. We went looking at houses together. And it was in an Edinburgh estate agent's that I suffered a cruel put-down. The chap behind the desk was charming as we asked to see the details on a quaint home. He asked: 'What do you do for a living, sir?' I replied: 'I'm a schoolteacher.' He gave me a look as he slammed his book shut, and said: 'I don't think this will be for you, sir. I think it might be a bit out of your range.'

It was the moment of truth. Being a teacher was considered the kiss of death in terms of purchasing power. I realized there and then that I could never provide this woman with the standard of living she had been used to. I also knew that marriage could turn into a misery for us and I couldn't live with that. I had learned this lesson from my father.

My mum had come from a wealthier family than my dad. I had always been aware, even as a kid, that my father could never earn enough money to keep my mother in the manner to which she had become accustomed with my grandfather. I never wanted to get into that position, where you were financially impotent and couldn't give your wife and kids what you wanted to give them. I never wanted the shame of saying to a wife or child: 'Sorry, I can't give you it. I can't afford it.' I knew what it was like coming from people who never had enough.

That's why even to this day I am careful with cash. I don't take money for granted. Also, being brought up during and just after the war had an effect on my psyche. I don't like waste. I regard it as a major crime if you throw away half a loaf. I simply don't throw food away. I know what it's like not to have any to go on the table. These days nothing annoys me more in restaurants and cafés than the old have-a-nice-day-and-enjoy your-meal brigade. For me, bad food is a crime. I hate the French, but I love their grub. Vivé la république! When I get indifferent food in the UK I want to shove it up their bums, I really do.

My first wage packet was £4, so I know what it's like to scrape for cash. I was also unemployed and know what it's like to have no cash at all. I solemnly believe these Government Ministers who moan about the level of state benefits should be made to spend two or three weeks living on very little cash. They could never fully appreciate the lack of self-esteem or the uncertainty about the future, but it would give them a little understanding.

Even though now I can earn in a day what it used to take me ten years to make, I still go on about telephone bills to my wife Sue. It is not that we can't afford them — it's more a case of old habits dying hard. To this day I appreciate the fact that I can afford things. I don't take things for granted.

I recall as a child not being able to visit my Uncle Tom and Aunt Eva in Chelmsford by train. We had to go on the bus because it was cheaper. It was a full day's travelling. There were no motorways and it was very hard going. My mother and father never had any savings when I was a child. They never had bank accounts. They got their weekly wages on a Thursday and by the following Wednesday they had spent up. I know that even today there are lots of families in that position — struggling to get by on the breadline. And they're the lucky ones with jobs. I remember my mother crying, because on Wednesday, the day before my father got paid, she had exactly one shilling in her purse. A shilling!

Don't get me wrong, my parents looked after me as best they could. They provided everything they could, but in those days there just wasn't any extra money for fun. I never really went hungry, it was just that people of our class were not supposed to have fun. I remember once having a journalist round at the house and making two cups of tea, using the one bag. He joked that I was a bit of a tightwad for someone who'd been so successful on *Coronation Street*. I told him to think himself lucky he was in Lancashire — if he'd been across the Pennines in Yorkshire they'd have hung that teabag on the line to dry and got another six cups out of it. Deep pockets and short arms in Tykeland, and not without good reason.

With my background and knowledge of what it's like struggling to make ends meet, there was no way I could marry this lass, who had enjoyed such a privileged upbringing. But our relationship continued. We'd had some great parties and tremendous fun. In those days the pubs shut at 10.30 p.m. and our local boozer was by the city's *Scotsman* newspaper offices. Every night at 9.30 p.m. there would be an influx of totally sober journalists. They would then embark on some of the most ferocious drinking I have ever seen. Pints of heavy, which is like English bitter, and whisky chasers went down their necks one after the other. In the space of an hour they had done the job; they were virtually all falling-down drunk.

Unable to get a mortgage on my meagre teacher's salary, we were still intent on moving out of the shared city-centre flat. After hunting round for a rented house with a garden we found an ideal home at Corstorphine, just on the fringes of the city. Our life together was bliss, but in the back of my mind I knew I still wanted to work in the theatre.

Then out of the blue I got a phone call from my old pal Andy Smith. He had written a play called *Heroes of the Iceberg Hotel* and asked if I'd like a part. He had secured a seven-week run for it at the Half Moon Theatre, which was a few hundred yards from the Tower of London.

I wanted to do it, but knew the woman in my life had no intention of moving from Edinburgh. Although I was enjoying the teaching, the salary wasn't enough to buy a house. I faced an awful dilemma. I was in love with this woman, but I was being offered a job that in my soul I knew I must do if I was to fulfil myself. I was terribly torn. I couldn't ask her to go with me. What would I have been asking her to do? Go and live in the back of a car.

She was unaware of what was going through my mind at

that time. I had to resolve the problem on my own. I kept delaying the decision, but after much heart-searching I resolved to go. I was destined to do it, but it was such a horrible period. Still I kept postponing telling her. Finally the day came when I did two things.

First I wrote a letter of resignation and put it in an envelope. For about forty minutes I hesitated with it in my hand beside the pillar box. 'I have a good job here, a pleasant place and a great woman. Am I doing the right thing?' The question went through my mind again for the thousandth time. Even as the envelope dropped out of sight I was racked with worry. But as it nestled in with the other mail out of my reach in that letterbox I knew there was no turning back. 'This is it; you've gone and done it now,' I said to myself. It was honestly the hardest decision I have ever had to make.

Then I went home and took her out for a drink. The really hard part was telling her. I said: 'I've got something to tell you.' She looked at me. 'I'm going to have to go and do this job in London.' She asked: 'How long will it be for?' I replied: 'Seven weeks.' But deep down we both knew it would be a lot longer.

The day came for me to catch the train to Chorley en route to London. She came down to the city's Waverley railway station to wave me off. I waved her goodbye and off the train pulled. I went and sat down in a corner of the carriage and started thinking again: 'I've just waved goodbye to this woman, who I could have lived with for the rest of my life.' I sat in silence all the way to Carstairs, past the lunatic asylum, still wondering if I'd done the right thing or whether I should be incarcerated for my madness. When I arrived in Chorley Mother had no qualms; she certainly believed I was barking mad, giving up my profession for a seven-week spell on the · stage. She also thought I was bonkers giving up the girl, but I was kidding myself that I hadn't done that.

I kept ringing her up at the house in Corstorphine at every available moment; I was missing her that much. About a fortnight later she dropped a bombshell of her own. It began with the old chestnut that always spells trouble: 'I've got something to tell you.' I'd used it on her and now I was getting a taste of my own medicine, but I wasn't prepared for what came next.

She said: 'I've actually been going out with somebody else, so I don't know what to say, really. Anyway, I'm thinking of moving in with this guy. Do you think you can come up and take whatever stuff you've got left in the house?' It was all very sudden. I said: 'Yes.' I went back into rehearsals and I had gone really white. They asked if I was all right. I looked in the mirror — it was as if I'd seen a ghost, I was that pale. The colour had just drained away. I was in total shock.

All those thoughts I'd had before came back to haunt me. I had left teaching and was stuck in the middle of London with nowhere to go. I'd just been given the bullet by the woman I loved. I didn't blame her. I just thought: 'What have I done?' I asked myself that question over and over.

A month later, when the show finished, I went back up to Edinburgh. She was still in the flat, but set to leave the next day. She had made the transition from being my partner. It was like talking to someone totally different. It was her and yet it wasn't her. We went out for a drink. As we got back I said: 'I'll stay in the other room tonight then?' She said coldly: 'Yes.' As I went to say goodnight to her she was getting undressed. I'd seen her gorgeous naked body hundreds of times, but she turned and said: 'Do you think you could shut the door? You are embarrassing me.'

I closed the door and went into the spare room. I didn't sleep all night. I lay totally awake until the following morning. What had happened was really surprising to me. In a way it is what I deserved. I'd left and pretended to myself that I would go back. But women know better. They are very intuitive. When I'd left seven weeks ago she knew I was no longer part of her life.

In the morning she got into her little red Mini and said: 'I'll see you then.' She drove off down the road. The bloke we rented the house off turned up a few minutes later. He went through everything, telling me how many forks and knives were missing and that the bin lid was broken. I felt like thumping him. He accepted the keys and said: 'I suppose it will be all right.' I walked down the street thinking it would never be all right again.

I then faced a four-and-a-half hour drive home in my battered red Fiat 500 Estate loaded with all my personal belongings. I pulled up into my mother's drive, applied the handbrake and the pressure pushed the floor out of the car. This had happened before and it reminded me of that old saying about Italian cars: 'You pay for the mechanics and get the body for free.' They had terrible rust problems in those days.

I have never seen my Edinburgh girlfriend since, but the strangest thing happened about three years later. My mother was in town shopping and she ran into this woman with a child in Chorley. She had married the bloke she left me for, got a job in the North West, and they had bought a house in Whittle-le-Woods, near where I live now. I never thought she would ever leave Scotland, and I now know she has moved back again.

Not so long ago I was doing a personal appearance up in Aberdeen and I felt compelled to drop in and see how her parents were doing. They had a huge farm on top of a hill, which had been extended and rebuilt since I had last seen it. I pulled up in my Pontiac Trans-Am and knocked on the door. I wondered if they were still alive. It was answered and straight away I was invited in. Her parents both seemed well. They told me she was still married to the same chap and they had a daughter and a home south of Edinburgh. All of a sudden, a door opened and a boy walked through. He looked just like her brother, but I realized he'd be much older now and that this lad was his son.

I thought of her father again only the other day on the fiftieth anniversary of the end of the War. He was a good man, taken away from home to fight for the old country, and he had seen unspeakable things done to his friends and enemies alike. Like all his comrades, he was affected by it. He had been out in Africa and had seen all his mates blown up. He used to disappear in his room for days on end when the memories came back to him. He was still suffering from it through the 1950s and 1960s. It is something that will probably never go away. Mental scars like that remain with people forever. People always go on about the Germans and the Japanese apologizing, but who keeps buying their bloody cars and televisions? My only regret is that the nuclear bomb didn't arrive earlier. There is no point in fighting with one of them, as we all now know.

We had a good chat and I passed on my regards to their daughter. I often think of her even now. When she knew me I was very slim. I bet she watched me on *Coronation Street* occasionally and thought: 'Well, you bald fat sod, you got there in the end.' I did, but it wasn't all plain sailing. I was entering uncharted waters.

7

Stage Struggles

Heroes of the Iceberg Hotel was never a hit, but it helped me enormously. Tickets for the play were 50p — imagine trying to get into a theatre these days for that. It can cost you more than that to spend a penny in some places. Our old pal 'Lew' Lewis turned up for a performance and a pint afterwards. When he heard about my predicament up in Edinburgh he very generously allowed me to kip down in a room in the house where he was staying in Mitcham. Wild parties ensued, in which we sought enlightenment with the help of cannabis and the old mind-bender itself, lysergic acid diethylamide, generally referred to as LSD. Like the Vikings of old, we used to collect magic mushrooms and have a fry-up. Boy, did we laugh!

It was at one of these parties that I first had the hallucinogenic drug. I got chatting to an attractive Asian lady, a doctor at a London hospital. She said: 'Have you ever tried LSD?' I said: 'No.' She said: 'Would you like to try it?' And before I could reply she had offered me this tiny microdot. I reckoned it was too small to do me any harm, so I swallowed it. It was little more than a pinhead in size. There was no immediate effect. She went off to the bathroom and on her return I said: 'Hey luv, that tablet you gave me is a load of crap. Have you got another?' She smiled knowingly. Then about twenty minutes later it hit me.

I turned round to see that the paintings on the wall were moving. And that was it — I was out of it for twelve hours. I was hallucinating non-stop. I could hear conversations out in the street. I could hear people at the bus stop over the road chatting. I was losing contact with reality. My brain was in overdrive. My imagination had clicked in and I couldn't distinguish between what was happening and what was a hallucination. I was watching the TV, but didn't know what was on it.

My sense of smell was heightened as much as my hearing. I could smell all sorts of things coming out of the pores of my new Asian friend. I could smell herbs and spices and in her voice I could hear the lilt of Africa. It was most peculiar. I lost all my inhibitions — not that there were many of them to start with. But I didn't have a clue about what was permissible and what wasn't. I suppose in a way I was out of control. I told the Asian doctor I had a lovely body and she gave me the opportunity to examine hers. The sex we shared on LSD was absolutely out of this world. I wanted to sing and dance as we did it.

I had tried the drug out of a sense of cosmic nosiness, and it was such a mind-blower that I tried it again once more in the company of my doctor friend. But that second trip was a nightmare. One of the terrifying things about the drug is that you lose touch with reality. It is awfully powerful, but takes about twenty minutes to take hold and get into your system. This delayed effect can be dangerous, because people sometimes try more. But once you have taken the drug you are locked into the trip. If it is a bad trip then, believe me, it's very bad. It is a drug that takes you to the very edge of your knowledge and experience, but if you used it regularly you would lose your grip on reality.

After what happened to me I can see why they use it on psychiatric wards. I drifted into a twilight world, somewhere between dream and nightmare at first. The walls started to bend in on me and nothing was as it seemed. There was no going back. It went on for twelve hours and for ten of them it was like being locked in a house of horrors. I would not encourage anyone to experiment, because drugs can kill. As a parent myself now I would be horrified to discover a child or young person using any illegal substance. Reg says don't do it, too. It's not like having a large brandy, when you feel the effect straight away. It was a period of deep introspection, and having been through it I wondered why I bothered. You can't really beat a pint of bitter ... it's cheaper and it's legal.

But the Asian lady was a new experience. My last night with her marked the start of one of my best weeks for bedding different ladies. I achieved a state of near Nirvana by having intercourse with five women in one week. It was almost a case of going back to the glory days of my first year up at Northumberland.

The doctor was my first dark-skinned lady, but I followed that up the next day with a black temptress from St Kitts in the Caribbean. She lived round the corner and I got chatting to her in the park. I invited her round for a cup of tea and before I knew where I was I had removed all her clothes.

But she did have a surprise in store for me. I ran my fingers through her hair and it came away in my hands. She had been wearing a very impressive black wig, and underneath her hair was cropped very short. But in a matter of moments we had got over that embarrassment and on to other things. I was given a demonstration of West Indian lovemaking at its finest. I actually fancied doing it all over again wearing her wig, but I didn't have the courage to ask on what was, after all, our first date.

The next day I started in a new theatre production called *The Motor Show* and afterwards there was a big party. I got chatting to this statuesque blonde, a stunning six-feet-tall beauty.

After the bash I offered her a lift in my cab. We got to her flat, which was in Swiss Cottage, and she said to me: 'Will you be going home tonight? Or would you like to stay the evening with me?' I said: 'It's very kind of you.' I couldn't refuse an offer like that, could I? She worked as a set designer and her flat was impeccable. There were curios and artefacts everywhere and superb paintings on the walls.

We had a coffee and a piece of cake. She excused herself and nipped into the bathroom adjoining her bedroom. About five minutes later she reappeared from the bedroom, naked except for a pair of high-heel shoes and a Victorian corset. With her long blonde hair cascading down her shoulders she looked a picture, but sadly I didn't have a camera.

But if you've ever seen a bouncy castle erected in the space of thirty seconds, then you'll realize what had happened to me. I actually burst out laughing at the ingenuity of the woman, her sensational style and sense of humour. After our first night of passion I wanted to see more of her and I did.

I'll never forget the times she stayed at my house: after a night of eroticism I'd wake to find her sitting starkers at my baby grand piano, playing Chopin. I used to look at this woman and think, 'Where could I ever find a fantasy like this?' She was particularly fond of receiving it while on the telephone to others. They would all be saying to her, 'Hey, you sound really relaxed.' Not surprising with the old cock of the north working through a heavy bout of foreplay.

But shortly before we parted company she made me howl with laughter. She was a very staunch left-winger. She visited China and gave me a little grey Mao Tse-tung cap to wear one night as we made love. Soon afterwards, she invited me up to her parents' house in Dorset when they were away on holiday. We headed off in my convertible Chevrolet, but nothing prepared me for the house she called home. It was a huge place with a garage for six cars. There were gardeners everywhere and they kept coming up to her and saying: 'Good afternoon ma'am.' She'd reply: 'Hello Smith.' She addressed them all by their second names. When in London she was a raving leftie, but when in the country she was to the manor born. Her parents were rolling in it and before long we were rolling in a king-size double bed. She was treated to one of my top performances outside of the theatre.

We got back from this trip and she disappeared for a few

days. She came to see me and I asked: 'What have you been doing?' Very honestly, she replied: 'I've been having it off with a young boy.' I said: 'Oh, have you?' Then something just snapped — call it dented male pride — but I said: 'Oh right, well you'd better go off and shag him some more.' One of my friends at the time said: 'Where on earth are you going to find another one like that?' He might have had a point, but us Morleys won't be crossed. When we fall out we fall out for ever. It was a trait of my father's and I seem to have inherited it. My pride would never let me approach her again.

But back to my week of near heaven. Conquest number four was an incredibly attractive lawyer. Our first night of passion led to lots more, but I'll come to our relationship proper in due course.

I bagged my fifth female at the weekend. It was a quite incidental, off-the-cuff arrangement, on the Saturday night. She was an intelligent young woman with a slight facial disfigurement after an accident. I saw her inner beauty and gave her what she desired. In the free-wheeling café society of London in the 1970s this kind of one-night stand wasn't considered out of the ordinary. There was no reason why we couldn't just do it. The arrival of God's vengeance, in the form of AIDS, however, was to change all this inside ten years.

After moving into Lew's house in Mitcham I decided I needed an agent. I'd already picked up a few hints, but being a methodical person I acquired a long list of casting agents and approached them all. About a fortnight later I got my first TV advert through a lovely casting lady called Marilyn Johnson. It was 1972 and I was picked from hundreds to appear in the advert for Guinness. It was a cracker, a real stroke of genius. The public response I got from that advert was incredible.

But it wasn't all positive feedback. I had people coming up to me in the street and aggressively saying: 'Nobody tells me what to drink.' In one pub in Leyland I was enjoying a quiet pint when this bloke bellowed: 'Hey, you're the bloke in the Guinness advert.' He then bounded around the bar, pushed his face right up against mine and said: 'Shove your Guinness up your arse.' I tried to defuse it by saying: 'Well, why not? I've tried everything else.' But the rapier wit was lost on him. It was a very scary situation because I didn't know what he was going to do next.

Another time I was out with a friend of mine in Oldham, having seen a play at the famous Coliseum, when a gang of lads started running up and down the main street shouting about Guinness. It was winter, but all they had on their backs were short-sleeved white shirts. They ran past us and ducked into a shop doorway. Then they jumped out in front of us and the leader of the pack suddenly shouted: 'Course I can drink ten pints of Guinness. What do you think I am — a poof?' Yet by and large the recognition was rewarding.

The problem, as I've subsequently found out, is that when you achieve stardom, you do so by sacrificing your own identity. You become the product, but you've lost yourself. You become an object of people's desires. But on the down side you also get the jealousy. Some people just want to have a go at you for no other reason than the fact you are famous.

But back in those early days fame wasn't really a problem. I was struggling from one job to the next, although I still managed to keep relatively busy. I landed my first TV role in 1972 on the popular drama *Crown Court* — the wage slip was £8. I also played Aladdin's mother in panto — my first performance as a dame. I'd never have guessed then, picking up less than £40 a week, that just over twenty years down the line somebody would offer me lots of lolly every week to play another panto dame. But after years of hard graft and learning the trade, this Christmas that's what I'll be getting for my comic role in the panto *Sleeping Beauty* at Sunderland's splendid Empire Theatre. As Fred Pontin used to say: 'Book early.'

I don't remember the exact pay cheque for my part in *Aladdin*, which was staged at Shepherd's Bush next to the BBC. Someone from the Beeb spotted my performance and from there I was invited to do a comedy show for the corporation, called *Parrot*. I was very flattered when this BBC chap told me I was immensely talented and very funny as he offered me the part. It was a TV show written by the guy who produced the Jimmy Savile show. It got mixed reviews. If it had been successful, it would have kicked me upstairs to stardom, but sadly it wasn't.

I then did *The Motor Show*, a satirical comedy about the oil crisis and the development of the motor industry. That toured all over England. I was that hard-up that I slept in the back of my clapped-out Ford Cortina instead of spending cash on guest houses.

After that I was on tour again with the Oxford Playhouse Theatre, playing in a four-hander which featured Harry Landis as Einstein. Harry was big in the 1960s doing *The Army Game*, which I'd watched avidly up in Lancashire. It was a great thrill to be working with him.

During this whole period between 1972 and 1974 I was very involved with the Half Moon Theatre Company. One of my friends at the time was Maurice Colbourne, a strapping 6ft 3ins tall guy, who originally hailed from Sheffield. They were real hippie actors at the Half Moon. They used to share everything and would walk round with no shoes and socks on. It was like a commune. They did some really brilliant productions. I remember one in which the whole stage was like a book. To change sets they would turn these giant pages over. There was some great experimental theatre. But as well as the abstract, they also did more conventional stuff, traditional Shakespeare and pantos. We had brilliant times and we used to laugh a lot.

I had many laughs with Maurice, who was from a working class background like myself. He'd got into showbusiness after a chance meeting with the celebrated actor Tom Courtenay. Maurice was a waiter at the time, but Courtenay, who came from Hull, persuaded him that the time was right for Northerners to break into acting. I saw him play Falstaff in *Henry IV* — he was excellent. His break into television came with the BBC series *Gangsters*, in which he played villainous John Kline. After I'd seen him for the first time on TV I said to him: 'Maurice, you've cracked it.' He had a string of leading TV parts in major shows, including *The Onedin Line*, *Shoestring* and *Dr Who*.

But it was the glossy Solent sea-and-sex saga *Howard's Way*, in which he played the central character Tom Howard, that made him instantly recognizable. But when he suddenly found fame, to my complete amazement he dropped his left-wing politics. He bought a little place over at Dinan, near Rennes, in France and regularly took holidays there with his family. I was shocked when I discovered he'd died there on 4 August 1989, aged just forty-nine. He was always so healthy-looking, but he had apparently suffered a heart attack and passed away in the arms of his second wife Jeany, with whom he'd had a daughter called Clara. He also left two grown-up daughters from his first marriage.

But in the 1970s, just as Maurice was starting to make his name, I was still very much a jobbing actor and very new to showbusiness. I displayed my naïveté one day as I was preparing to go on stage for a performance of Bertolt Brecht's *The Resistible Rise of Arturo Ui*, which draws an analogy between an American gangster who becomes very big time and Adolf Hitler. The renowned actor Simon Callow — who has since starred, among other things, in the hit movie *Four Weddings and a Funeral* — was playing the leading role of Arturo.

One night, as we were changing in the dressing room, someone pointed out Simon's photograph in a gay magazine. Now Simon has one of the deepest and loudest voices since Noah shouted: 'All aboard.' I had not realized he was homosexual — he didn't have the manner of a gay person. But suddenly this gay magazine appeared and there was Simon spouting about gaydom. I was in the mixed-sex dressing room when I just blurted out: 'Fuck me, Simon's a fruit.' They all said: 'What a thing to say.' Or: 'What a dreadful thing to say.' They were so ridiculously precious. I said: 'I'm sorry.' But I was laughing. I couldn't believe it, I just hadn't realized. It would have been more diplomatic to keep my mouth shut, but I was a typical Lancashire lad who spoke first and thought about it later.

Linda Marlowe — who wasn't big then, but is now — was also in the play. She is the long-time partner of playwright

Stephen Berkoff, whose plays *East*, *West* and *Decadence* have all achieved critical acclaim. Linda recently popped up on TV as Ester in Lynda La Plante's ITV series *She's Out*.

But when I met her in that play with Simon I was still wet behind the ears as far as your fruits were concerned. I'd never met a gay person until I left Chorley and arrived in cosmopolitan London. I, like many blokes, have always found there is a comic element to homosexuality. The man with a high voice and feminine gestures is great fun. However, if you are an out and out gay it can be quite dangerous for you, particularly in a rough area. You'll get one of two reactions; either people will laugh and titter, or they'll want to batter you for being a pervert. There are also certain jobs that discriminate, like the British Army, which regards homosexuals as beyond the pale. But in the theatre world gays are embraced.

My next gay incident was in 1973 while I was making my first professional performance at Edinburgh's world-renowned drama festival. I had a part in another Brecht play, *Drums in the Night*, which is about the struggle between the left- and right-wingers in Berlin just before the outbreak of the Second World War. It was on at the Traverse Theatre Club in the city's lively Grassmarket — tickets cost just 35p for matinees and 75p for evening shows. It was in a pub after one of these performances that a guy came up to me and said: 'Don't I know you?' Shaking my head I said: 'No.' He said: 'You're an architect or something like that.'

I replied: 'No.' And then this refined gentleman, dressed in tweed, said: 'Do you go down at all?' I was stunned. He said: 'Rumpy, pumpy.' I told him no thanks — I certainly didn't fancy one up the tradesman's entrance, as we say in Chorley.

Yet my only truly gay experience came later at an all-night party at a place in Peckham, London. I was quite intoxicated when this dark gentleman from the West Indies offered me what looked like a cigar. It was only when I came to light it that I realised what I'd got in my hand. He withdrew the offending item very quickly as I explained there'd be none of that Royal Naval lark with me. And I'd already eaten!

After Edinburgh, I got on the payroll at Watford

Corporation in October 1973, on a basic wage of £20 a week. I hadn't become a council gardener — it's just that the Watford Palace Theatre, where I was performing in *The Tempest,* was local-authority-run. The wage wasn't great, especially when you consider I had to pay my agent ten per cent. I played the part of Trinculo and Colin Prockter, who recently appeared in the *Street* as the stand-in bar manager at the Rovers Return while Bet Gilroy was away, played the lead role of Prospero. Philip Jackson, who later played Poirot's sidekick in the hit TV detective show, was in it as well. Marianne Faithfull was doing a play afterwards and, in the light of her Mars bar experience, we bored a hole in the partition door to view the lady in the flesh. I had red eyes for weeks.

In the same period, I was asked to do *Rainbow* — the kiddies' TV series. It was the British equivalent of the Yanks' *Sesame Street* and proved to be a big hit for Thames. I went down and met the star of the show, Bungle, and his puppet pal Zippy. The show was great fun. It was originally set in a farmyard and, off-camera, the great joke was that the farm creatures would be screwing each other daft. I was there one day and even Zippy was at it with one of the goats — the dirty so-and-so.

The puppeteers sat on very low chairs and held the puppets up above their heads. The guy who played Bungle was working at the Royal Shakespeare Company in Stratford-upon-Avon at night, but during the day, he'd be dressed up as this big hairy bear. He was covered from head to toe by this furry costume and it must have got absolutely sweltering inside it during the summer months.

One day at the studios, I was walking down the corridor with the director, who asked if I'd ever met Morecambe and Wise. I said 'No' and with this he opened a little door into this studio. Right in front of me stood Eric Morecambe and Ernie Wise. I just froze. He said: 'Hello Eric, hello Ernie, this is Ken Morley.' By the way, Ken Morley, at this point, was a nonentity. But they both said: 'Hello, mate.' I was speechless, having been suddenly confronted by two of the telly world's comic greats. They were icons of British television and for me it was like being introduced to the Pope or Marilyn Monroe, or, come to think of it, both of them together. I was completely dumbstruck. I really wish I had said something to them about how fantastically funny they were, but I was gobsmacked.

When you meet somebody like that, you can get overawed. It is a really big psychological thing, having seen somebody on the box and then meeting them in the flesh.

It has happened with me since achieving fame through *Coronation Street*. Not so long ago, I was having a pint in a local pub when a bloke I used to work with at Hill's Bakery came up. He said: 'Hello Ken, would you mind speaking to my wife? She's a really big fan of Reggie — she's crapping herself in the next room and won't come out.' Her anxiety was sparked by the prospect of meeting me. I went and had a few words with her, but there was that look in her eye of awe and she wasn't really up to chatting. I knew how she felt. From personal experience I was aware it would have done no good saying: 'Calm down, it's only Ken who used to work with your husband at Hill's.' I had been exactly the same on that day with Morecambe and Wise.

But the work that really kept me ticking over during those early years in acting was the adverts. I did one for Sharp's Extra Strong Mints with the renowned comedienne Sheila Burnett, others for chocolate eggs, washing machines — you name it, I did it. I was going for two or three a week and getting them. I was flown out to Italy for a scissors advert. I also did ads in Holland and Germany. Though by then, ads had come a long way since the first one I'd ever seen, which was for Brooke Bond tea. Later, I even got a part with the chimps in a Brooke Bond PG Tips advert. Well, actually the part was as one of the chimps. I stood in for them while they had their tea break, so the production crew could line the cameras up. I must be one of the few actors in the world who can boast he was once a stand-in for a monkey!

One of the adverts I did for *Yellow Pages* became quite controversial. It involved me asking where various shops were and being continually hit over the head with the *Yellow Pages*. As I was bashed they used the line: 'Get it in your head.'

Unfortunately, it was quickly withdrawn after an idiot boy copied it and cracked his dad on the skull with a plank.

But I still endured periods of 'resting' — the actor's term for being out of work. And it was during one of these spells that I met a woman called Evira Goldcorn, who had been a student at Manchester University. I had been toying with the idea of going to university to study the history of theatre and she suggested I write to a guy called David Mayer up in Manchester, where she'd studied English and Drama. I did just that and he wrote back and invited me up for an interview. I saw him and got accepted for the course.

I was still living in Mitcham and so I applied to Surrey for a grant — they told me to bugger off. It was just at the point when local authorities were getting a bit careful. But I decided to ring up Lancashire, who'd given me my last grant for the teaching course. The phone was answered by the same woman who'd told me there were no jobs for teachers a few years before. I told her how I was now an actor and asked her: 'Have you seen the Guinness advert? Well I'm the bloke with glasses in it.' She had and she told me it would be all right for me to study drama, and with that I got another grant for three years.

Incidentally, three years later, after finishing university, I rang up the Lancashire education department to ask after a teaching job. The same woman, who I'd spoken to every time I rang the office in the past decade, answered the phone and said: 'There's no work here, luv.' It was the same line she'd used in 1968. It really tickled me to get the same response nearly ten years on. I wondered how people became teachers in Lancashire — there was I with six years' education paid for by the county and they still wouldn't take me on.

I'd thoroughly enjoyed my time with Lew in Mitcham, but one irritation had been the local crime. I had two motorbikes — a Yamaha and a Suzuki — nicked from outside the house. I put an advert in the paper to try and get one of them back and a woman rang to tell me where the local kids took the stolen machines. I set off to these woodlands and sure enough found a motorbike. It wasn't mine, but it was brand new. I picked it up, walked it out of the woods, parked it by a telephone kiosk and called the police. I gave them the registration and told them I'd leave it by the phone box for collection. I went back at about five o'clock and it had gone. I was quite pleased with myself for rescuing it from the thieves, but when I got back in the wood I found it again — only this time burnt out. The police hadn't been fast enough off the mark.

Several months after the theft, I rang the police in Mitcham to see if my bike had turned up. I was told it hadn't because it wasn't on the computer. Then, twelve months after the crime, I got a call from the cops in Merton telling me they had an engine and gearbox with the serial numbers of my bike and they had been there nine months. I was a little irate, and told them I'd only called Mitcham a month or so before.

I really enjoyed buzzing about London on the motorbikes. I knew my way round quite well, because I'd landed a job driving a mini-cab. Sadly, I hadn't gained 'the knowledge' — I didn't know my bum from my elbow. But all the same I was dropping little old ladies off at bingo along with longer trips to the airport. I remember once phoning home in a state of amazement after a fare had tipped me a fiver for taking him to Heathrow. But on the whole the work was hard and the money wasn't great. The airport was the closest I got to a foreign holiday at that stage.

I did take one break out of the city, though, when Pete and Monica went down to Cornwall. I caught a train to Exeter, taking my moped with me, so I could surprise them at their campsite at Lizard Point. The crash helmet was reminiscent of World War One and their faces were a picture when I roared across the campsite shouting: 'Hi-de-hi, campers!' Monica was well used to my practical jokes by now — I'd often ring her up and do some heavy breathing before announcing myself as Aunty Kenneth. Once she got a real mucky call in which the pervert said: 'Do you fancy a big one, because I'm coming round for you now.' Monica thought it was me and said: 'OK, I'll leave the back door open.' Thankfully the telephone pervert didn't show. She got quite a shock when she discovered it wasn't me and I toned down my phone pranks after that. I'd nicknamed Pete 'Liberty' Smith from an early age and it was the first moniker that stuck to him, the second being his wife.

My own overriding love interest during this time and throughout the mid-1970s was the sultry lawyer, who I mentioned earlier as a notch on my bedpost during that heavenly week. But she was much more than that and my mother even hoped she might have been my bride one day. But marriage wasn't something that happened in the circles I moved in during the 1970s. I was slightly indifferent about the institution anyway.

But I was far from indifferent about her. She was a real lady. She was public-school-educated and from a very civilized family background. Her mother was from a very wealthy Australian family. Before I left London for Manchester I was living with her and we were to maintain the long-distance relationship through my university years. Once again, however, my love life was going to get hectic and complicated, as you'll discover.

8

The Two Degrees

I packed my bags and headed off to Manchester. I got a place in a flat not dissimilar to the hovel that millions of TV viewers saw years later in the BBC's hit comedy show *The Young Ones*. Ironically, the stars of that show, Rik Mayall and Ade Edmondson, were at Manchester University at the same time as me doing the same drama course. Their inspiration must have come from a similar squalid bedsit to mine. My place was a filthy pigsty and after tolerating it for several months I quit in disgust during my first year. I moved back in with Mother, up in Chorley, thirty minutes' drive away.

But the observations in *The Young Ones* were very true to life, if perhaps a little exaggerated. Lots of the older houses in the student bedsit land were owned by Polish landlords, or characters of dubious origin. They would do next to nothing for the tenants, simply appearing to collect the rent in between trips to Kraków, or wherever. Alexie Sayle played the bolshie landlord to a tee. I laughed when I saw the show — it brought so many memories flooding back. It was fantastically funny and deserved its success. Both Rik's parents were schoolteachers and he'd perfected the art of playing the spoiled bastard. And it was good to know both he and Ade had hit the big time. Another great talent at Manchester on the same course as us was Ben Elton — a brilliant comic in his own right. His stand-up sketches could be superb. I saw him once years later at the Comedy Store and he was seriously funny.

But enough about them ... this is a book about me. In the finest traditions of student life, I managed to make sure my time was usefully spent ... drinking and rogering. Of course, you'd generally done so much of that in the first six months that you'd neglected studies, so from there on in it became a real hard slog.

I tried to keep up my acting work as well, principally in the lucrative field of advertising. I could take a day out and do the filming in London without interfering too much with my course work. I needed cash from somewhere to finance all the fun I was having.

I also did a string of summer jobs. The Salford Skin, Fat and Bone Company was one of the strangest places. The chap who ran that was a real Holdsworth. He'd watch the workers coming in at the gate and would make an extravagant movement with his arm to look at his watch when the stragglers arrived. He'd boom at latecomers and boom down the phone. There was a lot of him in Reg — the sweeping arm movement to look at the watch was a throwback to those days.

On trips back to London at the weekends I would tumble back into the arms of my lawyer friend. But through the week I was still sowing a few wild oats. At Northumberland I'd managed to plant several fields of barley and in London I'd achieved at least a few hectares, but in Manchester I probably only managed a couple of acres. My sexual appetite was settling down. I was in my mid-thirties and realized more than ever before that it was quality not quantity that really mattered.

I was also very keen to make a success of the course. I had jacked in a lot of work just to go and study the history of the theatre. I wanted to read about theatre down the ages: the Greeks, the Romans, medieval theatre, Shakespeare, Jonson and Marlowe. But my biggest sacrifice was yet to come. I went down to the BBC for an interview with the playwright Alan Bennett. He had produced a very funny five-hander and they wanted me for one of the roles. I wanted to do it, too, realizing that it could be the stepping stone to stardom.

I thought the script was superb and was hoping to do the work in my holidays. But it didn't fit in with the beginning of the final university term. I discussed the dilemma with Mother, whose common sense and sound advice had helped me see my last three-year course through. After much heart-searching, I decided to stay at university. It turned out be a good move in more ways than one. The BBC production flopped. A long time afterwards I met the director and I asked him what had gone wrong. He explained that one of the actresses involved had frozen on set. They discovered she couldn't walk and talk at the same time. He told me it was such a bad experience that on the strength of it he had gone back to being a lighting cameraman.

That was a close shave for me. And, of course, if I'd taken the plunge I'd never have met my darling wife Sue, who was doing a four-year double honours degree in Drama and English. It was in the third year that we met.

I was the number-one bicycle sniffer on the campus. I could tell a lot about a lady by the smell of her saddle and Sue's smelt scrumptious. We were on the same course, but we never met until 1977, when I was in my third year and she was in her fourth. She was incredibly bright and is a very, very intelligent woman.

I was walking along the street when I saw her for the first time — a vision. She was wearing black leather boots, black culottes and a black top ... as you may have guessed, black was extremely trendy at the time. When I saw her I simply thought: 'Good grief, she's gorgeous. I've got to get to know her.'

Apparently she had been aware of me for a long time at the university. She tells me it was hard not to be aware of me, as I wore a fur coat back then. I was also very much larger than life, extremely solvent, having worked, and not one to make a virtue out of poverty. I looked like Elton John, which although no help with the ladies, gave me a somewhat glamorous aura. It was known on campus that I'd been in a commercial and in the *Punch Review* with the late, great Bill Grundy. I simply didn't conform to the average student stereotypes.

I got to know Sue by asking her for some help with an essay. She was a real hard worker and quite an expert in the subject by her fourth year. I was questioning what I had been told about the seventeenth-century French playwright Racine. We clicked pretty quickly. Sue found me very amusing and loved my spectacular Lancashire ability to get to the very heart of the matter. She liked me for saying what I meant.

But it was when my car broke down a short time later that we bumped into each other again. She said for a tenner I could spend the night at her flat instead of waiting in the cold with the car. I loved her sense of humour. We sat up chatting half the night. Like me, she was from a working-class background. Her father, Harry, was a surveyor turned decorator and her mum, Vera, a housewife.

We never looked back from that night. I went out with her continually from then onwards. For me it was love at first sight and she obviously found me just as irresistible. I'd take her on dates around Manchester and would find her reactions to things fascinating.

She and her friends had heard of Manchester's thriving gay community, but had never dared call in at the trendiest homosexual haunt, the city's Grand Union pub. I took them along there one evening for a laugh and they were flabbergasted by the rock-on Tommy flamboyance of some of the transvestites. These chaps would have tattoos of the *Ark Royal* on one arm and mother on the other. They'd be dressed up like *Come Dancing* contestants with sequins and diamanté everywhere. The bull dykes were also a leg-warming sight, ripped denim jeans and brass wear being all the rage. The ladies' loo apparently was covered in a hideous mosaic of snot, blood and graffiti, which nobody had the guts to wipe off. With all these butch lesbians on the prowl I had to ensure none of them tried pinching Sue's bottom.

I also introduced Sue to curry. She'd heard other students talk about the famous Plaza Café — a very basic curry house — but had never been there. Once again I broadened her horizons. It was essential that you went to the Plaza plastered — if you went in sober you'd probably never sit down. It was one of the ingredients of a great student night out, the other two being eight pints of lager and a legover. The strenuous sex often helped keep the figure in trim by shaking the curry and lager round so much in your stomach that it made you sick. The Technicolor yawn was often an indication of a good night out. Being experienced I managed, by and large, to keep my curries down, but this had the side-effect of making me fatter.

Those who'd overdone the drinking often overdid the curry. Charlie, the boss at the Plaza, was a Nigerian gentleman, and he served up a dish called Suicidal. You needed a cast-iron stomach and an asbestos mouth to withstand it. Not many people had a combination of the two, but after twelve pints of Guinness guys get brave. One of Sue's friends sampled it, against my advice and, suffice to say, he couldn't stand it. Those who did, not only got the burning sensation on the way in, they got it on the way out as well. Toilet rolls in student households were often housed in the fridge to help cope with the after-effects.

Sue was like an innocent abroad among all this revelry, but really warmed to it. In no time at all she knew her way round curry menus and the city's seedier pubs. Her parents wouldn't have thanked me for it, but I saw it as all a part of her education. Anyway, drunk or sober, curried or not, she was a bit tasty between the sheets!

Despite our term-time bliss, though, we both had weekend worries. Mine was my lawyer friend in London and Sue's was a boy called Dave, who lived in Oxford. She had been with him since starting at university and he had left the year before. The distance between both of us and our other partners helped us to get together. I was having the best of both worlds with Sue in the week and my other girl at the weekend, but I knew this wondrous arrangement could not go on for ever.

It ended rather oddly one weekend, when I was in London at my lawyer girlfriend's place. I told her I was going out for a pint with Lew and she said: 'You go out of that door and you don't come back.' I didn't. We were to remain friends, but our romance was finished. Later she told me she had

had enough of the rat race and cashed in her chips and moved to Australia.

I still had Sue, and had probably grown closer to her anyway. We had similar backgrounds and interests. Amazingly, at exactly the same time her relationship with Dave ended equally amicably. In effect we'd both been cheating on our partners while our fledgling relationship found its wings. Soon we were soaring together to the heights of passion without the hindrance of another soulmate on the scene.

I spent a lot of time round at her flat. I was like an odd-job man, always fixing their hair dryers and servicing Sue in whatever fashion she desired. She said she liked me because I wasn't pretentious like a lot of the other students. I was thirteen years older than her, but we established a tremendous rapport. I was very down to earth, feet fixed firmly on the ground, head on occasion in the clouds. I had to work really, really hard at exam times, but Sue seemed to sail through. She was a natural and loved being a student and all the studying. I was yearning to return to the real world. I had lots of ideas, but found it hard structuring answers to questions like: 'Discuss Ibsen's theory of heredity', or some such!

Sue tells me that at college she knew I was going to be famous. She also saw the same spark in Rik Mayall. She said people would gravitate around us, because we had the ability to make others laugh. Others with a gift she noted were Ben Elton, Ade Edmondson and a chap called Phil Bretherton, who hails from Preston, and is a friend of ours to this day. Coincidentally, *Coronation Street*'s casting director James Bain was on the same course as Sue. She recalls he was the envy of his contemporaries when he got a job in TV with Granada straight after university.

I was awful for ribbing the lecturers, particularly the somewhat eccentric American, David Mayer. His daughter Lise was around at the same time. She's now dating Angus Deayton, presenter of BBC 2's show *Have I Got News for You*. Not long ago I saw Rik at Granada Studios. I said, 'How you doing?' and, grinning from ear to ear, he said: 'You know who I shagged?' When he told me, I nearly gave him one of my medals. Back then, as far as I could see, a good number of the lecturers were leering after the students. They were as shagged-out as the rest of us in the mornings, because they'd spent their spare time either rogering the students or trying to roger them.

To give Sue her due, she had brightened up my time at university immensely. Despite the odd romantic interludes in the first couple of years, I was never truly happy at Manchester. In fact, I was pretty unhappy. I had gone from the glamour of the theatre business to an austere department. I hadn't realized at the beginning that Manchester was essentially an academic course. It was the theoretical study of written dramatic literature, with virtually no practical theatre work.

I was miserable, but Mother sorted me out. She said, 'Listen, you fat sod: if you leave now, you can get out of this house and don't bother coming back.' She made me realize I was feeling sorry for myself, so I returned to university and got stuck into my studies. At Northumberland I had wanted to leave after a couple of my pals were booted off the course. We had been on a fieldwork course and were staying in a youth hostel. We'd been out and had a good drink. At one o'clock in the morning this chap attempted to have a pee through the window. He was that drunk he didn't realize it was shut. Someone found the puddle in the morning and he was unceremoniously turfed off the course.

The lecturers were a weird bunch, mainly ex-university types. One, though, had been at the British Museum and he was so boring it wasn't true. Whatever the level, education is about communication. The best principal ever was a lovable English eccentric Jack Shemilt who was a wizard of a teacher. He was so good that I hardly took a note. He opened my eyes to how government and Parliament were run. The greatest dictator in the world is the British Prime Minister. He can get rid of a civil servant, he can get rid of a Cabinet Minister. The Prime Minister can hire and fire at will. Prime Minister's question time, he said, was absolute rubbish. All the questions are submitted beforehand and he only has to answer those he likes the look of.

At Manchester University I discovered that it was a British Prime Minister who had legislated against the theatre, because he didn't like political satire. What would he have made of *Spitting Image*? Walpole was the man who in 1736 introduced the Theatre Act, which meant theatres in this country had to be licensed and all plays had to be submitted to the censor. The playwright Henry Fielding had written a couple of very strong plays about Walpole and they had incurred his wrath. The Act ran for over 200 years — and it caught on with films as well — virtually up until I started in the theatre.

As a result of the censorship the legitimate theatre died. Light comedy and vaudeville was really all that was allowed. For decades nothing serious happened in the theatre until the nineteenth century, when Shaw and Ibsen came along. British people were denied serious theatre at the whim of Britain's Prime Minister, the first among equals!

All writers reflect the society they live in. In Charles II's time the plays by Dryden, Vanburgh, Etherege, Congreve and Wycherly were about court life, the life of a perverse and privileged stratum of society. The British monarchy at its finest. After Cromwell died, Charles II came back from France with his court. What an unusual sight they must have been: all these blokes wearing make-up, high heels and periwigs as they minced past 15,000 members of Cromwell's New Model Army on Blackheath, London. They stood to attention and he took the salute, close to where our London home is today. He got back and suspended Parliament for eighteen years. Having just escaped with his life during the Civil War, old Charlie boy was determined not to go on his travels again.

At the beginning of the nineteenth century, he was followed by the absurd and frivolous behaviour of George IV, the Regent who went round wearing pink trousers and a pink wig. He in turn was followed by what we have today: a proper secure-looking monarchy. Well, they were secure until Diana and Charles split and he confessed his adulterous liaison with Camilla Parker Bowles.

After that lot the Royals plunged in the popularity stakes. I for one wouldn't be sad to see the expense of the Civil List put to some worthwhile cause. Sir Reginald ... in keeping, certainly.

Anyway, back to university life. As I mentioned earlier, I was a student in the art of saddle sniffing. It was a tradition to run one's nose along the bike seat. I had a relationship with one woman singled out in this fashion. She was an outstanding beauty, and to cap it all she never wore any knickers when she rode her bicycle. She said she liked to be close to the real thing. In fact she was close to the real thing for the following three months.

She came to visit me at my mother's house when we were on holiday a short time afterwards. She screamed so loud during one session that the neighbours thought she was being murdered. In the throes of passion some women aren't very loud and some women are. The louder the better for me, but this girl was so loud that the neighbours came round. I answered the door and this chap said: 'Are you all right?' I apologized and told him I was just practising some very high Wagner notes. He left and I went back to it. But not before I'd given the lady a couple of socks to stuff in her mouth to prevent the neighbours hearing that same old chorus.

Two types of women were available at university. There were very young virginal types who had left home for the first time. They were very prim and most were, unfortunately, unpractised in the ways of the world. As a result of that I only bedded two of them in the first six months. But there was a residue of previous graduates who were still living in the area doing various jobs. They would come to the student parties, discos and everything. They were much more attractive, because they were experienced and wanted some fun. The lady who nearly screamed the roof off that house was one of these ladies.

Another bizarre trait she had was stripping stark naked and nipping into the garden. She did this when she visited me in Chorley and I had to tell her in no uncertain terms that she had either to come in or get dressed. Chorley folk weren't ones for wandering round in the knack, certainly not in the daylight anyhow. If a story of that kind of carry-on had got back to my mother she'd have been less than impressed, to say the least.

These kind of midweek sexual athletics went on right up until the final year, when I curtailed my activities to the two women in my life: my lawyer girlfriend and Sue. I began courting Sue more seriously as our relationship developed. I took her for dinner at the swish Casa Españã restaurant, which was way above budget for most impoverished students. I also wanted to be with her as much as possible.

I recall one evening going out with Sue after one particularly painful trip to the dentist. Most people would have gone home and wallowed in self-pity, as I'd probably have done if it hadn't been for Sue, but I was in love and desperate to see her. I reached the restaurant where she and her friends were dining and asked the waiter if he could put some warm water in a lemonade bottle. I sat through the meal with this bottle held against my cheek to ease the pain. A lot of people might not have bothered. I was sat there in my tee-shirt and everyone else was in their best, but I was in agony and hadn't thought about changing.

Sue's flat in that final year was in a shared house in Victoria Park, not too far from the wonderful Indian restaurants along Manchester's curry alley at Rusholme. Earlier she'd lived in Whalley Range, in the heart of Manchester's red-light land. She made me chortle with stories about going to use the local phone box. Especially hilarious was her first trip there to call home shortly after arriving. There were queues of women outside and Sue joined the line, unaware that the girls were all hookers plying their trade. Nobody was using the telephone, which Sue, thankfully, noticed after a short time. The ladies of the night simply stood by the phone box in case the cops came, so they could pretend they were waiting for a call. Some even kept a small dog on a lead, hence the expression, 'walking the dog'.

Sue soon became streetwise and had a ready put-down for any kerb crawlers who made a mistake. Despite all the hookers, Sue never met Hugh Grant. He had a great hit with *Four Weddings and a Funeral*, but he managed to hit front pages on both sides of the Atlantic thanks to his little indiscretion. I, unlike Hugh, have never paid for sex, but I don't think the episode will do him any harm. As somebody said, there is no bad publicity, only publicity. Without it showbiz would struggle. I don't live in an ivory tower and fully understand that publicity is the lifeblood of *Coronation Street* and all successful shows.

Many people now see Hugh in a whole new light. He's no longer just a foppish Englishman. Some probably quite admire him for being a real man and going out and giving a good-looking woman a seeing-to. You may not agree with the morals of going with a street-girl named Divine — but he is human, after all, and one man's meat is, well, one man's meat. What he does with it is his business.

But the incident on Sunset Boulevard reminded me of a quaint story involving my dear innocent mother. It was right at the beginning of the AIDS epidemic. She was watching a news programme as Sue and I were busying ourselves in the kitchen. The newsreader was explaining the ways the HIV virus could be transmitted when Mother shouts: 'Hey Kenneth! What's this oral sex?' Sue and I shot looks at each other before I replied: 'I've no idea, Mother. It must be something dentists do.' She was satisfied with the explanation. Mother still likes to think of me as an untainted four-year-old in short pants.

Sue's mum Vera is probably a little more streetwise, having lived in London. There is always a difference in attitudes between the generations, but Vera was horrified when she visited Manchester to find her daughter living smack in the middle of all the prostitutes and pimps.

I adored Sue's splendid mixture of innocence and intelligence. Sue told me later, much later, that I was regarded as a TV star back then. She also confessed that there were occasions she tried to impress me. I was constantly doing my best to impress *her*. She told how after one student production she'd attempted to be ever so sophisticated and poured a whisky and soda. She didn't know when to stop with the soda, so filled it to the brim. The drink was weak as dishwater.

But, apart from her heavenly looks, the thing that had impressed me most about Sue was her sharp mind. She was the ideal sparring partner for my rapier wit. I recall telling her about the hilarious antics on campus the day some work had to be handed in for assessment. It was 30 April 1977, if memory serves me correctly. But some of the lads hadn't finished it. They sneaked up to the lecturer's office, locked him in, and left him there until the work was complete. He was banged up for three hours, shouting and screaming. When they'd completed it they slipped the work under the door and let him out. He never guessed who'd locked him in.

One of those lads is now a lecturer himself at Salford University. I often remind him of that day, saying: 'Steve, do you remember locking the lecturer in his room and shoving your stuff under his door?' Of course he recalls it, but I bet he'd be none too pleased if some pranksters tried the same on him.

At the end of the final year the students' theatrical company was set to stage Shakespeare's *Winter's Tale*. It was mounted at the Stephen Joseph Theatre. Joseph founded the drama department in Manchester and later moved on to the Alan Ayckbourn Theatre in Scarborough. It was one of several venues in the city in those days.

The Bernsteins were still running Granada TV and they had funded the drama department in its early days. Granada used to encourage young talent and had a place called the Stables Theatre on the site, where *Coronation Street*'s studio stands today. Maureen Lipman and her husband, the very talented writer Jack Rosenthal, were regulars at events in the theatres.

In *Winter's Tale* I was stuck with the leading role of Leontes, King of Sicily. I was very unhappy. It was a big part and it took a lot of learning. I was cast against type. I was a lightweight comedy actor in a heavy role. Needless to say, and rightly so, the laurels went to the comedy guys — Rik, Ade and Ben. They were brilliant.

But the production just showed how much talent there was in Manchester at that time. Another course member who went on to be famous was Maggie Philbin. She was in my tutorial group and was one of the sweetest, most innocent girls you could wish to meet. She went on to do the four-year course and got her MA. She was the type of girl who wouldn't know the difference between a screw and a nail. Suffice to say, I never nailed her.

Surprisingly, despite her complete lack of knowledge about anything mechanical, she went on to present *Tomorrow's World*. That for me was like asking a chimpanzee to fly a Boeing 747 across the Atlantic. But she managed it well enough.

Only a couple of years ago I had the misfortune to meet her ex-husband Keith Chegwin. He was just beginning his dawn capers on *The Big Breakfast* show when he decided to hammer on my front door and wake the household. It happened on the day before I was supposed to be doing a live broadcast for the Channel 4 morning show. The telephone rang at 7.30 a.m. and this squeaky little voice said: 'Have you looked through the curtains?' I looked out and there was a crowd gathered and a camera crew. At first I thought I'd got the booking wrong. Then I saw Chegwin, the toad, grinning from ear to ear. The sight of that is enough to put most people off their breakfast, I can assure you. Then he started shouting for me to come downstairs. Swiftly into my dressing gown, I was on my way. I grabbed four empty milk bottles, opened the door, handed them over and said: 'Two pints and a yoghurt please.' I did an ad lib routine for him and that, thankfully, was the end of that. For weeks after, I had the two-gallon bucket at the ready in the bedroom just in case he returned.

One of the happiest bits about university for me was leaving it. When it came to the degree ceremony, I went out and bought a cap and gown. Lots of the other students refused to wear them. Mother was very proud of my achievement. But like everything, I left getting there until the last minute. We arrived just in the nick of time. I strode up to receive my award from the Duke of Devonshire, still wearing my shades.

It was a very impressive gathering: all the tutors were there in their different caps and gowns. Those who'd graduated in the States looked a bit like cheerleaders. I saw David Mayer, the man who had accepted me on the course, and recalled once asking him about the philosophy of the department. He said: 'Fly like a bee and sting like a butterfly.' Another gem was his line about the difference between us and the students at the nearby Royal Northern College of Music. He'd say: 'There, it is all talent and no intelligence; here, it's the other way round.' He could be a charmer.

Sue's parents came up for the ceremony and met my mother. They all had a grand day out. Afterwards, we all went up to Chorley. Sue and I posed for photographs in the back garden. We were a picture ... the two degrees. Three years had passed by in the twinkle of an eye, but what a twinkle!

9

Fat's Life

Having made the break with my lawyer girlfriend, I moved to London with Sue and set up home in Tooting, not 100 yards from the lunatic asylum. *Citizen Smith*, starring Robert Lindsay, was big on the box at the time, so my fur coat went down a treat on the streets of the 'People's Republic'. We moved into the upstairs of a very run-down, semi-detached house owned by an Asian dentist who was a refugee from Idi Amin's Uganda.

The downstairs was home to a very odd couple indeed. He was an Argentinean academic and his wife a physiotherapist. Occasionally he would disappear off to Nepal or wherever, to research music. When he was home it was like being in the rainforest at times with all these bizarre noises belting through the floorboards from below. There were also constant horn sounds invading our home from his mini-didgeridoos.

But I gave him his decibels back in spades by turning the stereo speakers upside down and letting him have *The Ride of the Valkyrie* or Meri Wilson's August 1977 top-ten hit, *Hey Baby I'm the Telephone Man* at full blast through his ceiling. That record, with its awfully catchy lyrics, was a precursor of the dreaded Tweets 1981 hit *The Birdie Song*, which was played in discos from Barnsley to Benidorm to get drunk Brits on their feet and acting daft. It was a bit of traditional British revenge. Four years later we beat the Argentinians again down in the Falklands; fortunately my war with the neighbours was a bloodless affair.

The flat was frequently uncomfortably cold and I used to buy Calor Gas heaters. I was used to warming places up, since from the age of about nine in Chorley my job had been to rush home from school and light the coal fire in readiness for Mum and Dad's return from work. These days, giving kids matches to light fires is virtually unthinkable, but in those days it was the done thing. I piled balls of paper, firewood and coal on top of each other and then placed a small metal shovel in front of the grate, which was covered with a sheet of newspaper. This drew a draught upwards and fanned the flames until a great roaring inferno was achieved — all this by an unaccompanied ten-year-old. We only had the one coal fire in the house and if that wasn't lit the place would be very cold. I'm very pleased to say my parents never had to dial 999.

But down in Tooting, Sue once summoned the Fire Brigade after losing her key. She telephoned them to help her get back in the flat. But she was horrified when a full engine, klaxon wailing, blue lights flashing, came to her rescue. She had expected one man with a master key. They should have charged her for the call-out, but very kindly let her off. I found it hilarious when she told me.

I was working at the Half Moon Theatre at the time on a couple of plays by my old pal Andy Smith. One was *Cool Million* and the other was *Free Chicken Dinners*. They allowed me to display a whole range of talents, including singing and dancing. I was playing larger-than-life villains and idiots, and I loved it. *Free Chicken Dinners* was staged as a lunchtime play at Soho Poly and was a very witty piece about three chickens who escaped from a battery farm. It looked at humans through the eyes of these chickens, who got into all sorts of scrapes. One day after the performance I rode my motorbike home wearing the full chicken costume. But Londoners are so drugged and obsessed with feeling each other up on buses and pavements that they didn't even notice.

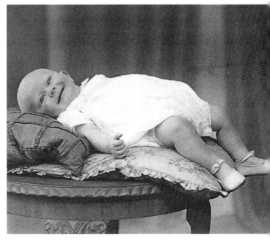

Top: Whittle-le-Woods' wedding of the year, 1941. My mum and dad Phyllis and Frank get hitched as bow-tie-wearing grandad Israel Owen looks on. And no, I'm not in the picture.

Left: Splashing time – me and Mum on our big holiday at a Blackpool boarding house, just twenty miles from our Chorley home. Note the beach wear.

Above: I was a beautiful baby, but even at birth I was bald and fat.

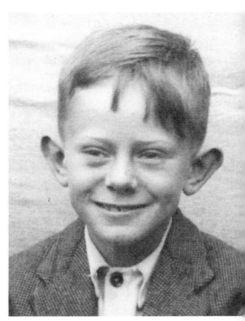

Top left: Class act. Even at primary school I'd entertain fellow pupils with stories.

Top right: Ear we go – age seven I display the smile that was to become famous.

Above: Look at those legs – it's Pete's wife Monica displaying her pins in a mini-skirt. Meanwhile I'm at the back trying to pull the barmaid in this Chorley hostelry.

Height 5 feet 10 inches   Green Eyes   *Ray Rising 1973*

KEN MORLEY

1973:
Manke in Brecht's
DRUMS IN THE NIGHT
        Traverse and Hampstead Theatres
Trinculo in
THE TEMPEST
        Watford Palace Theatre

HAZEL MALONE MANAGEMENT   01-499 0951

1659

op: No it's not hair on my shoulders. It's my fur coat – it ripped from top to bottom hen I bent to tie my shoelace in Leicester Square.

bove left: An early agent's card on which I displayed my wares.

bove right: Whacko – I spanked my pupils with a ruler and whistled the death march class. Try doing that today!

Top: Edinburgh days. I dreamt of stardom as I taught drama … and it sent me cross-eyed

Above: *The Incredible Adventures of Sherlock Holmes* – I played the psychiatrist who looked as though he needed a shrink.

tage fright – I look a shocker in this early snap from my thespian days.

Top: Passion wagons. I show off a couple of Austin vans … I lost my virginity in a back of an Austin 7 that I bought for a tenner. That's money well spent.

Above: Stud and student – I was in legover land as I studied at college and university. If you didn't get a leg over in the 1960s then you didn't have legs.

Top: On the prowl – Pete even has hair, so it must be the 60s. I'm the handsome one with glasses and a trendy quiff.

Above left: Get it in your head: an early ad for Yellow Pages was banned after a boy mimicked it and belted his dad's skull with a plank of wood.

Above right: What a spectacle! From an early age I wore NHS glasses and stood out from the crowd.

Top: Cheek to cheek – and there was plenty of that with the gorgeous Sarah Lancashire

Above: Grope on the Pope – the tantalizing Tanya on telly, but actress Eva Pope was even more fun off-camera.

During this period I also starred as Frank, a security guard approaching retirement, in a play entitled *Frank and Rosa*. It was a clever piece about this couple in their sixties reflecting on their lives. We only had eight or nine days to rehearse it, but it worked out fine. It wasn't savaged by the critics anyway, but I've always been quite fortunate in that department.

Another couple of projects around this time got good write-ups. First, I was touring with Alan Bennett's play *Habeas Corpus,* in which I was playing the very apt part of a corset salesman. We did a run at Sheffield's Crucible Theatre, and it was here that I met Mel Smith for the first time. He was assistant director at the theatre and a very funny man indeed, as fans of his hit TV shows *Not the Nine O'clock News* and *Alias Smith and Jones* will agree. Mel, whose face resembles something the dog sat on, had this amazing ability to pull women. Nothing overt, they simply walked towards him. You may not have noticed, but Mel Smith has an identical profile to the late, great Alfred Hitchcock. Now he's following in the old man's footsteps and is in Hollywood doing great things as a film director.

I also adapted a work by the Greek playwright Aristophanes with Andy Smith and the play, *The Poet and the Women,* got some great reviews. The renowned critic Bernard Levin wrote: 'The finest production of a Greek comedy I have ever seen.' High praise indeed. It was all about the one day in the year when the women of ancient Greece were given power. They ran the show and became judge and jury over the men who handled the affairs for the rest of the year. The blokes in the play, myself included, were all fitted out with these huge rubber penises that hung down to their knees. The extensions tell the audience: 'These men are big pricks.' It was a short play, revolving around them getting their come-uppance.

Sue, meanwhile, had started off working at a rather swish employment agency in London. She didn't stick it very long, because she had decided to go on and do her MA at the University of Kent. She would commute to Canterbury, where she was getting stuck into Elizabethan and Jacobean studies. She did a remarkable dissertation on *The Role of the Revenger in Elizabethan and Jacobean Theatre* and graduated with flying colours from the MA in 1979. I mentioned earlier that she was a very brainy lady.

But she had some very funny stories to tell from her short spell at the employment agency. I'll never forget her coming home to tell me about the boss of a Japanese company who had called looking for staff. He told her the age of the people he wanted and then said: 'No kneeglos.' Sue asked him what he meant and he repeated: 'No kneeglos.' Then the penny dropped and she told him straight he couldn't say that, because it was racial discrimination. The Japanese was being very blunt in saying exactly what he wanted. He couldn't see the problem with it.

This reminds me of one of Mother's early visits to London. I'd taken her shopping to a large store in Brixton called Morley's. Now in Chorley there aren't many black people, but in Brixton there are quite a few. Anyway, Mother took a garment up to the counter and said to the assistant: 'Do you have anything like this in a nice nigger brown?' I wanted the ground to open up and swallow me. I said: 'Mother, you can't say that here.' Incredulous, she said: 'Say what, Kenneth, I only asked for something in nigger brown.' Fortunately the staff were friendly and understood it was just Mother's way. But I had visions of her sparking a race riot. I was very careful when we went out shopping after that.

Sue tells a great story of how Mum really put a London butcher in his place after she'd asked for a particular cut of meat and he looked at her blankly. She'd asked for 'a good bit of skirt'. The butcher couldn't believe his ears — he thought Mother might have been an ageing lesbian on the pull. But the confusion was cleared up when Mum, one of only two female butchers in Chorley, explained how to make the cut. She left the shop shaking her head and telling Sue she didn't reckon much to southern butchers.

Cleanliness is next to godliness, so they say. Well, if that's the case my mother's not far off either, because she is very close to cleanliness. She's obsessed with keeping things neat and tidy. She used to lecture Sue on the dangers of sharing a

Hoover. Mother would confide: 'I knew people who shared a Hoover. It was disgusting: they all had each other's muck going in their homes.'

Mother was down on a visit when we went house-hunting in London. She came with us and started inspecting everything, looking in all the nooks and crannies for dirt. Sue couldn't believe it: Mother had also suddenly turned into Chorley's answer to Sir Christopher Wren. She was tapping walls and stamping on floorboards. We went to one house owned by several nurses and she was horrified. She announced in front of the estate agent: 'Does nobody own a brush in here?' Quickly followed by: 'Look at the state of that bin.' Then she finished off with the one that got up Sue's nose: 'Oh! I suppose it is London and that's how they like living down here of course.'

Mum is a firm believer in the North/South divide. Civilization is centred around Chorley. She couldn't believe it when Sue took Humphrey, one of our Lancashire heelers, to an animal psychologist. Mother saw that as the ultimate in Southern lunacy. But Humphrey needed help, because he had become incredibly protective of Sue. It reached the point where he would growl and bark at me any time I went near her. Thankfully, since he was gelded his obsession is cured these days. But back then he used to get hold of one of Sue's slippers and guard it with his life. He's a very curious hound, is our Humphrey. I'll tell you more about the pets later.

But back to Mother, who is a great teller of stories in her own right. One that had me and Sue hooting was about a proposed holiday to Perpignan in France. Mother used to offer bed and board to foreign students doing courses at the local college and was regularly horrified by the filthy state of their rooms. However, one guest from Perpignan took a real shine to Mum and invited her over to France. But Mother had heard somebody say that the old ladies in that area dressed in black shawls, and she somehow got it into her head that these women were part of the white-slave trade. She decided against going, saying: 'I won't be going over there to risk being taken off by white-slavers.' Mother was aged seventy-five at the time.

Anyway, the white-slavers still haven't caught her, but if

they did they'd soon discover she's worth her weight in gold. Even to this day she insists on ironing my shirts, which suits Sue down to the ground. Unlike Mother, Sue detests housework and chores like ironing. Mother isn't over-impressed with Sue's domestic abilities. When we decided to buy a dishwasher, Mother said: 'Sue, you don't want one of them — they're for lazy folk.' Whenever Mum is having a gentle dig at Sue, she uses the phrase 'lazy folk'.

Sue admits she probably fits into that category and feels very comfortable there. She doesn't mind Mother being highly critical of her. Sue once got told how Mum took her grandmother on a day trip to Blackpool, but the old lady couldn't be doing with sitting on the beach. She said she'd rather be back home using the soap stone to white her front doorstep. In the old days householders used to take white polish and put it on the steps with a stone. It was damned hard work. Mother is a firm believer in the virtue of hard work. You've got to remember that Sue was born on 24 October 1954, and Mother was born over forty years earlier, on 22 March 1914. They are light-years apart in terms of their ideas about how to do things, but I love them both.

Sue was there the first time Mother saw me on the stage. It was in 1979 at the now defunct Round House Theatre at Chalk Farm. The play was *The Strongest Man in the World*. I played the Red Army sergeant trainer of the man in the title. It was a play about world-beating Russian Olympic champions and what happened to them with drugs and steroids and things. There was lots of choice language, four-letter words and barrack-room references to parts of the body.

Mum was accompanied to the performance by my Aunty Eva. Sue told me that Mother was mortified. She was disgusted and didn't care who heard it. Apparently she said very loudly: 'Why are they making our Kenneth do that? I hope they don't think I've brought him up like that. It's horrible.' She was very annoyed. The play got rave reviews. I got an earful from Mum, who isn't afraid to speak her mind.

A few months after leaving college Sue had suffered her own personal trauma — the death of her father, Harry, at the early age of fifty. He was a smoker and on a Saturday morning he had a heart attack. He initially put it down to indigestion, as many people do. That morning he'd had a letter from the Inland Revenue saying they would like to see him. He had it with him in the loo when he collapsed. By the time they realized what was happening it was too late. Having lost my own father, I knew how Sue felt. I was there for her when she needed me and she knew that.

She didn't drive and I made sure she had cabs coming to pick her up and take her across the city to her mum's. She didn't need the hassle of buses and tube trains at a time like that. I also encouraged her to come along to the rehearsal rooms with me, just to give her something to help take her mind off what had happened. She was only just twenty-one and a lot of her friends didn't understand what she was going through. Some of them were very dramatic and it wasn't helping Sue. Young people often don't know how to react to death — it is so alien to them.

Losing a parent is an awful experience — for so much of your life it has been you and them. The only way to come to terms with it is to face up to it on your own. Nobody can truly comfort you, although Sue told me later I was a tower of strength through those dark days. She said she felt she had benefited greatly from my calm sympathy. Hot on the heels of this, my Uncle Tom died. My mum saw his body lying in state and told me how the undertakers hadn't combed Tom's hair properly. I suppose viewing the body helps people come to terms with the death and allows them to grieve more openly, but for me it brought back sad memories of my own father's death. As I'll explain later, I still find that terribly upsetting.

But on a much lighter note, back in the late 1970s Sue and I watched a lot of videos. We'd get an assortment of five a week and never knew what was going to be in the batch. Some of them could be slightly erotic. My mother was visiting once when a new set arrived. She flicked through and found one called *The Ace of Spades*. Mum liked the sound of the title and thought it would be about a game of cards, so she asked Sue to put it on. Sue slipped it in the video recorder and left the room.

When she got back she realized it wasn't a film about a card game, but a blue movie. She dashed over and switched it off, dreading what my mum would say. Mother immediately went into hysterics and said: 'It isn't one of those cheeky films, is it?' She's pretty hard to shock.

So am I for that matter, but I've been shocked a few times in my life, mainly by the ridiculous questions medics have asked me. There was the army doctor in the 1960s whose first question was: 'Have you ever had VD?' As if you would admit that to a stranger. I felt like saying: 'Well actually not once, but several times.' And then at my medical for university this woman asked: 'Mr Morley, have you always been obese?' Most people wouldn't know what the word meant. It was the first time I had heard it used in relation to me, but sadly not the last.

The next time was when I was in a room in Soho with a group of other hopefuls auditioning for an advert. A woman assistant to the director came to an adjoining door and said: 'Could we have the fat actors in please?' Everybody looked round at each other, wondering who on earth she could mean. There was a group of about six who looked like beanpoles and another six of us all wearing glasses and overweight. They know precisely what you are in the advertising world. Fat and cuddlies in the left-hand corner. She said it again: 'Can we have the fat actors in?' We looked round again for the fat actors.

Then this woman caught my eye and nodding her head as if I was an imbecile, she said: 'Yes, you.' It was another moment of truth. Yes, I was a fat bastard and there was no escaping it. The six of us were singled out and left the room. In the middle of a normal conversation people don't say that to you, but in the advertising world they categorize everything by size and shape. Fortunately for me, the cheques were fat as well.

One of the fattest was for Kronenberg, shot in Portmeirion in Wales, where the cult 1960s TV series *The Prisoner* was filmed. Imagine getting paid good money to drink beer — it's probably one of the best jobs in the world.

During filming, one of the cameramen told me of the fun and games they'd had making an earlier advert in Germany.

Diana Dors's husband, Alan Lake, was in the frame to play the part of the composer Schubert. The ad was about him writing his unfinished symphony, but Alan turned up absolutely plastered. He started drinking to calm his nerves about flying and had to be poured off the plane. He was rolling drunk, so they took him to the hotel in Munich and put him to bed.

They reckoned they wouldn't see any more of him until the next day, so the camera crew and some Kronenberg executives went off to a black-tie dinner in the hotel. There were hundreds of people there when the doors on a balcony above swung open and a steaming Alan appeared. Everybody turned to look at him, because he made such a clatter. Then, in his loudest stage voice, he said: 'OK, where's your fucking leader, Adolf?'

The cameraman said you could hear a pin drop. He had just silenced the entire restaurant. He said after that Alan was sloshed every day and couldn't manage the one line he had to say. He was playing Schubert and somebody walked past and said: 'Hey Schubert, what about your unfinished symphony?' He is then supposed to raise his glass and reply: 'What about my unfinished Kronenberg?' But he kept slurring, spilling the beer and saying: 'Fatt about my funfinished Froninkroog?' This went on for a couple of days until in the end they had to to put guards on him to keep him off the sauce. Otherwise it could have turned into Kronenberg's unfinished advert.

I met Alan Lake a few years later when I was appearing in a dramatized documentary. I was playing the part of a photographer. I was looking for this wharf in London's Docklands and stopped a policeman to ask directions. I was driving a black, old and very small A35, and the copper said: 'I'll jump in and show you.' We pulled up on the quayside and there was quite a crowd watching. Some wag shouted: 'Bugger me, I knew the Met were short of money, but I didn't think it was that bad.'

When the policeman saw the stunning women on this boat he decided to stay. He provided instant crowd control, but his tongue was hanging out at the sight of the models in their bikinis. He generously offered to join us on the boat — wasn't that good of him? My job was to stick my camera right in among all these half-naked women. Believe me, it was no hardship. When he saw this he cried into his helmet.

During breaks in filming I got chatting to both Diana Dors and Alan, who was a reformed alcoholic at this stage. The pair of them had numerous spectacular bust-ups down the years before getting back together again. He finally got off the booze by booking himself into a monastic retreat. When I told him I'd heard about his exploits on the Kronenberg advert, he held his hands up. Laughing, he confessed it was all true. From seeing the pair of them together it was apparent that Alan was head-over-heels in love with Diana. He hung on her every word. It was a total, genuine and all-consuming love.

A few years later I was starring in Jonson's outrageous *Volpone* at Birmingham Repertory Theatre with Robert Brown, the chap who played 'M' in the Bond films. He came along and said he'd seen Diana Dors the week before and she'd told him she had the big C. It was an awful shock to know such a vibrant woman had been struck down with cancer. She died not long after, in the summer of 1984. Poor old Alan only survived five months longer. He found he couldn't live without her and blew his brains out with a shotgun in the bedroom of their sumptuous home at Sunningdale in Berkshire on 10 October of that same year. It was a real tragedy; he left behind a fourteen-year-old son, Jason.

I was struck a body-blow shortly afterwards. Sue dumped me. Our relationship, which had started as bliss, became a real bumpy ride in the mid-1980s. I was wracked with insecurity because Sue was so much younger than me. All the usual fears that older people have about younger partners went through my mind. She was a gregarious, attractive girl, open-minded, and loved meeting people.

It was the second time we had split up. The first time was December 1982, when we succumbed to the stresses and strains of where we were going to spend Christmas. Sue had started working at Blackheath High School and the pressure of work was tremendous. Single teachers always get landed with the school play and I'd warned Sue to try and avoid that at all costs. It is hundreds of hours of unpaid overtime and masses of relationship-wrecking aggravation. She got lumbered. She was leaving home at dawn to get to school before 9 a.m. Her previous job had been with the BBC and start times there were much more flexible.

But because she was doing the school play she wasn't getting home until very late in the evening. We were supposed to be going North for Christmas, but before then we had a massive row. We had built Christmas up into such a big thing. After that row we didn't speak for a month. Sue spent Christmas in London and I went to Mother's home, alone. We were both miserable, but putting on brave faces. Sue was telling her friends: 'It was a case of good riddance.' When I called her she was very cool. 'Fancy hearing from you,' she said. But afterwards she admitted it was brilliant hearing from me. She accepted that she had put on a silly performance. We met up for a drink and we were together again.

On the second occasion a few years later, the inevitable happened as a result of my working away from home. She met somebody else. I was with the Cambridge Touring Theatre Company at the time, travelling the length and breadth of Britain and going two or three weeks without seeing Sue. It was just the sort of stuff that splits couples up. We got to the stage of thinking: 'Is it worth carrying on?'

And then Sue found a toyboy. We split. I went and started a relationship on the tour. The break was complete. I was really quite chuffed and took a perverse delight in discovering her new beau was a handsome young rock singer. If she had gone off with some ugly swine I would have been mortified. The old ego would have been crushed. It was a backhanded compliment. He was in his twenties and looked a bit like James Dean. I don't know what I'd have done if he'd looked like Bernard Manning.

But a few weeks further down the line, things changed. Her relationship had petered out and so had mine. At this point I realized Sue was the person I wanted in my life and we got back together. I phoned a few times and she kept telling me what a wonderful time she was having. I told her I was doing fine, too. But deep down we were both pining to get back together. I invited her out for a drink and we clicked straight away. They say absence makes the heart grow fonder. On both occasions we separated, it took just one drink for us to realize we were meant for each other. We've been together ever since and she still means the earth to me.

Yet throughout the 1980s I had two birds in my life. I loved them both, but in different ways. One was, of course, Sue, and the other was a sulphur-crested cockatoo called Pete. And he, like Sue, had a mind of his own.

He was given to me by the widow of teacher Blair Peach in 1979. On 23 April of that year, New Zealander Blair, thirty-three, was injured in a police baton charge at an anti-facist demonstration in Southall, London. He was a member of the Anti-Nazi League and was demonstrating against the National Front. His death a few days later made him a household name, but it was very sad that his skull was thin and that's why the blow proved fatal. His first wife, Sue, lived just up the road from us in Mitcham. In July 1988, the Metropolitan Police paid his family compensation of £75,000 for his tragic death, without accepting liability.

Sue, who was going back to New Zealand, said to me one day out of the blue: 'Would you like Pete? You know he has a real liking for you.' From that day on, Pete became a constant companion of mine. I'd take him to the park for a fly around while I learned lines. He was that tame that I could perch him on my shoulder and he'd come down the pub with me. When I was home in Chorley I'd take him for walks. But he hated being locked up in his cage. Every night when I put the blanket over his cage to help him sleep he'd start cursing. He knew some great obscenities and would shout them for all he was worth.

Sometimes he suffered from nightmares and would fall off his perch. He'd wake up cursing. In the mornings he'd shout hello. If nobody uncovered him he'd do it again. He'd shout it louder and louder, until it became an ear-piercing shriek. He'd spend his days munching through twigs. I'd give him four small branches and he'd chomp through them — I guessed they were the cockatoo equivalent of twenty full-strength Capstan cigarettes.

But he could also be very intimidating if he didn't like somebody. He would jump on their shoulder and stare them right in the eye with his beak open. He was almost growling at them. But as well as his wicked temper he also had a terrible sense of humour. He really upset my mother one day when she fell off a chair at lunch. He wouldn't stop laughing — she was shouting at him to shut up. But the more she shouted the more he laughed. It was hilarious. She got very angry. He once bit her simply because she'd kissed me and he was jealous. Chimpanzees apparently get very possessive of their owners as well.

Another time he laughed his head off was after a party where he'd been smoking cannabis. Obviously, he wasn't rolling his own, but there was so much of the stuff around that it had a tremendous effect on him. I was driving home and he was perched on my shoulder, laughing uncontrollably for twenty minutes. At first I thought he had gone stark raving bonkers, but then I realized what it must have been. So I started laughing along with him. People who saw us pulled up at traffic lights laughing like hyenas must have wondered what the joke was.

One of the funniest incidents with him, though, happened one night as I was driving home from London to Chorley to see my mother. I had to make the trip on urgent family business in the early hours of the morning. I decided to take my Ford Cortina, although it had an out-of-date tax disc and a somewhat balding tyre. I'd got as far as Staffordshire on the M6 when the car got a puncture. It was winter and it was absolutely freezing. Within two minutes the Gestapo Range Rover had arrived, lights flashing, on the hard shoulder.

Immediately, I thought about the tax disc. The officer was out of his car and striding up to me. He said: 'Having trouble, sir?' I nodded, thinking to myself, 'I will in a minute, when he gives me a ticket.' But as he walked to the front of the car he spotted Pete inside and asked: 'Is that a cockatoo?' Obviously it was and he asked for a closer look.

As I reached in to get Pete out he asked his junior to change the wheel for me. And then he put Pete on his shoulder and proceeded to hop along the middle lane of the motorway Long John Silver-style shouting 'Aye, Jim lad,' and 'Pieces of eight.' There I am on the hard shoulder of the M6 without a valid tax disc, one policeman auditioning for *Treasure Island* with Pete and the other one changing my wheel. I couldn't believe my luck. Before they waved me off, this chap had asked to buy Pete, but I turned him down. I remember driving off thinking I'd just been in a *Monty Python* sketch and nobody would believe the story.

I'll never forget another mealtime when we had six friends round for a curry. We had just got all the dishes out when he jumped on to the table. I made a grab for him, but missed. Pete then ran through the vindaloo, over the poppadoms, back through the rice and then into a bowl of custard. We had a vote on it and decided to eat the meal anyway and not the parrot. Pete was given an early night and locked in his cage in disgrace. He was shouting and swearing — almost as much as we were after plucking his feathers out of the food. A couple of people round the table would have quite happily wrung his neck after that exhibition.

But he survived and lived until he was about eighty-odd in parrot years. He only died after I got the part of Reg in the *Street*. At first, I gave him to a friend, Michael Hughes, who had a female cockatoo. But after weeks of rejection and having bitten my friend's mother-in-law on the nose — for which he received a chocolate biscuit — he had been returned. I then sent him to my cousin, Margaret, who had a small farm in Walton-le-Dale, near Preston. Years later, he had a heart attack and was rushed off to the vet but, despite the old injection and every care, after a couple of hours he went off to that great perch in the sky. Unbelievably, when my cousin returned home she found his four-year-old female companion dead on the bottom of the cage. Both birds had died within half an hour of each other. Mind you, Mother didn't mourn him — she had never forgiven him for laughing at her the day she fell off the chair.

In the business they say don't ever work with children or

animals. But I really never had any problems with Pete. I even took him down to rehearsals at the Beeb. I remember once I was standing in the loo with Pete on my shoulder when Ernie Wise walked in. Straight away he started to laugh. It turned into a fit of uncontrollable laughter — it was a far cry from our first meeting years ago. This time I think I left an indelible impression on Ernie. Now how many times have you seen a cockatoo in the gents? If you'll pardon the expression.

10

Working Towards Reggie

I had to pinch myself. I'd just been offered serious loot to fly to the other side of the earth and mow a lawn. I was about to become the highest-paid gardener in Australia, thanks to lawnmower manufacturers Flymo.

The capers that went on with that Flymo ad were astonishing. Saatchi and Saatchi were the advertising agency and their executives and some Flymo people went ahead to Sydney to scout out a garden. We had to fly to Australia to film the advert because it was winter here, and there are only two other places on earth with the same type of grass. Australia was one and South Africa the other. After being assured it never rains in Oz they chose Australia.

They had whittled the audition hopefuls down to just two. After the top executives returned from their reconnaissance mission, myself and the other chap were summoned to London's Battersea Park. They wanted to see if we could use the lawnmower! I got hold of the Flymo, pushed it about three or four yards, and that was that. About a week-and-a-half later I got the call: 'We'd like you to do this ad, Ken. Are you available to fly to Australia?' I thought they were joking, but they weren't. It was January and it was freezing in Britain. But I'd just landed a flight to Australia with a large amount of dough waiting at the other end.

Sue was green with envy. It was a great job, but the flight out was horrendous. I got sandwiched between two Chinese people on the way there. Nerves had brought on incontinency, and after fourteen hours of their continual farts and belches and grabbing the sick-bag, I was enormously thankful when they staggered off at Singapore. To add insult to injury, before we entered Australia the air hostesses came down the aisles with these little spray canisters and started squirting stuff all over us. I couldn't believe it — they were spraying us to kill off any bugs we might be carrying. I complained, but to no avail.

When I arrived I was greeted by one of the advertising bods, who said they had a problem. The chap who owned the garden they had selected months earlier had left his grass uncut. It had grown into a jungle. There was no way the Flymo would manage it at that height. They had to call out a chap with a heavy-duty agricultural mower to slice it down.

The next day we all traipsed up to look at it. But after it was cut the grass had turned all yellow and brown — nothing like the green, green grass of home they'd envisaged on their advert. So they called out another chap with a tractor and some fifty-gallon drums of green paint. He then proceeded to paint the grass with a spray gun. When he'd finished it looked absolutely crisp and green. Ideal for filming the advert. We were set to return the next day and do the ad.

But the following day it was chucking it down. It was like being back up in Lancashire. I said to the chap from Saatchi's: 'I thought you said it never rains in Australia.' It ended up raining for ten days on and off. We were supposed to be there for four days and ended up out there for twelve.

I wasn't really complaining. We were staying in the swankiest place in Sydney — the Sebel Town House Hotel. It was like being in a living Madame Tussaud's. The place was packed to the rafters with international stars and then there was me — a virtual unknown who appeared in adverts. Bob Dylan, Michael Parkinson, Billy Connolly, Lauren Bacall, Phil Collins,

Griff Rhys Jones, Mel Smith, Val Doonican, and Mark Knopfler and the guys from Dire Straits were all there. It hit me every morning when I went down for breakfast — here I was tucking in with some of the world's great celebrities. It was a very laid-back hotel and very luxurious. After setting eyes on all the stars I couldn't wait to tell Sue who was staying at the place.

I had already met Mel Smith up at the Sheffield Crucible, so I sidled up and gave him a squeeze from behind. At first he didn't know who it was, because all his party were in front of him. He was over watching a performance of a play he'd written and starred in with Bob Goody in London called *The Gambler*, and also to promote *Not the Nine O'clock News,* which was taking off in Australia.

But one guest I wish I had chatted with was the legendary Hollywood sex symbol Lauren Bacall. I came face to face with her in a hotel lift. I was knocked out when I got into the lift and saw the ultimate siren of the 1940s standing there. I smiled. She was really cool when a waiter arrived with a trolleyload of dirty plates, she just shook her head and said: 'I don't think we'll have that, if you don't mind.'

He obeyed and then the doors closed. I was locked into what must have been the beginning of many a man's fantasy. Her fame is like that of royalty. Everyone in the world knows your face and you take on a certain aura. She looked at me and straight through me. I just thought: 'Oh God.' It was like a rerun of that first shock meeting with Morecambe and Wise all over again. Now I really regret not having said anything to her. I had thirty seconds alone with Lauren Bacall and never managed to make a single witty remark. I should never have let that opportunity slip by. The *Street*'s Reg would have managed a quip — even if it only succeeded in making him look a plonker.

I wish I'd given her my best Bogart impression and said: 'Of all the lifts in all the world it had to be this one.' But I guess she'd probably heard that one before. I later discovered she was appearing in a play over there, produced by one of the late, great Robert Morley's sons. I never bothered her for an autograph, but one of our party was a big-name hunter.

The guy who was with us from Saatchi's was an out-and-out Bob Dylan fan and approached him for an autograph. But Dylan just brushed him aside, saying: 'I'll sign after my dinner.' He told another three people: 'Not while I'm eating. I'll do it later.' The man from Saatchi and Saatchi was most upset, but that was Dylan's way of dealing with unwanted attention during his meal. The moral of this story is, if you want someone's autograph in a restaurant at least leave it until they have stopped eating.

After the filming I set off to visit relatives, who had emigrated to Oz in the late 1950s. Lots of people went over on £10 one-way tickets back then. My immediate family almost joined the exodus, as I mentioned earlier — we were just a fortnight off sailing. My Uncle Frank, who got on that boat, and his family, were staying at a place called Lake Eucumbene, which is on the border of New South Wales and Victoria State. It only looked about an inch or so on the map, but it was hundreds of miles. I drove from noon to midnight without seeing a soul. The tarmac just ended and I was on a dirt road, then before long the radio crackled and faded away.

I stopped the car and suddenly realized I was in the middle of nowhere. It was a harrowing experience to stand there in total darkness with just the noise of the animals round you. The stars were twinkling and shining and as I turned round I stumbled. I had completely lost my bearings, engulfed in the dark.

I arrived at the lake shortly afterwards and there were only a handful of caravans there. I got out of the car and this voice from the darkness said: 'Hello lad?' It was my Uncle Frank. I hadn't seen him for over twenty years. He asked: 'How's your mother going on?' I said: 'She's in fine fettle.' He said: 'Christ, I haven't heard anybody use that word for twenty years.' It was quite an emotional thing for him — meeting someone from back in England. We went out fishing together for a couple of days then I turned the car round and headed north to see his brother, my Uncle James, in Queensland.

I had embarked on yet another marathon drive. All day and into the night, a hell of a slog. Once again I stopped the car in the pitch-black and listened to the sound of dingos on the hunt for food. Not fancying the idea of becoming a dingo's dinner, I jumped back in the car. I thought to myself, 'If the car has a breakdown, I'm done for.' I pressed on, keeping up a steady seventy miles an hour.

About sixty minutes later I arrived in a town with a slightly run-down hotel, but one of the best rock bands I've ever heard playing in it. I decided to have a couple of pints. That was a problem; the aggressive Aussie barman said: 'We've no pints here, mate. We have minis and schooners.' Being a man, I opted for the schooners. I had a couple and went up to bed. I faced another mammoth drive in the morning.

I headed off relatively early. I must have got 100 miles into the middle of nowhere when I ran out of petrol. I wasn't best pleased. But it was when I got out of the car and the sun hit my legs like a blowtorch that I realized I was in serious trouble. I thought, 'I'll fry and die out here', because I hadn't seen a soul on the road since leaving town. I quickly got back in the car. The heat outside was so intense that it was like stepping into a furnace. The air conditioning had by now gone off in the car. All I could see was endless mountains. There was no sign of life anywhere. I began to sweat.

After about five minutes of abject terror, I saw a cloud of dust in the distance on the horizon. I thought, 'There is a God after all'. I'd been saying my prayers. I couldn't believe it when the guy who stepped out of this car in the middle of the Bush was a priest from the village of Adlington in Lancashire, just a couple of miles from my home town of Chorley. It was the most amazing coincidence imaginable. He took me off to get some petrol. The fuel stop, fortunately, wasn't that far away. It is illegal in Australia not to stop and help a stranded motorist and after my experience I could see why.

I returned to the car, filled her up, bade the kind priest farewell and continued on my way. At the end of another exhausting day I entered into the paradise that is Queensland. It's like Las Vegas and California rolled into one. My Uncle James lived at Southport on the Gold Coast, a glorious spot. I had fixed to meet him at a golf club, but when I arrived he wasn't there. I thought he'd forgotten about me until somebody pointed out that I should have put my watch back an hour when I crossed into Queensland. He turned up at the right time.

His beautiful busty, blonde daughter told me during my stay: 'I'm looking for a man who doesn't drink, doesn't smoke and has no vices.' I had to tell her the truth, and said: 'I think you will find, darling, they crucified him two thousand years ago.'

The trip was a dream, just like my cousin. And amazingly, twelve months later, Flymo asked me to do it all over again. I could hardly refuse, could I? Only this time I decided to have a bit more of a holiday out there and stay with a guy who I'd worked with on the first trip. I'd invited this Aussie to stay at my place any time he was in England. Inside the year I got the call: 'G'day sport, I'm at the airport with my girlfriend. How do we get to your house?' They stayed for a month and we had some fun. I got invited to his place if I was ever back over there.

But when I called he'd moved. I tracked him down through a theatrical agent and discovered he had left the business to operate a dude ranch in New South Wales. It was basically somewhere that townies could visit in the middle of the back of beyond and ride horses and trail bikes to their hearts content.

It was there that I had a terrifying run-in with a kangaroo. I had gone with my pal to feed some kangaroos he'd been keeping in a tennis court when suddenly one of the beasts got angry. It leant backwards on its tail and stood up on its hind legs and gave me the eyeball-to-eyeball. I read its mind: 'Make a move, you Pommy bastard, and you'll be picking your tripes up off the deck.' After they've leant back like that they launch forward and bring their massive feet down the front of your belly. Whoops!

It continued staring at me and one wrong move would have prompted an attack. My pal told me to freeze. He knew a nasty incident might be about to happen. Fortunately, it was defused without any bloodshed. But after that I had a tremendous amount of respect for the 'roos, as they called them. I kept well out of their way.

On one expedition from the ranch I visited a tiny hamlet in the outback. Right smack in the middle of this small settlement was a stone monument with twenty-five to thirty names on it. These men were all lost in the Great War, probably many at Gallipoli, where the Australian army got a real hammering. I remember standing there and thinking that the number of names on the stone must have meant a whole generation of males from this tiny community had died. These blokes had travelled round the globe on a boat for seven weeks on a trip to meet their maker. It was awfully sad thinking of all those husbands and sons buried in Europe.

I remember a chap who worked in Hill's bakery telling me what the First World War was like. He'd been shot in both legs just two days after arriving at the front at the Battle of the Somme. He was stretchered off to the top of the hill, and all the way down the other side and up and over the next hill there were wounded men six deep. As far as the eye could see, there was row upon row of casualties — and they were the lucky ones! A lot of their pals lay dead on the battlefield. Yet here I was in Australia, thousands of miles away, and that war had even touched these people.

I stayed in Australia for about a month on that second trip and had a fabulous time. However, the jaunt had started quite oddly with me being propositioned within a couple of hours of touching down. It was by a hooker. I must confess I was very surprised by the prostitutes in Sydney. I was standing in the King's Cross area of the city in broad daylight when this girl came over and said: 'Hello, are you looking for a young girl at all?'

I wasn't — I'd just stepped off a plane after almost twenty-four hours in transit. I'd only gone for a short walk to get a breath of fresh air. But she was such a pretty girl I could see how the chaps were tempted. I later got talking to a policeman, who explained to me how they were more concerned about keeping homosexuals off the streets. Gays would gather down at Sydney Harbour, but the cops would go down and do their bit, throwing them in the water. They called it: 'Flicking poofters'. In the early part of the 1800s, homosexuality was rife due to the fact that very few of the convicts transported out there had been women. Sydney Harbour on Friday nights had been like an uncontrollable orgy of naked bodies, drunk and writhing in every corner. Phew!

The second advert followed on from the first, in which I had been asleep on a deckchair with this bulldog on its back asleep beside me. I was supposed to be mowing the lawn, but we are woken by a car horn going beep. I jump up, spring into action and in a flash I've finished the lawn thanks to the Flymo. The wife asks: 'Have you done the lawn?' I reply: 'Yes, my sweet.' In the second one he's sat in the deckchair having done the lawn, but his plants get a grip on his wife's ankles and do her in! Lovely!

But out in the sticks it was really weird. A lot of them wore the corks on their hats to keep the flies off — regular Crocodile Dundees. Yet as soon as I opened my mouth in a bar, conversations would stop and everyone would turn round. I was classed as a whingeing pom — a legacy of history. The Brits had of course shipped many of these people's forebears over there as punishment for some crime or other back home.

One of the most beautiful areas was the Tweed Valley, near a place called Murwillumbah. It was just as scenic as the Lake District, very lush and green. Before I flew back I scaled the peak of Mount Roberts on the Macpherson Range overlooking the coast. I thought to myself, 'If only Dad could see me now.' He had so much wanted to visit Australia and there was I being paid handsomely to go there. I was on top of the world. The view was magnificent. I found out later that the very next day another famous actor climbed the same summit. Gavin Richards, who played Captain Alberto Bertorelli in 'Allo 'Allo, took in the view before leaving for Britain.

He had hired a BMW during his stay and the day after coming down the mountain he lost control of it in the desert. Apparently it happened at a crossroads and it spun off the road and on to its roof. He decided to leave the car and stuck a message on the windscreen. He had to walk four miles to the nearest town and made his way from there to the airport. He phoned the car-hire people just before he jumped on the plane

— I bet the face of the person he told was a picture.

But by the end of my stay I was looking forward to coming home. No matter how far you wander, there is no place like home. One of my uncles made me very aware of that when he came to visit a few years ago and just wanted to stay. He'd been away for thirty years, but knew deep down that Lancashire remained his home. The weather out there is incredible, but it was really too hot for me. I was desperate towards the end of the stay to get back home. Sue, the woman who meant the world to me, was after all waiting back in dear old Blighty.

And I really fancied a pint in our long-time local, the Duke of Devonshire, in Balham, just round the corner from our London home. We'd have regular nights out down the 'D-o-D', as we called it.

And it was in that very boozer that I almost died. I was drinking a pint when a crazed youth burst in and shot me in the head. Being shot with a .22 air pistol was a strange sensation. I suppose it was a bit like being hit over the head with a rolled-up newspaper. When it happened I looked round and saw this guy standing in the pub doorway with a gun in his hand. It didn't occur to me immediately that I had been shot.

The gunman had a horrified look on his face. He must have seen the blood pouring down my face. When I felt it dripping down my neck my first reaction was to go after the man with the gun. He ran outside and jumped into a waiting RAC van. I had a pretty good description for the police and the RAC. I believe the van driver got sacked, and rightly so. Outside, I put my hand to my head and felt the warm blood pumping out. I couldn't believe what had happened. There I was, enjoying a quiet pint, and I'd become a victim of violent crime.

It turned out the gunman was a racist and had been after a group of black people who were sat behind me. The police arrived, along with the ambulance, and I was taken to hospital for treatment. A doctor removed the .22 pellet that had been nestling against my skull. I was very lucky, because an inch further forward and I could have lost an eye or, even worse, been killed.

After that we decided to move out of the area. But before we left the patch I had another run-in with the law. Only this time, I was on the wrong side of the fence. I had taken a wrong turn at some lights and been stopped by a policeman. I was asked to produce my documents at the station. I turned up the next day and handed them over, but there was a deathly silence as the desk officer studied the MOT.

He looked me up and down and showed the certificate to a colleague. I had started to shuffle from one foot to the other with nerves, because I gathered from their expressions that something wasn't right. Then number one said to his colleague: 'Do you want to do it?' I was very apprehensive and puzzled. But before I could pipe up with a question, they said: 'Kenneth Morley, you are under arrest for the possession of a stolen MOT.'

Immediately I started to squeak about how I'd had the MOT done by some local lads, but they treated me like a criminal. They took me into the cells, took my shoes and braces off. All the time I was bleating about being a teacher, a respectable member of the community. It was sheer naked fear when they slammed the cell door on me. I was there at their mercy. I was given a real grilling. Fortunately, I was released after a couple of hours when they caught the lad who had given me the MOT.

As an actor, the experience was to prove invaluable to me. Only a couple of years ago it helped me on *Coronation Street* when I acted out Reg's Christmas arrest at Bettabuys. We had done all the filming and I was getting carted off into the police car when *The Sun*'s lightning-fast photographer Jim Clarke sprang out from nowhere and started taking photos. He surprised all of us, but managed to capture Reg's look of absolute bewilderment before we realized what was happening. The press often had a field-day at Bettabuys, because it was an outside location. I remember being a bit peeved that the pictures might go out too early and take the shine off the scene. As it was, people who saw the picture in the paper kept coming up and asking when it was going to be on the telly, so it wasn't that bad.

But press photographers never really invaded my space

during the 1980s. I was for most of the decade still a struggling actor, although I knew, deep down, that fame and fortune couldn't be too far away. Or at least I hoped they weren't too far off.

Meanwhile, I ploughed on with stage work, adverts and small parts on TV. One production I entered into was *Comic Cuts*, which also starred Barry Foster, who had become very big in the lead role in the TV crime series *Van Der Valk*. The play we were in had been done three times before and died a death every time. I travelled down to Southampton for the show and we were rehearsing while the panto was on.

Barry had incredible blue eyes and his hair appeared slightly pink. Earlier in 1983 he'd been banned for three years for drink driving. He had stupidly got in his car after a couple of glasses of wine. Anyway, we all drove down together and after a wet and miserable start ended up having a great time. We were all staying in digs in Southampton and enjoyed a glass or two together after rehearsals. Barry was a brilliant jazz pianist and we'd get smashed every evening after work. Everyone got on really well and got stuck into this play together. We turned it into a smash hit.

Funnily enough, Barry came to rehearsals one Monday raving about a stunning performance given by a great hulking guy in the Steinbeck classic *Grapes of Wrath*. He'd seen the performance at Bristol Old Vic and had been knocked out. He said this actor, called Lew Lewis, had reduced him to tears. I told him Lew was a big pal of mine and I'd shared his house for four years. He went on to say the performance was absolutely riveting for the whole audience and Lew had earned a standing ovation.

I finished with *Comic Cuts* after helping to make it a great success. But I admit I was a bit upset when I heard it was going on tour without me. Victor Spinetti had the lead role and I must confess I smiled wryly when the production died on the road after three weeks. It was later pencilled in for a long run in the West End, but that bombed as well. Five failures and only one success: when yours truly was involved!

One of my favourite stage productions, though, has to be

Jonson's *Volpone*. I starred in the title role in that on numerous occasions and worked with a host of very talented actors all over Britain. One production was particularly memorable because Sue had brought a coachload of 'A' level students along. She was at a girls' school and was teaching *Volpone* in the final year.

I failed to mention that during one scene my trousers were dropped and my backside was bared to the audience. I knew it would embarrass Sue and she was furious at me for doing it. Afterwards, she told me she was cringeing, but all the girls thought it was hilarious because they had all seen Miss Staples's boyfriend's bottom.

A lot of the ghosts from my past have popped up at Granada. Not long ago I was walking along the corridor there when I saw Nichola McAuliffe, who plays one of the surgeons in the hospital comedy *Surgical Spirit*. She was striding towards me with a group of actors and her director and her producer.

Well, without so much as a word to the others, who didn't know me from Adam, I said to her: 'Excuse me, would you mind?' She said: 'Not at all.' At this I lifted her off the ground and she wrapped her legs round my waist. There and then for a few brief seconds we simulated sex in front of them. And then I put her down and said: 'Thank you, that's been a huge relief for me.' She said: 'Fine, any time.' Then she gave me a kiss and walked off as if nothing had happened, hotly pursued by a gobsmacked ensemble all asking: 'Who was that?' Theatre folk are like that, you know.

There's another girl at Granada, who starred in *Children's Ward*, who I know from the stage. We did a rape scene together that featured in *Volpone*. She was very into the part and so was I. Manfully I grabbed her and threw her on to the bed, but as I did so I nearly took her leg off on the side of the bed. I was so wrapped up in the frenzy of the character that I proceeded to hammer into her. And to give her her real due, she was that engrossed in her part that she didn't realize half the screams were for real until afterwards.

When I appeared in *Volpone* at Croydon's Warehouse

Theatre during the month of May one of the company was Berwick Kaler, who went on to play Jimmy Nail's anorak-wearing sidekick in *Spender*. He is a smashing chap. He was in panto at York one year and told them he could do a better job of writing the script. He ended up writing the panto for the Theatre Royal in York for years after that.

I also appeared in Joe Orton's play *What the Butler Saw* at Croydon and this production got tremendous reviews. One of the reviewers was a chap called Lahr — his father, Bert Lahr, had starred as the Cowardly Lion in the *Wizard of Oz* alongside Judy Garland — and he gave us a wonderful write-up. He'd written Joe Orton's biography and paid me the ultimate compliment when he said: 'You are the best actor I have ever seen in a play by Joe Orton.' High praise indeed.

Another part I played was that of a psychiatrist in *The Amazing Adventures of Sherlock Holmes*. It was never a blockbuster, but it helped put the bread and butter on the table. Round this time I also had a good role in a show called *The Tax Exile* alongside Maynard Williams, the son of actor Bill Maynard, famed as Selwyn Froggitt and more recently Greengrass in *Heartbeat*. One night we had both his father Bill and Mr Theatre himself, Harold Pinter, in the audience.

After the show, Pinter said to me: 'A brilliant performance.' I said: 'Stylish actor yourself, if you don't mind me saying so.' He was a top international playwright, but a smashing chap. He said: 'I believe you are into American cars.' I told him I was and that I had a Pontiac. I asked him what he had. He said: 'I have a very old Mercedes Benz.' He was wearing a rather old-looking leather jacket, so I retorted: 'You got the suit with the car?' He was very sharp and saw the funny side.

But through all my years in theatre I still never ceased to be amazed at some of the antics of individuals in audiences. You get lots of jokers who don't realize the noise they are making is coming out above the play. One such plonker was Mr Neil Kinnock, who was then the Labour Party leader, who had turned up to watch me in *The Ragged Trousered Philanthropist* at the new Half Moon.

He had taken some children with him to the theatre and had

members of the audience laughing into their hands as he tried to explain what the play was about. Everybody could hear him. I could hear him on the stage, my wife Sue in the audience could hear him. Sue was doubled over as this baritone Welsh voice competed with the actors on the stage. I honestly don't believe he knew his stage whisper could be heard by most of the theatre. But after that I thought he must be pretty thick-skinned not to have realized. Still, he would know all about theatre, being in Parliament.

On 11 June 1987, Kinnock helped reduce me to tears. It was the day of the General Election and I had voted against the Labour Party for the first time in my life. It was a very emotional moment for me as I stepped out of the polling station. For the first time in nearly thirty years I had not voted Labour. I thought of my father, a life-long socialist, and suddenly felt I had betrayed my class. I walked down this alleyway after coming out of the polling booth with tears streaming down my face.

I was so guilt-ridden. I went back to the house with a cloud over me. I had voted for the SDP–Liberal Alliance, because I could not agree with unilateral disarmament. When I got home a Labour Party canvasser called. She said: 'Can we count on your vote?' I replied: 'I don't think you can.' She said: 'They aren't going to get in. I've been to twenty houses and even the people who normally vote Labour aren't behind us.'

At this point I was living in a ground-floor flat in Forest Hill, which had one room that was awfully cold. I was convinced it was haunted and the heat returned after I hung a crucifix on the wall. I was never truly happy in the flat and twice during my time there it was burgled.

The first break-in happened in mid-January, and the policeman who attended told me it was the 329th case of burglary in the area that year. We were surrounded by flats and houses, but nobody had seen or heard anything. Or if they had, they were too terrified to go out and get involved.

On the second occasion, they came in the middle of the day and just sledgehammered the front door down. The police later told me I was lucky to have been out, otherwise I might have suffered some serious damage myself. You feel violated when your home is broken into. For weeks after, every bang in the night has you running scared.

After that second burglary I started looking for a new home. I looked at Rolf Harris's old place in Sydenham. The estate agent's blurb read: 'Bars to all windows.' They made it sound like some sort of desirable extra, but I imagined it would be like living in a prison.

I like London because it is such a vibrant city with a tremendous nightlife. One of my favourite pastimes was taking my inflatable motor boat out for a spin on the Thames in the summer. It was an Avon dinghy which we called 'The Rubber'. I remember returning home in it after going out for a drink with Alex Norton, an actor friend, and getting buzzed by a police helicopter.

We were by the Houses of Parliament when the helicopter came right above us to check we weren't terrorists. In no time at all they decided we were just a couple of boozers. A lot of Londoners were amazed to discover we didn't need a licence to take the boat on the river. I just put it in the boot of the car, drove down to the water and inflated it with a foot pump before bobbing up the Thames to Henley, or Windsor, or wherever.

Our old university chum Phil Bretherton and his then girlfriend Charlotte Attenborough, daughter of Sir Richard, were always great company on a trip down the river. The Thames is a very romantic place — away from the traffic and down among the waves. At full tide the river has the look of a huge lake. With the Wren and Vanbrugh buildings you would swear on a midsummer's evening that you were in Venice. Then within half an hour the tide turns and off we would go back down the river to Greenwich.

It was the same year, 1987, that I landed the part of Flockenstuffen in the BBC's hit comedy 'Allo 'Allo. Strangely enough, one of the stars of the show was Gordon Kaye, whom Sue knew from her time up in Manchester. The role started off quite small, but grew and grew.

And it was here that I met up with Gavin Richards, who had

climbed that same Australian mountain just twenty-four hours after me. *'Allo 'Allo* was great fun, though it could be very nerve-wracking as it was filmed live in front of an audience. It ran for a remarkable eighty-three episodes, plus a Christmas special, between 1984 and 1992. Incidentally, it lasted eight years — longer than the Second World War.

In 1988 I landed a cracking part as Toad in *Toad of Toad Hall* at the Bristol Old Vic, which is a marvellous theatre. Later that year and into the next I started getting a more prominent role in *'Allo 'Allo*. But 1989 was to be a momentous year for me for other reasons.

Sue finally put her foot down and told me that, after twelve years together, if we were to have a future as a couple then we should get married. She was right, of course. But neither of us wanted the big traditional church wedding. I am a Protestant and she is a Catholic, so sorting out a church might have been a problem. Also Sue's mum had remarried after her father's death and we didn't think it was fair to expect her to stump up for a wedding. The tradition that the bride's family pays the bill is the last vestige of the dowry.

So we sloped off and got wed on 27 July 1989, at Woolwich Town Hall. Sue looked stunning, but she always does in my eyes. I wore my best suit and tie. Lew Lewis acted as my best man, Andy Smith was there and a friend of Sue's from the prestigious French school she was working at, and that was that. We didn't tell another soul. After the ceremony we went to a Greek restaurant in Blackheath and had a meal. Then on to the airport to catch a flight to Zante for our honeymoon.

It was from the airport that I rang Mother. I hadn't expected the reaction I got. I said: 'Mum, I have something to tell you.' She said: 'I hope it's nice.' I said: 'I'll let you decide that. I've just got married.' She slammed the phone down on me. I couldn't believe it. Apparently she nearly had heart failure. She went and sat in the lounge shaking her head. Her cousin Eva was with her and thought something awful had happened.

About an hour after that first phone call I rang back and Eva answered. She said: 'I don't know what has happened, but your mother has nearly had a heart attack.' When I told her, she congratulated me, but I wanted to hear those words from my mother. At first she refused to come to the phone. But she eventually did and I said: 'Look, I'm coming home on Sunday, I'll explain everything then.' She said: 'There isn't any explaining to do. You've done it now.'

I only found this out recently, but my mother lost a stone in weight after getting that call. She didn't eat for days. Mum went right off her food. Eva said she was in a state of shock. Even to this day I know Mother hasn't forgiven me for getting married without telling her. I always said I'd have a no-fuss wedding, but I know she'd have wanted to be there. To this day we have never had a wedding present from her. She says she could never bring herself to buy us one after what we did. I only found out as I gathered information for this book just how profound the effect was on her.

She felt she had lost a son. Mothers often have deep-seated resentments towards the wives. They are the other woman who has taken their little boy away. But as far as the son is concerned he is always that little boy while his mother is around.

After those difficult phone calls, we jumped on the plane to go and enjoy ourselves on the romantic, sun-kissed Greek isle of Zante. Strangely enough, it was raining when we got there, so I spent a day rambling round with a bin bag on to keep the water off. The food was great, the sun was hot, the sea and the sand were super ... and the sex, well, Sue knew just what to expect. My finest performances ever were probably given during that week. There were plenty of encores ... it was, after all, our honeymoon.

11

Bettabuys — My Big Break

I was expecting an audition. Instead, it was a casual chat with two blokes in a tiny room in October 1989, not too long after my return from honeymoon. They'd seen me as a birdwatcher called Eric in the Granada TV comedy series *Watching* and thought I looked OK for the part of the bumbling Bettabuys boss Reg Holdsworth. They asked me if I could do it, I said yes, and that was that. When I didn't hear anything for weeks, I forgot all about it.

Then out of the blue they rang my flat in Lee, London, and said: 'Can you come up and start filming on Sunday?' It was only a six-week contract, but I had a feeling Reg Holdsworth could work out as something special. I put the phone down, clenched my fist and punched the air as I whooped 'Yes' at the top of my voice.

On the Friday, I filmed *'Allo 'Allo*. Saturday was spent preparing for the morrow — I wanted to make a good impression. Then again, who wouldn't? I was about to star in the biggest and best soap on television. On Sunday morning I arrived at the Granada studios in Manchester without a clue what to expect. As I drove into the car park at 7 a.m., a huge grey Mercedes swept up, a door opened and out stepped Liz Dawn wearing a long coat, wide-brimmed hat and expensive jewellery.

She looked every inch the Hollywood star, a Greta Garbo figure. I thought: 'That can't be Vera Duckworth!' I expected her to give a royal wave of her hand and say in a very posh voice, 'Oooh helloo dahlling, how are yoouu?', or some such drivel. Instead, as I stood there gaping, she turned and said: 'You all right, luv?' Her broad Northern accent was as down to earth as a *Coronation Street* cobblestone. That was my introduction to the *Street* and for a Lancashire lad like myself, it was like coming home.

I'd been in the theatre for so many years that I had lost touch with *Coronation Street*. I had approached the soap from an odd angle. I'd been doing Shakespeare and classical theatre as well as bits of TV comedy. Sue and my mother both watched the *Street* avidly, but I didn't have a clue who any of the newer characters were. When I saw that I was filming opposite a chap called Kevin Kennedy, who played Curly Watts, I didn't even know what he looked like.

But when he turned up for filming I knew they had provided me with the ideal comic sidekick. Kevin is such a long, thin, pipecleaner of a person that the mere sight of him next to my short and fat bulk was bound to get a few laughs. Little did I know just how much we'd make them laugh, or how soon the laughter would start.

Curly was Reg's trainee, and seeing him there, so young, so nervous, so pale, suddenly brought a host of images back from my past. Hill's Bakery bosses sprang to mind as I saw myself standing there, as a nervous fifteen-year-old on his first day at work. I remembered all of those blustering and babbling buffoons who ordered me round for £4 a week. I recalled Murphy the jobsworth prat from Radio Relays and the tyrant from my university summer job at the Salford Skin, Fat and Bone Company. I vividly recollected him looking at me with disdain as he made a sweeping arm movement before ostentatiously looking at his watch as I nipped to the loo.

An amalgamation of all these managerial misfits was being

born on the aisles of Bettabuys. I had to rehearse the scene in front of the crew on my own at first, and it was quite nerve-wracking. In *'Allo 'Allo* we rehearsed for four or five days and then performed live before an audience. But when Kevin walked in to do the filming, he proved an inspiration. I thought, 'I can play this bombastic fart' and Reg came to life. A star was born and we knew it in an instant.

In the first scene, I was walking down the supermarket aisle, lecturing Kevin and laughing to myself, then suddenly I stared into the distance at some unfortunate worker. Snapping out of the stare I carried on laughing and said to Curly: 'Right follow me and do as I do!' Reg and Curly were in business. When we finished the whole crew were laughing. Kevin turned to me in surprise and said: 'You know, they don't usually laugh like that. I think we're on to a winner here.' We definitely were ...

But I had still kept my hand in supply teaching. I had been working on and off at Archbishop Tennison School, near Kennington Oval, South London. I needed something on top of the acting to help pay the bills. I was teaching the kids in the daytime and then they were going home in the evenings and watching Reg on TV. They were always interested in what was going on behind the scenes and who was sleeping with whom. They never had any inhibitions about sex like adults do. They were always dying to know what Curly gets up to. They got straight to the point with the questions. My answers had to be diplomatic.

I've loved the challenge of teaching since I went to Brixton on supply work and another young teacher warned me: 'For God's sake don't go into room 304. It's like Rorke's Drift in there with all these kids jumping up and down going "ooooh aaaah" like Zulu warriors. And don't try using the old ploy of picking on one of the little ones at the back to scare the front row.' He said he'd tried that and 'the little one at the back was 6ft 2ins when he stood up. He hurtled to the front, got down on the floor, did twenty press-ups, flexed this great balloon in his arm, and roared "musce-ell". At that point all the other kids in the class started jumping up and down like agitated tribesmen.'

It was that horror story that made me realize teaching was the ultimate challenge. The lifts to the top floor of the six-storey school were switched off shortly after 9 a.m. to prevent them being vandalized, so teachers had to traipse down twelve flights for their mid-morning break. The lifts only went back on for fifteen minutes before lunch, the same after lunch and then for a similar short spell at the end of the school day. The librarian used to keep his library locked; it was a siege mentality and he was on the staff. He used to say: 'If I open the doors they just run in like animals and knock the books off the shelves.' It was strange. It would have made the perfect setting for a sitcom. Months later, after slapping a boy for spitting at him, the librarian was forced to take early retirement. Apparently, defending yourself was considered politically incorrect.

I'll never forget Ken, the headmaster of that school, taking early retirement at fifty. He sold his terraced house in London for £185,000 and moved back to his homeland, Jamaica. He said: 'When I go back to the Caribbean I will be living like a king. I will get a big, big house just outside Kingston and live on my pension without any problems. It's going to be a lot of trouble round here. Now's the time to get out.' He knew what he was on about and got out at the right time; shortly after, the housing market crashed and the words negative equity became part of common parlance.

Back in 1990 the *Street*'s producers and scriptwriters saw the potential for Reg and Curly. To their eternal credit they extended my six-week run in the show. The magic of Holdsworth is that everybody knows one. He is the archetypal talentless, ruthless worker who has risen from the shopfloor and who is happy to stab his old pals in the front as well as the back to make sure he stays in management. Holdsworths even run the country these days — they are spotted by their lack of forward thinking, their desire to get somebody else to carry the can and eagerness to avoid difficult decisions and hard work. I keep thinking of designing a game about the Government called 'Spot the Holdsworth'. The promotion of the inadequate often makes those above them look much better than they really are.

We all know bosses who should never be there, who are to staff management what King Herod was to childcare. The family-owned factory, or business, is often the perfect place to find the Holdsworth. TV anthropologist Desmond Morris could produce a documentary on the Holdsworths and the way subservient staff interact with them. Kowtowing to their faces, sniggering at the prats behind their backs. All human life can be found in a factory, or a supermarket, or even an office block.

My father suffered at the hands of Holdsworths who had him working twelve hours a day for next to nowt, coming home after work absolutely knackered and collapsing into a catatonic sleep in his chair. As soon as anybody made a noise he would wake, raging about silence being golden or something similar. He was that tired out that he had no time for life outside work after he'd finished. He'd be stuck in his section of the factory without windows for six days a week. Unremitting toil had totally broken many of them by the time they reached fifty-five. Hard work never killed folk, but judging by my father it didn't half turn them into a funny shape.

That is the type of family that *Coronation Street* was initially about. The workers who slaved all their lives and really got nowhere other than the same dingy two-up-two-down terraces they were born in. Lots of work, but bugger all to show for it. The real world as it was in the 1950s and 1960s. The people in charge of them were the predecessors of the Holdsworths. They voted Conservative, dressed well and ate even better. I came from that *Coronation Street*-type community. I understood the show and what it was about.

Reg was to add a little extra menace and malevolence to the lives of the workers. He was the smiling hatchet man who wants to keep everybody in their place. But at the same time as being a monster, there is something eminently watchable about a bloke who has climbed up the greasy pole. Basically, he is still a peasant himself and whatever he does his roots show through.

The scripts were of a very high standard, very tightly written and with gags that had beautifully delivered punchlines. The viewers warmed to him, and it was only a few weeks after my first TV appearance on the *Street* that I got recognized from the show. I was driving my car along the fast lane of the motorway, and another car drew up beside me. The windows came down and a group of lads chanted: 'Curly Watts!' I thought it was quite funny.

But eight weeks later another car drove up and someone shouted: 'Oi, Reg, over here!' I actually looked round to see who they were shouting at, then realized with a jolt that it was me. It was on the M1 near Hemel Hempstead — it is a moment I'll never forget. I was absolutely thrilled; Reg had been recognized; I had finally made it. The next two days were packed with people chanting 'Hello Reg' or shouting 'Reggie'. From that day to this it has been Reggiemania. It was fast, furious and fun.

He became 'Randy' Reg soon after as a result of his continual stalking of female members of the cast. There were probably only Ivy Tilsley, Vera Duckworth, Mavis Wilton, Emily Bishop and Betty Turpin that he hadn't tried it on with among the ladies in the show. But we'll discuss Reg's wicked womanizing ways later.

Not long after joining the *Street*, my days as 'Randy' Reg looked numbered as I endured a nightmare cancer scare after finding a lump in my groin. There I was on telly chasing all these desirable women and in real life worried sick that I might have to have a testicle or two removed.

I heard a radio report about cancer of the private parts just before I discovered this lump on my own. I was in the bath at the time and the chap on the radio had found his growth as he soaked in a tub. He talked about what he'd had removed. I gave the old plums a quick feel and guess what? Bingo! I jumped out of the water, dried myself down and immediately went to the doctor. He examined me and said: 'I don't like the look of this. You'll need to see a specialist.'

I started to worry. The usual fortnight wait for the specialist doesn't calm anybody's fears. And sure enough, when I was able to get to see him he didn't calm anything. He said the same: 'I don't like the look of this.' Imagine somebody saying that about your wedding tackle — it's very upsetting. It was the first time it had ever been said to me; as you are by now aware, lots of women had got to see my private parts in the past. Time was going by and I was getting more and more worried. I thought, 'If the worse comes to the worst — he ain't going to be "Randy" Reg any more.'

The specialist sent me for an ultrasound scan, operated by an Italian. I got the same lines, but with an Italian accent: he put some jelly into my groin to enable the monitor to move around, and then he said: 'Eh you gotta a lumpa here, ah donna lika the looka that.' By this stage, I just knew I was going to get the bad news. The lump was 2cms by 4cms and as I am looking at this thing on the television monitor, the door opens and a woman cleaner is standing there. She stares at the screen with a picture of my privates on it and says: 'Incredible, those things, aren't they?' There I am with my trousers off thinking, 'You don't know the half of it, love.'

But a few days later, I got the all clear. The specialist told me it was a benign cyst, and that I'd be better off leaving it where it was — I could have hugged him. It is the first time I felt like kissing a fella. At about the same time Sue and I had started to plan a family. It only took one try. Sue, being the analytical type, decided to improve her chances of things happening. She lay down with her bum on a pillow. It did the trick. There was I looking forward to months of rampant practice and we'd gone and done it first time around. It just goes to show that Ken, or for that matter Reg, is so virile and potent that intercourse with a roll of linoleum would produce a carpet.

I got three months off work just before the baby was due, but Roger decided to leave his appearance until the last minute. He weighed in at 7lbs 14oz, two weeks late, on 11 November 1990. The boy is just like me, late for everything. They passed the baby to me and he looked just like a drowned rat — he had the Morley looks even then. Within an hour a nurse came round to say that the gynaecologist wasn't sure if he'd left a swab inside and it was necessary to have a quick X-ray. They were extremely apologetic, but as I pointed out, these things do happen. I asked as she switched the machine on: 'Will you keep your eyes peeled for an 8mm ring spanner — I've lost it somewhere.'

I had to leave the next day for a two-week stint filming in Manchester. It was murder having cuddled my new baby and then having to go away. It is one of the hardest things I've ever had to do. I so much wanted to stay there. If we'd had a few days together as a family it wouldn't have been so bad.

I rushed home to see them as soon as I could, but once again I had to go back to Granada. And during this trip North I was expected to attend a glittering celebration of the show's thirtieth anniversary. It was a real star-studded bash and Cilla Black was hosting the party live on TV. The Queen had sent a good-luck telegram and Cliff Richard sang *Happy Birthday* via satellite, live from his concert at Wembley Arena.

But all I could think about was Sue stuck at home with Roger, watching the splendid occasion on the box. She would dearly have loved to have been at my side and I would have been happier with her there.

We got served traditional hotpot at the bash, which suited me down to the ground. And we all got a glass of champagne to toast veteran actress Doris Speed, who played the original Rovers landlady Annie Walker. Doris was almost ninety and got a standing ovation when she walked out on the stage. Sadly, she died on 17 November 1994, at the grand old age of ninety-five.

She was a remarkable woman, having already had a career and retired as an office worker before she broke back into acting via *Coronation Street*. The show's creator, Tony Warren, had written the part with Doris in mind after working with her on a BBC radio *Children's Hour* play years before. She ruled the Rovers Return with a rod of iron in her day.

Initially, though, I wasn't filming in the *Street*, I was just doing scenes at Bettabuys — which were all recorded at a Morrison's supermarket in Eccles in Salford on a Sunday when the store was shut. I only met those members of the cast who were involved in scenes at the store, so there were a lot of big names I'd not seen. But Kevin had been going into the studios and telling them about the new boy.

My first day in the studios proper is etched on my memory for ever. Thirty of the most famous faces on television swivelled to the dressing room door when Kevin Kennedy uttered the immortal line of introduction: 'This fat bastard is Ken Morley.' But after the initial show of apathy and some 'blowing off', the remainder of the cast returned to chomping their sandwiches and reading their scripts.

I was totally blanked. I understood the mentality, because nobody knows in a show like *Coronation Street* if the newcomer is going to become a regular or another never-has-been. When Kevin made his announcement, I thought, 'Now *that's* an entrance.' But it was met with deathly silence. It simply didn't arouse any real interest.

I could hear the lettuce rustling in the sandwiches as the rest of them carried on with their lunch break. I realized at that moment that I hadn't arrived. It was very much like the first day at a new school. You walk in at the bottom level and all the established fourth-formers treat you like dirt. They are all terribly confident and you are the new boy. But to be fair to them, having a new actor in a long-running series is a pretty regular occurrence. So you only ever really get to know the people you are working directly with.

The room I walked into on that first day was in an old bonded warehouse and had a row of about thirty telephone-cubicle-style boxes, about five feet tall, along one wall. Poking out of the top of each one was a renowned actor's head. It was like walking into a room full of celebrity battery hens — only this bunch got a lot of corn for being there. It was very bizarre, suddenly being confronted by thirty famous heads.

But after a while I was allowed to kiss several hems and that continued right up until my last day on the show. That awful nickname Kevin gave me also stuck — only it got adapted to 'bald, fat bastard'. But I always corrected them: 'rich, bald, fat bastard'.

Coronation Street's cast have a very racy, punchy, no-messing-around sense of humour. Actors say things to each other that other people wouldn't dare say — whether it be about smells, lack of taste or the hump on your back. Actors will deliberately bring it out to break down embarrassment, because the TV camera focusing on you shows you warts and all.

On-screen, Jill Summers plays blue-rinse battleaxe Phyllis Pearce to a tee, but away from the cameras she is a bundle of laughs. Jill said to me one day: 'They've just been telling me you are a fat bastard. Is that true?' She said it completely straight-faced in that deep gravel voice of hers — I was taken aback.

But she is also extremely elegant, so I couldn't resist the chance to try out one of my favourite gags on her. It happened in the posh executive dining room at Granada, where we all sat down for supper one night. The tables were set with silver cutlery and a magnificent chandelier hung from the ceiling. Jill walked over looking immaculate, and I pulled out a chair for her like a true gentleman.

She said: 'Oh thank you, Ken.' But as she sat down I slipped a massive whoopee cushion on the chair. The most enormous farting sound filled the air and everyone froze with an 'oh dear, the old dear has gone incontinent' look on their faces. There was a moment of silence, then Jill turned round and laughed: 'Oh, you swine.' Now who could imagine Phyllis Pearce in that position? It just shows what a great actress Jill is. She reminds me very much of my own mother Phyllis and is a similar age. They both look very good for their age and I was amazed to find out Jill is actually three years older at eighty-four.

But everyone on the set enjoys a joke. I remember Bill Waddington, who plays Percy Sugden, rolling up at the studios in his Mercedes and asking me if I wanted to buy it. I told him, 'I bet when you were knocking ten bells out of them in 1945 you never dreamed you'd be driving one of their cars?' Only shortly before I left the show he had to use the same line on screen when he slagged off Jack Duckworth for test driving a Mercedes after his £30,000 windfall.

Bill took it in good part and I followed through with 'Have you had a legover in it?' He replied, quick as a flash: 'You'll not find a mark in that car.' Later in 1993 those same sentiments about the striving of the nation through the war years came back to me when the closure of the giant Leyland truck plant in Lancashire became a possibility. Leyland DAF had gone bust, redundancies were on the cards and I just kept thinking about all the people, like my parents, who had worked round the clock at that place to keep the war effort afloat.

It was heartbreaking for me to think the government was prepared to stand by and watch a near 100-year-old industry die. Britain is losing its manufacturing base and, as a third-generation engineer, that really guts me. Throwing 2,500 people at Leyland on to the dole to collect benefits didn't make economic sense to me. Surely the government should have stepped in, but nobody in power had the will to do it. Where will the country be in a few years' time when all the engineers are gone? Fortunately, a management buyout rescued some of the jobs at Leyland.

But we are already swamped with Japanese cars, Italian washing machines and German fridge-freezers. The vanquished in the Second World War have emerged the victors. We just need a Japanese cradle and a coffin to complete the cycle. It really saddens me when I think of the deterioration in our manufacturing sector.

On that note, I had to have a go at Kevin Kennedy when he squandered a substantial portion of his ill-gotten gains on a new black Japanese Mazda sports car. As I pointed out to him: '£18,000 is a lot to pay to sit on top of a light bulb.' Shortly afterwards, he jumped in it and started revving the beast, but it wasn't going anywhere ... not surprising really, considering we had jacked the wheels up off the floor. Sometimes, to get his own back, when we were filming Kevin would pass me a cup of tea with half a pound of sugar in it. Oh, I did enjoy that one, having to carry on with the lines while swallowing a bag of sugar.

Oh yes, Kevin and I had some great times larking about together. The pranks we played have certainly provided some of the most memorable moments for me during my six years on the *Street*. One of our favourites was stuffing packs of frozen peas down the dresses of the shop assistants. And we were forever filming scenes, totally straight-faced, with sausages poking out of our trousers.

On my first day of filming at Bettabuys I knew I was working with a natural clown when Kevin accidentally walked into a camera and knocked over a cameraman during filming. Not long after that I made a prize prat of myself during a lunch break in a pub near the Morrison's store. We'd only popped out for a quick pint, but I spotted this piano and told Kev I'd give him a quick blast.

I tinkled the ivories for all I was worth. The whole pub was silent and everybody was watching me. I thought to myself: 'You still know how to stop them dead, Kenny boy.' I gave them a racy version of *The Man I Love*. When I stopped I waited for the applause. There was none, but I simply thought it was a tough pub and they didn't want to show their appreciation. Smiling and rather proud of my performance, I said: 'Well, what did you think of that, Kev?' He didn't reply, just stood there staring at me with a hint of trepidation in his eyes. Again I said: 'What did you think of that?'

He replied, shaking his head: 'Not a lot, pal — you've just played right through the Remembrance Day minute's silence.' Timing: you've either got it, or you haven't; obviously I hadn't got it on that day. I wanted to vanish. The pair of us slunk out of the pub, fifty pairs of astonished eyes watching us. I've done some embarrassing things in my time, but that takes the biscuit. With hindsight it might sound funny, but at the time I felt about an inch tall. We had lots of other innocent laughs in Bettabuys, opening doors during takes and walking into darkened rooms full of sides of frozen beef.

But after joining the *Street* there was one hunk of beef that I already knew in the soap ... Britain's answer to Bruce Willis, the delectable Des Barnes, alias heart-throb actor Phil Middlemiss. Now not many people know this, but Phil used to abuse me on a regular basis. Every night I'd be dressed up with my false boobs in place and up would pop young Phil for a grope. No, we weren't customers at some gay bar — this was behind-the-scenes high jinx before curtain call at the panto *Pinocchio* at Stratford in the late 1980s.

I was playing dame Lily Piccalili and Phil was playing the amorous Arri Verderci. It was great fun, but what the audience at Stratford East didn't know was that every time just before the curtain came up, Phil was manhandling me. He would pop out of nowhere, get me on the floor and give me a good squeezing. The whole cast found it hilarious. Then, as the curtains opened, he'd run off into the wings, leaving me like a prat on the stage floor.

Every night like clockwork I'd feel Arri's slippery hands groping my ample curves right on curtain call. No matter how guarded I was against him — Phil would just spring out and give me a tweak or two. That lad is so good-looking I could pull his face off and wear it myself — the girls would be screaming for him every night. Imagine what his *Coronation Street* postbag is like — he gets a sackful every day.

My own fan mail, I hasten to add, wasn't so bad either. There are lots of unofficial Reg Holdsworth Appreciation Societies dotted round Britain in pubs and clubs. I've been invited along to many a do and there was even a football team who called themselves something like the Reg Holdsworth select eleven. They asked me to turn out for them, but I thought I'd spare my fans the sight of my muscular thighs. The very mention of them has been known to send women weak at the knees.

But one woman I'd probably never be able to send weak at the knees was Hylda Baker. Before landing the *Street* role I'd done a series about the legendary funnyman Jimmy Jewel's life. I got on really well with Jimmy and we chatted about his career. He told me some astounding stories about Hylda Baker. The pair of them had a smash-hit comedy show when they played a brother and sister who ran a pickle factory, but hated each other off screen. Incidentally, *Coronation Street* scriptwriter John Stevenson was one of the writers on *Nearest and Dearest*, which was produced and directed by the *Street*'s legendary godfather, Bill Podmore.

But back to Jimmy, who recalled how one night Hylda turned up at a black-tie dinner with a toyboy. He was a Spanish waiter and they'd been having a great time together. Well,

Jimmy told me how in the middle of this meal she stood up and announced to the room: 'I'm just going upstairs now to get laid.'

To look at her, you'd think butter wouldn't melt in her mouth, but in the flesh she was so unpredictable. He told me working with her was a nightmare, but he had the dilemma that the show was a success and he didn't want to leave it. His advice was that if it ever happened to me I should put the boot in, or I'd end up suffering just like he had done. He wouldn't have shed a tear when Hylda died in May 1986. Yet to the world they were still the stars of *Nearest and Dearest*.

But by and large the women I worked with at Granada were, fortunately, nothing like Hylda Baker. It was my delight to work with the splendid actress Sarah Lancashire, who plays Raquel Wolstenhulme with great aplomb. She came into the show as Miss Bettabuys and obviously before her arrival Kevin and I were mad keen to know everything about her; important things like: 'Has she got big knockers?'

When she arrived at the end of 1990 we were both knocked out by this beautiful leggy blonde. The first time I ever saw her, she was being shown round the set by the director. He was being very professional and polite, obviously out to create the right impression as he pointed out all the technical aspects of the studio. I was with Kevin, and the second we walked through the door and saw her, we brushed past him, threw our arms round her waist and howled: 'Come 'ere, come 'ere. We like you — will you be staying with us?'

The director grunted and said: 'Please ignore them — they're just animals we've hired for the week.' To her credit, she wasn't fazed at all. She just threw back her head and laughed, playing us at our own game. Kevin and I had a field day when she landed the title Miss Bettabuys. She was to be filmed in a skimpy swimsuit, so we'd put our hands in the deep-freeze compartments until they went blue and as the cameras rolled we'd put our arms round Sarah. Every time she would hit the top C — the shrieks were hilarious.

But she'd always get her own back whenever we filmed in the Rovers. She'd dip her fingers in the beer and walk up beside us and start to massage our necks. It was very nice until you realized what it was that was running down your back. She remains one of the sexiest women on the *Street*, wearing the tiniest of mini-skirts and the highest of heels. But we've frequently informed her there is a price to pay for being beautiful. And the price is a groping. Anyone wishing to grope Raquel Wolstenhulme, please send a tenner to Reginald Holdsworth's Hands On School for Young Gropers, Weatherfield.

After a couple of weeks in the show I told Sarah she was set to become a cult figure in the soap, but she said: 'No, no, I'm only here for a few weeks.' How wrong can you get? She might play the dumb bimbo on the screen, but away from the cameras Sarah is pin-sharp. She is a devoted mother with two young sons and spends as much time with them as possible. Her brains are partly inherited from her father Geoffrey, who was one of the original scriptwriters back in the early days of *Coronation Street*. He is very proud of her and I'm told he'd love to write a script for her *Street* character.

When she landed the part of Miss Bettabuys she was popping up to see him in hospital after he'd suffered a stroke. He later revealed in *The Sun* newspaper how Sarah holding his hand and telling him funny stories from the studios helped him win his battle to live. He was the proudest man alive when he watched her *Street* debut from his hospital bed. He had been one of Granada's top scriptwriters and had devised the hit comedy shows *Foxy Lady* and *The Cuckoo Waltz*. The headline on the story was smashing: 'MISS BETTABUYS MADE ME BETTER'. And speaking of hospitals, her brother's a doctor.

But not all headlines can be so kind. I once got in a lot of bother after *The Sun* ran a story which screamed from the page: 'BET WAVED HUGE CUCUMBER ROUND AS I SAID MY LINES AND CHOKED BACK GIGGLES'. The Bet in question was Bet Gilroy, played by Julie Goodyear, who went ballistic when she saw the headline. But I was unaware of this when I was summoned to the producer's office. When I got upstairs to see the boss Carolyn Reynolds she was white with rage, livid.

Carolyn lost no time in telling me I had breached my

contract by discussing with a newspaper an incident that had happened behind the scenes. It struck me as very small cheese, because the bit about the cucumber was only a small paragraph in the whole article. But it was made very clear to me I had been an errant actor in discussing this vegetable. I soon discovered I was to be given a good thrashing. Not literally, you understand. Quite enough of the phallic imagery already, thank you very much!

No, the gravity of the situation was such that I would be disciplined in the form of the entire newspaper fee of £12,500 being confiscated and given to a charity of the producer's choice. This seemed to me to be grossly over the top, particularly as I had read several books by other members of the cast and the previous director, Bill Podmore, who had all relished discussing the careers of others in a more than frank and titillating manner. Nevertheless, after much to-ing and fro-ing involving Granada's legal department I decided against cashing the cheque and framed it. It took pride of place in the lavatory at our home in Park Road, where it now hangs beside a cheque from the BBC for thirty-six pence. I don't know which is worse.

At this point I felt a rift had been opened up between myself and the producer and certainly between myself and Julie Goodyear, who I understood had complained. After my caning in the producer's office Julie confronted me and blazed: 'What do you think you are doing? You don't discuss with newspapers what has gone on in the studios.' I told her I understood that now. It wasn't intended to be a vicious story — it was full of fun. Nobody I met, other than a couple of people at Granada, took it in any other way. I for one would love to be perfect.

Incidentally, here is the offending paragraph from the newspaper, so you can judge for yourselves: 'In another scene when the camera scanned off her and on to me she produced this massive cucumber to try and make me laugh. I kept a straight face, but it wasn't easy.'

The issue simmered on for quite some time. Stony silences ensued. It was all pretty silly, really. And the matter eventually subsided as all matters do. There were to be other petty problems, but the battle of the cucumber stood alone as the first case of much ado about nothing. Meanwhile, Holdsworth went from strength to strength as the scriptwriters and the viewers warmed to him.

Despite the bad feeling that later came about I will never forget my first ever scenes with Julie ... I was terrified. It was the first time I had set foot in the Rovers Return, and the script called for Reg to march in, grab Bet and Alma round their waists from behind and say: 'Can I buy you ladies a drink?' It was a dramatic entrance at the best of times, but faced with the vision of Julie with her famous bosom, piles of blonde hair and flashing teeth, it was all the more harrowing.

I really wanted to get it right, and I walked in there very strong and very positive. But halfway through the scene, the producer Mervyn Watson stopped filming and sent a note saying: 'You're playing it too posh.' I was absolutely furious, and right in front of Julie and Amanda Barrie, I lost my cool. 'What's wrong love?' they said. I replied: 'The bastard producer just told me I've got it completely wrong.'

Without batting an eyelid, Julie turned to me and said: 'Never mind, luv, go out and come back in again. It'll be all right.' That's just what I did — and it worked a treat. Later, after other scenes in the Rovers, she told me: 'You're a very frightening person to be with, do you know that?' I was stunned — it was a great compliment from the most awesome woman in showbusiness.

12

Street Strife

It had been a long day. Up before dawn to drive from our London home to Bettabuys in Salford for the *Street*'s regular Sunday filming. Two hundred miles plus on the road, followed by a full day in front of the cameras. The only break from the unremitting toil was the odd forty winks lying on the checkout desks, or even on a camp bed down the supermarket aisles. But by and large, no rest for the wicked and as I've already revealed, Kevin and I were wicked.

Filming finished late. But that was not unusual, because we only had the one day to record all the Bettabuys scenes. Every Sunday we took over Morrison's supermarket in Eccles. It had to be the sabbath as that was the only day it was closed to the public.

I was driving home listening to some late-1950s hits on the stereo when the inevitable happened. The clocks had gone forward at midnight, so I'd lost another hour of sleep. The M61 motorway wasn't the ideal spot to cat nap, but nevertheless I nodded off at the wheel.

I woke with a jolt — just after my beloved Cadillac Fleetwood hit forty concrete blocks on a pallet on the hard shoulder. A lesser car would have been totalled by the impact. I was very much awake as my machine took off. As I sat bolt upright there was nothing in front of me except sky, and there was no noise. Apparently the rumble of tyres on motorway ceases on take-off. It was the first time, and hopefully the last, that I'd ever gone flying in a Cadillac.

It's the lack of wings and joystick which gives you that sinking feeling as you sail through the air. I shouted inaudibly — I was in that much shock I couldn't get the words out. I was making Neanderthal sounds. You know it ain't going to be long before you return to terra firma … and, inevitably, you know it won't be a happy landing. It wasn't.

In a split second the horizon plunged, as the car went into a nosedive. It's funny how all accidents seem to happen in slow motion. The forty-five-foot drop from the embankment only took an instant. A parachute would have helped, but putting your feet on the brakes in mid-air is next to useless. Yet, instinctively, you do it all the same.

The next sensation is the smack in the nose as the steering wheel comes up to greet you. Simultaneously, the Cadillac smashed through a fence and hurtled into a field bordering the motorway. It was nothing short of a miracle that I got that far, because there must have been two tons of concrete on that pallet on the M61 on the outskirts of Bolton, Greater Manchester. If I'd hit that lot in a Mini, or any other car, I've no doubt I'd have been a goner.

I almost was. Blood was pouring down my face and I could smell petrol. I was in a good deal of pain after butting the dashboard, but I had to get out of the car. The chunks of concrete had ripped out the entire silencer system from the car and smashed the bonnet back in a V-shape, crushing the doors shut. I shouted: 'Give me a break, God. I am bad, but I'm not this bad,' as I desperately kicked my way out through a window. Seconds later the car started to sizzle — it was about to become a barbecue.

If I'd been a bit slower the newspapers could have had a field day: 'RANDY REG ROASTED ALIVE' — I imagined the front-page headlines the next day. Fortunately, other motorists had stopped to help and the fire amazingly never caught hold.

After stepping from the wreckage I just stood and gawped at what remained of the car. And then in the distance I heard a voice shouting: 'Are you all right? Shall I call for an ambulance?' I turned round and saw a lone man standing by a Volvo on the side of the motorway.

In reply I did an impressive jump in the air, a tap dance and then took a bow, shouting back: 'How does that look?' After escaping from the mangled motor the Good Samaritan must have thought my mind had gone. He did call for an ambulance, probably in the hope that men in white coats would come along for the lunatic who'd just had a crash and was dancing by the debris.

The police were the first emergency service on the scene. Miraculously, I had drifted from the middle lane, across the inner lane and over the hard shoulder without bumping into anyone else. The police officers who attended described me as 'very lucky'. They acknowledged my miracle escape, but it turned out I wasn't that fortunate. The boys in blue still booked me for driving without due care and attention.

Shortly afterwards an ambulance arrived. As the ambulanceman helped me inside, I noticed that my lips had swollen enormously. At the time I thought if they blacked me up now I could do a great Al Jolson. The only other time I have seen lips so inflated was after Lynne Perrie had her mouth stuffed with bits of her bottom. I'll never forget her appearance on the late night Channel 4 chat show *The Word* when she told presenter Terry Christian as he kissed her in greeting: 'You've just kissed my arse.' He didn't know what to say. When I later discovered it cost her nearly £3,000 to have the job done, I thought: 'If she'd asked me I could have showed her how to get the same effect for next to nowt. Take one large steering wheel and bash your face into it — hey presto!'

I arrived in the Bolton hospital's casualty department escorted by an ambulanceman. I had blood all over me, a swollen nose and giant lips. I reckoned it was the perfect disguise to keep the fans at bay. I was very obviously walking wounded, but the fact that I was a patient didn't prevent one determined fan approaching, pen in hand. Very politely she asked: 'You are who I think you are? Please can I have your autograph?'

I couldn't refuse, but fortunately the other patients and people with them realized I was in a great deal of pain and very kindly left me to suffer alone and get cleaned up in peace. It could have been the first autograph I'd ever signed in blood, but I thought the novelty of that might have caused a stampede.

I was given one pain-killing injection and the very next day I got a bill for £24 through the post. I was surprised when it dropped on the doormat, but apparently if you have a motorway accident you have to pay the medical bills because they are not covered by your fully comprehensive motor insurance.

Roughly six months later, on 25 October 1991, I found myself before the Bench at Bury Magistrates Court, Greater Manchester. I attended to take my punishment like a man.

I expected a big fine and a slapped wrist. Or maybe even two weeks on safari or a skiing holiday with the rest of the criminal community. But nobody had warned me that Hitler reincarnated had popped up in Bury. And the Justice of the Peace decided to make an example of me. A six-month driving ban was meted out. At one point I thought he was reaching for the black cap, but thankfully capital punishment wasn't a sentencing option on a motoring offence.

I was horrified. I had explained to the court that I had just nodded off for a couple of seconds and had no intention of doing the same thing ever again. I could have understood their action if I'd stood in the dock and told them I regularly kipped behind the wheel on the motorway and saw nothing wrong with it. Or if I'd told them that the M61 was an interminably boring road and every other driver on it was fast asleep, but that obviously wasn't the case.

I also explained my personal circumstances — that I had a wife and baby son in London and needed a car to visit them after filming in Manchester. But collectively the Bench was lacking a heart.

The saga didn't end there. Almost two years later, the Department of Transport sent me a bill for £211.88 for damage to the motorway fence. A hell of a bill for three strips of wood. They must have thought I was as thick as two short planks. I checked the damage. They only had to replace 12ft of fence and my local wood yard told me it would cost just £12 for three planks.

The damage bill was: nine metres of timber, £98.88; call-out charge, £81.11; general items, £14.40; plus a 'management fee', £17.49. The matter was resolved in the end, but the bill was scandalous. I guess the £14.40 for general items meant they used a lot of nails.

Incidentally, that was the second time I'd been asleep in a car during a crash. Only the first time, when I was seventeen, I wasn't driving. I was kipping in the back as my cousin Peter Riding chucked his MG Magnet round a rallying course. Anyway, he lost it at seventy miles per hour — somehow we both survived. The car finished up standing on end.

Peter was a renowned nutter. Once he failed to jack up his car properly and it fell on his fingers, severing them. On another occasion he injured himself after accidentally ramming my father's Saab. Another time he hit a bus at seventy miles per hour — once again, he was lucky to live.

But at the time of my 1991 court case, these accidents all paled into insignificance. At the time I had no idea how much heartache that driving disqualification was going to add to an already strained relationship. Long-distance love affairs are tremendously difficult things to cope with. But for Sue, having a young baby at home and a husband more than 200 miles away was no joke. Sleepless nights, piles of nappies — you name it, Sue suffered it.

Meanwhile, I was working hard as Reg and the character was really taking off. But the ban meant we had to spend up to six weeks apart as I worked six days a week at Granada. The more I think about it with hindsight, the more I know it must have been utterly horrendous for Sue. With Roger being our first, I had no idea just how much hard work a baby could be. At the time I had the blinkers on, simply slogging away at work and concentrating on my career.

There came a point when Reg was nearly killing Ken. I was

putting so much into the show that other things were going out of the window. I almost lost my family thanks to Reggie.

But Sue is a very intelligent woman and one day she just gave it to me straight: 'Either you take the relationship seriously or we will get a divorce.'

It was a bombshell. And her crisp and crystal-clear words shook me up enough to make me see sense. She told me firmly: 'We simply don't have a marriage any more, do we? You seem married to the job. There is no future for our relationship if you carry on living alone in Chorley for weeks on end. You have to either get a bigger house up there and we become a family, or that's the end and we get a divorce. It is as simple as that.'

I knew it was crunch time and realized the last thing I wanted to do was lose Sue and Roger. Her frank telephone call woke me up to the reality of the situation. I was living 240 miles away and suddenly it was made clear to me what my priorities should be. And that the facts of life are: family means being together. A marriage means being together — not miles and miles apart. I needed a family house in Chorley and immediately started searching for one.

I was living in a *Coronation Street*-style, two-up-two-down terrace in Hope Street just on the edge of Chorley town centre. It was a lovely cottage home and the neighbours were a great bunch, but there simply wasn't enough room for us to live there as a family. One room was used as an office and I couldn't turn that into a bedroom, as I needed somewhere to escape to learn my lines.

Thankfully I found a suitable house very quickly indeed. It was one of the big, four-bedroom, detached houses just up the road from my childhood home. That house saved my marriage. Sue gave up her teaching job in London and moved North. There are no regrets on either side. We agree that was one of the best moves we've ever made. Before that we were simply growing apart.

If that had continued, I'd have woken up one day minus a wife and son. And I'd been working so hard for them. Acting on *Coronation Street* requires total commitment to the job. The show is bigger than any one person and pushes other things aside. It means six days a week committed to work.

It was shortly after the spell when I hadn't been back for six weeks that things came to a head. It was 1992 and at the same time Roger had started to shy away from me. He would break my heart when I visited home by saying: 'There is a strange man, Mummy, who is he?'

I would come home and he would press himself against the wall and be terrified of me. My own son was recoiling from me, because he didn't know me. It was terribly sad and it was really getting to me. You don't want your children growing up not knowing you. It got worse before it got better. It got to the stage where I would come in and say 'Hello' and he either cried or ran away.

It was heart-breaking — there was just no sign of recognition at all. He was my boy, but I might just as well have come from another planet. The milkman and the postman got more recognition than me — at least Roger saw them every day. Things like that really bring home to you the predicament of working away from home. Most people have a desire to do the best for their kids, but I was perhaps doing too much. I had to slow down and get my life together.

Ever since Roger's birth I had been through a really grim time. I saw hardly anything of Roger for three or four months. Then I ended up getting a driving ban. Twelve months after my disqualification, Leslie Crowther, former host of *The Price is Right* and *Crackerjack*, suffered serious head injuries when his Rolls-Royce careered off the M5 in Gloucestershire. He was unconscious for seventeen days and his career written off by the crash, so I realized then just how lucky I had been.

After Roger's birth, Sue stuck in there and earned my eternal thanks. Any parent will tell you just how tough those early months are. The birth itself in London was a very traumatic time for us. His arrival was weeks late and Sue spent two days in hospital waiting for it to happen.

Roger finally arrived, as I said, the day before I had to return to Manchester to film the *Street*. I had to go off to Granada, leaving my wife and baby in the hospital. I left them knowing that I wouldn't be able to get back for at least two weeks, because of pressure of work. And as I've already outlined things got much tougher before we had any breakthrough.

Just as the strain on our relationship was peaking, I was undergoing another personal agony ... the death of my mother's companion Arthur Brown. I was barred from driving, so I was cycling to the railway station to get the train to the studios in Manchester. Then after work I'd get the train back and cycle to Chorley District Hospital to see Arthur and my mum — who were both stuck in there at the same time.

Mum was ill on one ward and Arthur was on another. He had been in hospital for quite a while. It was an awful time. Getting about took twice as long without the car and my time had to be divided so carefully. Mother had life-threatening stomach problems and needed urgent surgery.

Then things seemed to improve. Mum was on the mend and Arthur didn't appear to be getting any worse. My workload at the studios was very heavy and I was busy learning scripts.

I missed seeing Arthur for a couple of days. Nobody told me that during that time he had deteriorated and become very ill. He had throat cancer — they tried to replace it with a tube and found it was all over his chest. He didn't know.

But as soon as I found out, I walked out of filming at Granada TV to be by his side on the day he died. I had to be there, because I had made a mistake once by not being with my father on his deathbed. I wasn't going to make that same mistake again. I had basically bottled out of being with my dad and holding his hand when he passed away. I was still in my twenties and hadn't experienced death and, to be honest, I didn't want to. I fill up with tears now every time I think about it — even though it was over twenty-five years ago.

Not being with him is my greatest regret. I left him when I should have stayed. A few months earlier, he'd collapsed after carrying a huge toolbox across the workshop floor. He had a heart attack, but pulled round again. But what got him was his liver packing up, which was awful for a man who hardly drank. I'd told him to call an ambulance when he showed me liquid pouring from his pores.

On the night he died I got the call at 1 a.m. I went to the hospital in Preston and there was my father lying on this bed looking like an ordinary person who was gravely ill, not an image you ever really have of the parents who brought you up and were constantly there to support you.

Until that moment I had never realized I had limits. But I lost my bottle. I couldn't stand to be there with my own father. I ran out with tears in my eyes. I knew it was the end for him, but I lost my bottle and couldn't stay with him. I regret leaving him to this day. I weep every time I think about it, without fail.

I'm in tears now. They just pour down my cheeks. It is like turning a tap on. The legacy of grief is unbearable as the memories flood back about his early death at the age of fifty-seven. Thinking about the funeral makes things even worse for me, because in the North there is this tradition of bringing the coffin into the house on the day of the funeral.

I will never forget that day as long as I live. The coffin got brought in and then the lid was lifted off. There, under a white gauze, was my father. He was dead. There was no dressing it up — he was there in the box and everyone was filing past him.

I remember my mother walking up to the coffin, saying, 'Goodbye, love' and picking up his hand. That image breaks my heart — I'm sobbing now from the bottom of my soul. It is bloody twenty-five years ago, but I can still see it now. This awful emotion just comes over me; the tears are like a river running down my face. I will be all right in a minute.

When your parents die, it gets you. Nobody can prepare you for it. Your own children can't help you, your wife can't help you, your friends can't help you — it's just you and them. Death is one of the ultimate truths in life. It will happen to us all some day.

Every funeral contains that terrible truth — that we 'walk in the valley of death'. You don't analyse your life so deeply every day, so when you recall moments that really matter, it gets you.

When we were teenagers, Pete Smith and I took a couple of girls out for a goose at Goosnargh, near Preston. In the village churchyard we found a tomb with an inscription that stuck with us. It read: 'Remember man as you go by, as you are now, there once was I, as I am now you will be, so prepare yourself to follow me.' At the time we didn't realize just how spot on the words were.

Dad has already followed in those footsteps. He had suffered a warning heart attack a year or two earlier and had been hit by dreadfully painful rheumatoid arthritis before his death. He got the first heart attack when he was up a ladder doing some decorating. He was in the middle of a sentence when it happened.

He told me afterwards there was no pain. It was like somebody had switched the light off. He only remembered starting the sentence and then waking up afterwards in hospital with the surgeon telling him who he was as he was coming round.

He recovered and went back to work. It was then that he had the second heart attack. And it was then that he was given conflicting advice by a couple of specialists. The heart man told him not to take the steroids he was taking for the arthritis that had made his body swell so painfully.

But the arthritis specialist insisted there was no problem with the drugs. He took the heart specialist's advice and cut them out altogether — if it had been me I'd probably just have cut them down. But it is a sort of no-win situation.

With all this running round my mind, there was no way I could stay at Granada for the filming after getting a phone call saying Arthur was much worse. It was lunchtime on 21 February 1992, and I just walked out. It was something I had to do and Granada were very good about it. Arthur's death was one of those damned awful things. When I arrived at the hospital he was on his way out. I apologized to the guy.

He just managed to raise a hand. He was a bricklayer by trade and I couldn't help thinking how just three months earlier he had managed to build a shed with those hands. He had appeared so healthy as he was humping lumps of stone round. But there on that bed, he had a matter of a couple of hours to go. He was unconscious by the end. I just watched him becoming weaker and weaker and his breathing becoming slower and slower. It was the first time I had seen anybody die. I cried. You realize there is an end to life when you see it. It is like watching birth in reverse.

The worst part of it all is having to go away afterwards, pick yourself up and go and smile for the cameras. On the outside you are happy Reg Holdsworth, but on the inside you hurt like hell. Just hours after holding Arthur's hand as his life slipped away, I was back at the supermarket filming some of my funniest-ever scenes.

I was so sad, but I had to work. The show must go on. I was shaken to the core, yet I was filming the hilarious scenes where Reg realizes that the lovely Elaine Fenwick is the boss's daughter. I suppose life is like that for all of us — you get the laughter and the tears.

Arthur's death provoked a real mix of emotions inside me. He was like a father to me and was a great friend. I'll never forget the strange sensation I experienced when I first saw Mum hand-in-hand with him. It was total surprise when I clocked them strolling along a railway platform holding hands. I was suddenly the audience to an amazing love story.

Arthur had been the first love of her life over half a century before. But they split and both married other partners. Then, fifty years later, they bumped into each other again when my mum went for a cuppa in a café in Chorley. They hit it off straight away. She was a widow and he was a widower.

I remember once going home and catching them with their arms round each other in the kitchen. It was a very odd thing to witness — your mother in a love situation. It is difficult for children in that position. Arthur had asked Mum to go out with him, but before the romance developed she rang to ask me if it was all right. Of course it was — she'd been a widow for eighteen years. But it was funny as well as peculiar — imagine your own mother asking your permission before enjoying a date. I was very happy — actually overjoyed for her. Some people never find that great love — my mother was lucky enough to find it twice.

Those happy thoughts help you at a time of grief. There is solace in remembering the good things. But actors can also be a great comfort at times of crisis. A few days after his death I had the added trauma of Arthur's funeral. And right after that I went straight back into filming. The cast were wonderful. They all came up and gave me hugs.

I remember standing there on the set as they all came over and put their arms round me, thinking: 'If I worked anywhere else I'd probably get a few embarrassed mumbles or a pat on the back. These people aren't afraid to show they care — they're like a family.'

In August 1995 the whole cast rallied round again to give Sherrie Hewson support after her father Ron passed away at a MacMillan Nursing Home, following a lengthy battle against cancer. Just hours after his death, Sherrie was in the studios for filming. All the scripts revolved round the death of Poison Ivy Tilsley. It was all stuff about funerals.

I got in for a scene with Sherrie at about 11 a.m. As soon as I saw her I knew something was wrong, but being a true professional, she had turned in for filming. She was red-eyed and very distressed, as you are when a parent dies. I gave her a great big hug, offered my condolences and to help in any way I could. But even in the midst of all this grief, there was a comic element on the set minutes before we were to film. As we parted from the embrace Sherrie brushed her hand on the back of my head and displaced the wig.

She looked at me with my lop-sided toupee on and said: 'Ken, I don't believe it, I've knocked your wig off.' At any other moment just before the cameras rolled, we would have found it hilarious, but right then we weren't really in the mood for laughter, although Sherrie did have a twinkle in her eyes behind her tears. Other people came over and offered their sympathies after we'd filmed the scene. Everybody sympathized with poor Sherrie having to get involved in all the filming and dialogue surrounding Ivy's death after having lost her father in real life — and having a real funeral to prepare for.

That same *Coronation Street* family bond had been in evidence earlier in June 1991, when Bryan Mosley, who plays Alf Roberts, had a heart attack. The cast rallied round and got him a giant bouquet and sent their best wishes for a speedy recovery. We were all very concerned about him and a lot of prayers were said for him.

Bryan is a committed Christian and thanked God afterwards for helping him to pull through. Many of the cast went over to visit him at his home near Bradford, West Yorkshire, when he was released from hospital.

I was among those who popped over to cheer him up and let him know we were all missing him. We had a good chat and a cuppa. He was sitting in an armchair and we were talking quietly. Then, as I was leaving, I picked up a brolly from the hallway and waved it around my head. Without a second's hesitation, Bryan picked up a poker and fenced with me all the way down the hall.

We were thrashing about, like two ageing Errol Flynns, down the garden path when I suddenly realized what we were doing. The man was recovering from a heart attack and the pair of us were behaving like kids.

I thought: 'Oh God, what have I done? If anything happened I could never explain this to the doctors!' We've chortled about it since.

After what Bryan had gone through I thought about my own health — almost overnight my weight had rocketed. I decided to go on a diet, and announced this to my friends in the cast in total seriousness.

They were obviously all concerned — whenever I walked on to the set from then on, everyone started chanting in unison to the tune of *Knees Up, Mother Brown*: 'Who ate all the pies? Who ate all the pies? You fat bastard, you fat bastard, you ate all the pies!'

13

Raving in the Rovers

Coronation Street's millions of fans would love to witness the
fun their favourite characters have away from the cameras. And
boy do we have *fun*. Some of the scenes that are screened are
hilarious, but the unedited highlights are often much funnier.
Many fans split their sides at Reg and Maureen's attempted
romp on his waterbed. You'll remember that Derek Wilton
punctured their passion by drilling through the Kabin ceiling
into Reg's flat and putting a hole in his waterbed.

But away from the cameras there were even more chortles.
Sherrie Hewson, who plays Maureen, is a magnificent actress
and we hit it off as a double act straight away. She has a
marvellous intuitive talent and a brilliant sense of humour.
People say she'd need that to marry Reg. I was forever winding
her up.

During the legendary waterbed scene I hid a lump of rotting
cheese in my underpants. Never mind the funniest scene in
soap history — it was certainly the smelliest. Before the
director called action, I placed a pungent piece of Gorgonzola
into my briefs. It should have knocked Sherrie out — as she
had to crawl under the covers passing this over ripe cheese. I

was gagging, because the smell was that atrocious. But she never even wrinkled her nose. Little did I know that she had a terrible cold, so that prank backfired.

I was very peeved that I'd endured this smell and Sherrie had missed it, so I didn't tell her about it that day. It was three weeks later when the episode was screened that I confessed. She thought it was hilarious and she said: 'Serves you right, you fat bastard.'

Sherrie's strongest points are her tremendous timing and razor-sharp observation. Throughout the waterbed period I became very conscious about my weight. It was sparked by me catching a televised shot of myself draped in a towel — I looked as if I'd eaten an elephant. The cameras always exaggerate your size, but in those waterbed shots I was obviously obese.

Sherrie was a tower of strength. I asked her: 'Will you still love me when I'm old and fat?' Quick as a flash she replied, 'You are old and fat' and then she tapped me on the head and said: 'You're bald as well.' It really was a tonic, just what I wanted to hear, I don't think. I'd already suffered the embarrassment of having a towel drop by accident during the rehearsals. The recording of that was played out over all the TV screens at Granada, although it didn't get broadcast.

The lads behind the scenes are not averse to a bit of gentle fun either. They once omitted to switch the waterbed heater on before I jumped in for a scene. I leapt on to this bed and it was like jumping into the Atlantic — freezing cold. I still had to deliver my lines, but was absolutely frozen. I only had a towel on round my middle and it made everything stand up.

Talking of standing up, I remember another scene where I'd spent the best part of half a day in bed with Sherrie. The beautiful actress who plays my screen wife turned to me and asked: 'Is that your leg?' With a devilish look in my eye I replied: 'No.' She said no more, but kept firmly to the other side of the bed.

Sherrie has a real gift, but as well as her acting ability she has a very definite accident-prone streak. If a door can fall off its hinges, or a drink spill, then Sherrie will be there. She is an involuntary puncher, pincher, slapper and puller-off of wigs. Her real-life husband is a smashing chap called Ken and he sympathizes with the physical punishment her clumsy streak often inflicts on me. If somebody handed her a hydrogen bomb ... she'd drop it.

I recall once standing on *Coronation Street*, waiting for Sherrie and there was a cat perched on a pillar box beside me. Sherrie suddenly ran towards me and pushed the cat into my head — she didn't realize it was a concrete cast. It hurt like hell. She was ever so apologetic. She had meant it as a joke and must have thought it was a real cat. She almost knocked me out cold. I didn't laugh at the time, but I can see the funny side now.

Sometimes when she is having nightmares she shouts out, 'Ken!' and her husband wonders which of us she's talking about. He has to wake her up to find out which one she's shouting for. I have to say he is better-looking than me, but then again I am fatter than he is.

Sherrie and I share a lot of little secrets on the set. There was a time when I was worried about baldness and she was thinking of having a facelift. She cruelly suggested I could comb the hair on my bottom upwards and on to my head. I reckoned she'd save a fortune by applying a bulldog clip to the top of her head, or a two-inch self-tapping screw to the back of her neck which she could adjust every morning.

Of course the most famous facial surgery in *Street* history happened when Lynne Perrie plumped for lip implants. Her pumped-up lips gave her the look of a baboon on heat. As I've mentioned earlier, I could have attained the same amount of swelling for next to nowt by slamming a door in her face. Nobody could believe it when these remarkable lips walked into the studios, followed fifteen minutes later by the rest of Lynne's face.

We've all heard the expression you've got to be cruel to be kind; well, we were just cruel to be cruel. There was nothing anybody could say. She silenced the green room when she came in. Now that's what is known as an entrance in the business. At first people weren't sure it was Lynne behind the lips, but she's only 4 ft 11ins tall so through a process of elimination we decided it had to be her. The lips were that large that some unkind wags suggested she was in danger of toppling over, because they made her that top-heavy.

I don't think she honestly knew just how large they were; we all thought she was losing her marbles. Apparently, she'd had the first lot of implants done at the Christmas before and returned to work looking healthy after the break. Ironically, her first scenes with her new-look lips were Holdsworth's wedding, but she hadn't had too much fat pumped in.

She said later the only pain she had during the process was the twenty-four knives she felt in her back after leaving the green room. Well it was more like forty. Every time she left the room, somebody would pick up an old picture frame that was left lying around and pull the most hideous face imaginable. Or even more wickedly, bend over and shove their bottom through the frame. Everyone was trying to do the best Lynne impression. It was a craze for several days, if not weeks. But we all knew the bosses upstairs would not be best pleased with their new-look star.

Changing your appearance, so you only bear a passing resemblance to the character you were before, is one of the surefire ways of losing your job in a long-running soap. Can you imagine Holdsworth arriving at the studios after a spot of liposuction? 'No' is the answer; he is a hard-working fat bastard who wouldn't spend his cash on that. The fact that the surgery also left Lynne unable to speak properly didn't help either. Though to give her her due, those lips did deflate quite considerably after a few days. But the press still had a field day slapping her new face all over the newspapers.

But everybody was still stunned and quite a bit shocked when she did finally get the bullet on 7 March 1994. She'd given them twenty-three years. Nobody envied Carolyn Reynolds the job of telling Lynne, after all those years of learning lines, that she was no longer needed. No wonder she decided to publish a warts-and-all book, *Secrets of the Street*. When Granada tried to stop its publication, the whole cast was shocked. They dreaded Lynne, who always maintained she wasn't sacked, exacting her revenge on them. Books had been published before and if they'd had that book banned then where would the rest of us stand with tomes about our own lives? When they failed to stop it there was a sense of relief and many realized for the first time that the TV company couldn't control them for ever. Some, whose secrets were revealed in the book, however, had a different view of things.

I found it all good knock-about stuff. I first came up against Lynne when her character Ivy Brennan had a job at Bettabuys. Now in the show she was a pious Catholic woman, but in real life Lynne was a raucous, raunchy lady. I had a reputation as the show's blond-haired, blue-eyed sex god, so Lynne singled me out for some special attention.

She was a larger-than-life character. On this particular day, we were sitting in a trailer learning our lines when Lynne asked me out of the blue: 'So do you fancy me, then?' I replied: 'Of course I fancy you, Lynne.' Without hesitating she picked up a steel fork, walked across the room and used it to prod me in the nuts. Then she shook her head and said: 'So you don't fancy me that much then ... '

Lynne dressed like a Hollywood movie star of a bygone age — arriving in the morning in a convertible Mercedes, dressed in shiny sequinned dresses, bedecked in diamanté and gold jewellery. The whole set seemed so much quieter when she'd gone. I looked around the other day and realized the rest of us wear rather more casual clothes, and I thought of Lynne in all her splendour. I really missed her. I remember her once walking into my dressing room after I installed the ladies' loo sign on the door. I had the lights off and was sitting in darkness. I'd tried the prank on a couple of the other female members of cast and they'd run a mile. So I said to Lynne: 'Come here, little girl.' She came right for me and this time I was the one who ran a mile.

There are two types of actors and actresses in the business at the level of *Coronation Street*. There are those who have a sense of humour as well as a great talent and then there are those who have the talent, but are absolute shits as human beings. Lynne wasn't one of the latter. She was a lively, talented and attractive actress, who was great fun to be with.

But I must confess after her collapse in the green room on 7 June 1993, Lynne never seemed the same again. There was a definite degeneration and it happened very rapidly. I was very sad to see the changes in her after her illness. She did her best to beat it and had stopped drinking. Now when I first came to the show she could sup for Britain, but she knocked the brandy and Babycham on the head for the sake of her health. These days she hardly touches a drop. I hear she's healthier since she left the show and enjoying life more than ever, so her fans needn't worry that she's suffered since leaving the *Street*. Everyone chuckled when they saw her dressed up as a nun in a Sunday newspaper on the week her character was set to die on screen in August 1995. Some of her co-stars would have quite enjoyed her wake after what she said about them.

Amazingly, Lynne never seemed to like Liz Dawn, despite playing opposite her character, Vera Duckworth, for years. She said some very hurtful things about her on occasions, but Liz is a forceful woman and never took them lying down. This brings me to Liz's way of hiding her lines round the set. Now we all have different ways of concealing our scripts from the cameras. I fold mine in half and hide it in my breast pocket so I can sneak a look. Bill Waddington rolls his into a scroll, but Liz has her own unique method.

She meticulously cuts up her scripts into neat little squares, sticks them on to bits of cardboard and then hides them all around the set, so she can say her lines word-perfectly. You'd never guess her lines were hidden in between baked bean cans on the supermarket shelves, or under a teacup. This sums Liz up — everything about her is neat and immaculate. I love watching her arrive looking a million dollars, with wonderful make-up, designer clothes and perfect hair. Then she walks into the make-up department and walks out as down-at-heel Vera Duckworth. The blokes on the cast nickname make-up the cryogenic chamber, because of the way the women are transformed in there.

But Sherrie, who plays Maureen, looks a stunner before and after her treatment in make-up. I recall once having a very risqué chat — between myself, Sherrie and Kevin — tannoyed round the Morrison's store in Eccles during Sunday filming. Fortunately that was one broadcast that the viewers never saw. We were joking in the supermarket manager's office about the sexual positions you could try out in such a big shop with such a wide range of different counters. We started saying we'd really like to do it with Sherrie, so she answered back: 'I don't think I fancy both of you on the meat counter.' And we got much more fruity than that, believe me. It was only afterwards when we all walked out and the crew were laughing that we got told the whole conversation had been broadcast on the store intercom. The smiles soon vanished from our faces at the thought of the producer being privy to that little lot.

We're both lucky that Liz Bradley, who plays Maud Grimes, has a sense of humour, because we had some great fun with her wheelchair. When she wasn't looking we used to switch it to full power and she'd shoot across the set at top speed. One day she delivered her lines and pressed the chair's forward button expecting to roll sedately out of camera shot. Instead she raced across the studios like Damon Hill through shelves of stacked tins and other props. Her face was a picture. And her language wasn't what viewers expect from a grey-haired lady. Another time we pulled the prank in the Rovers Return and she shot straight past the camera crew.

When she first got the chair, it ran away with her. When we did the scenes in her house, they were filmed in the real-life home of a couple from Irlam O' The Heights in Salford. It was side-splitting stuff. She had only just been introduced to the wheelchair and she was ramming into the furniture at ten miles per hour, because she couldn't control it. The couple who owned the house were sat in the background, and every time she hit the furniture, there'd be an exclamation from them. She took lumps out of everything. Granada TV, of course, paid them for the damage, but to see Liz hurtling into the doors, walls, tables and chairs was high comedy.

Japes and high jinx are always at a premium in the festive season — a spirit of fun pervades every workplace, including Granada TV's famous Manchester studios. Some of the funniest scenes I did in Bettabuys happened at Christmas time with Bill Waddington dressed up as Santa Claus. Now there's probably nothing more improbable than *Street* grump Percy Sugden as Father Christmas and that's why the scenes were so funny.

The most hilarious were when he played Santa and Reg acted the part of a little girl on his knee. Percy said: 'And what would you like for Christmas?' I told him: 'One of those talking dollies, that speaks when you pull a string and cries when you turn it upside down.' Percy said: 'That's a lot of money. Are you sure you deserve it.' Reg then had to give him a rollicking, telling him that would frighten off the customers. I only hope my mind is as nimble as Bill's when I'm in my seventies.

He's one of the old school of comics with a list of gags as long as his arm and a memory to match. He's got a reputation among the cast for being slightly mean, but I've seen him hand over as much as twenty pence in one go. He's a bit of a gambler and likes racehorses. I also heard he'd been praying for a big win on the National Lottery, but after a couple of weeks he'd still not won. He said a prayer again and the clouds parted and a booming voice came down from the heavens, saying: 'Please Bill, meet me halfway and buy a ticket.'

When he got the job as a lollipop man, one of the behind-the-scenes wags set him up for a spot of fun by tampering with his prop — the lollipop stick. Bill walked out into the studios with it and everyone started laughing. Some joker had stretched a condom over the top of it and Bill hadn't noticed. It was very funny, seeing Percy stood there with a contraceptive on his stick. Needless to say the viewers never got to see that.

But as I've said, Christmas was often the time for fun and games. Yet one piece of tomfoolery I inspired landed both myself and Kevin in hot water with the producer. It was at the Bettabuys Christmas bash, being filmed at the posh Pott Shrigley Hall hotel in Cheshire. Fooling about, I made an entrance down a magnificent sweeping stairway and pronounced to the extras and waiting crew: 'I'm a little fairy and my name is Fair Enough. When I get down these stairs I'm going to kiss your muff.'

When I reached the bottom I realized there was a deathly hush and a sea of unfamiliar faces were staring up at me, open-mouthed. The worst thing about it was that I couldn't stop Kev, who was following behind in a similar fashion. He pranced down the stairs saying: 'I'm that fairy's sister and my name is Little Nell and when I come down the stairs I'm going to do it as well.'

At the bottom he too stopped dead. The hotel manager had a look of horror on his face. And the dozens of people we thought were extras were in fact hotel guests. We were immediately called aside by the producer and warned about our behaviour. It was a genuine case of high spirits in our usual bad taste — backfiring in a big way.

But on another occasion it was a *Street* producer who ended up looking a bit of a plonker. It was at one of the early Christmas parties and we were all in a big room in the studios, getting well oiled. One of the guys threw some soda water at Sean Wilson, who plays Martin Platt, but missed him and hit the then *Street* boss Mervyn Watson. Well, Mervyn swung round in a severe temper and offered to take Sean's mate outside for a thumping. The next day when Mervyn came in he was the subject of much ribbing. By that time he had been told the incident was a mistake and it was a case of him being jackassed. He took the ribbing in good heart, but soon after he migrated to the BBC. After a spell there, he returned North, to a top job with Yorkshire Television based in Leeds.

The incident with the soda siphon leads on nicely to the bizarre behind-the-scenes crazes that spring up at *Coronation Street* from time to time. One of the all-time favourites during my time was for the cast to carry water pistols and ping-pong-ball-firing guns around for spare-moment gunfights.

Some of the most moving scenes in *Coronation Street* in recent years have been played out by stars with plastic toy guns tucked into their trousers. The second the cameras stop, the firing starts, as all the famous names in the show pelt each other with ping-pong balls across the set.

Everyone on the *Street* loves a good gunfight. The trend started after we nicked a lot of pistols and water guns from the children who play the sons and daughters in the show. It got so bad that the bosses at *Coronation Street* built a dividing wall between the areas where the actors go for coffee and the children's area. They either sit with their tutors there or play. But we showed them that we were bigger kids than them with all our fun and games.

Yet the dividing wall wasn't enough to stop us. Phil Middlemiss went through a phase of dressing up as Zorro in a mask and cape and maniacally firing his guns. It could get you like that. Everyone else hid their guns under their waistbands or behind their backs during their scenes, because they knew they faced being zapped as soon as the filming finished.

The favourite guns were the ones with the ping-pong balls, but some of the others used had little plastic arrows with suction tops. Cast members used to arm themselves, then sit in the TV room watching the others acting out their scenes. Whenever there was a sad or traumatic moment, everyone would whip out their guns and we would shower the television with missiles. There's been many a famous or harrowing scene which has ended with the leading lady in the middle of the TV screen ... with a plastic arrow on her forehead.

This summer just gone, the craze has been cricket on the bowling green outside the studios, during the lunch break. The year before, we were even more upmarket with games of croquet. This year the fad has led to the emergence of a Coro XI cricket team. Charlie Lawson, who plays Jim McDonald, captained the squad and I believe they were not disgraced.

Talking of which, the most disgraced star in the cast has to be young Simon Gregson, who plays *Street* tearaway Steve McDonald. He is an extremely good actor with the potential to make it in movies — he's the soap's equivalent of James Dean. He held his hands up about his cocaine habit, but I must confess he never offered any to me, the miserable swine. But then again, show me an actor who hasn't indulged in something he shouldn't.

One of his finest performances was peeing off the balcony of a hotel in Majorca. It gave a whole new meaning to the term Spanish Fly when he unzipped his pants and anointed the residents below. For that he scored an eight out of ten in my book. We all must remember that Charles II and Samuel Pepys were up to the same tricks before him. Pepys was fined for doing exactly the same thing in London. And neither of those two did too badly out of it.

Young Simon has always had more fan mail than the rest of us put together, mostly from pre-pubescent girls offering to get their kit off for him. As I know, that kind of frenzied activity can be tiring, so I've often offered to help him with his fan mail and his fans. But I find that just reading the letters leaves my hands shaking too much.

Nick Cochrane, who plays his screen twin Andy, is the more settled and sensible of the two. He is a talented actor in his own right and will be around for a long time. Andy not only has integrity, but has a great sense of humour. On my fiftieth birthday he came up to me and said: 'You're fifty today, aren't you?' I said: 'Yes, I really am. I'm beginning to feel quite old.' At which he said: 'Never mind pal, let me give you this.' And at that point he stuck his tongue right in my ear. I've tried it several times myself, but people keep hitting me.

But one of the greatest young talents to walk through the doors at Granada in recent years was the perfectly formed actress Eva Pope, who played temptress Tanya Pooley. Now all the blokes at Granada drooled after Eva, along with all the red-blooded males who tuned into the show. She was superbly put together and knew she was phenomenally good-looking and loved the reaction she always got from walking into a room.

Eva used to suck her thumb, which made her look very young, sweet and innocent. I'll never forget the first time I met this stunning woman. I was standing in the green room during my tea break when I suddenly heard someone running up behind me. It was Eva, who launched herself in the air, landed on my back and wrapped her legs tightly round my waist. She shouted in my ear: 'Is this the fat bastard, then?' After that I too was in love. Millions of blokes would have given their back teeth to have Eva jump on them. She was forever sneaking up on male members of the cast and leaping on them.

The other *Street* star the blokes go mad for is Beverley

Callard, who is known on the set as the woman with the Betty Grable legs. Movie star Betty Grable insured her pins for a million dollars and with inflation Beverley's must be worth ten times that. Her flame-red hair and perfect complexion make her many a man's fantasy. She also has a very waspish waist and a wonderfully sexy wiggle.

Another young member of the cast with star quality is Chloe Newsome, who plays Victoria Arden. I have seen her develop into one of the finest young actresses on *Coronation Street*. She doesn't suffer from any nerves at all. She came in as a really young girl, chaperoned by her mother. But she went and played with great confidence opposite the very formidable Julie Goodyear and the stalwart performer Roy Barraclough, who played Alec Gilroy, in some very demanding scenes.

She has also turned into a real stunner and is very desirable. Recently she made my day when she came to work in a pair of skin-tight platinum lycra leggings. She told me: 'I've also got them in a different colour.' I asked her if she'd wear them the next day and sure enough she turned in wearing a pink pair. I was thrilled. At the moment her portrayal of the spoilt brat of the *Street* is a superb performance.

Angela Griffin, who plays hairdresser Fiona Middleton, has rightly been named Best Newcomer in a Soap. Her *Street* boss Denise Black, who plays Denise Osbourne, is another very talented actress. The scenes Denise did with Don during the sex-pest saga were superb. She introduced a great element of fear into the portrayal of the victim. And Geoff Hinsliff, as Don Brennan, was brilliant. He played the malevolent monster as well as the happy hopalong grandad.

Another couple of stars who have a hidden side are Eileen Derbyshire and Thelma Barlow — who play the show's screen prudes Emily Bishop and Mavis Wilton. Viewers might be surprised to discover that both of them are fond of a belly-laugh. Eileen is a very funny lady despite her reputation for being a very private person. She has a dry sense of humour and a great sense of the ridiculous. If your trousers fell down she'd be the first to laugh.

Thelma is another who enjoys a laugh. She is very keen on

organic gardening and has even written a book on the subject. But she burst out laughing when I asked: 'Isn't organic gardening what people do when they stop having sex?'

Granada is like Hollywood's old MGM Studios, with a collection of fine stars. More stars than there are in the firmament, as they used to say.

Of course, one of the *Street*'s biggest stars, apart from myself, was Julie Goodyear — who impressed with her performance and her two most valuable assets. Her breasts were nicknamed Newton and Ridley and they were a fine pair. They still are, I hasten to add, because I once had the pleasure of filming opposite them. My eyes were on stalks and these boobs were just eight inches away from my face. It took me two weeks to get my eyes back into their sockets.

It was one of the hardest scenes I have ever had to do, because of the enormity of what was in front of me. It was also a very funny scene, but because of the proximity of her bosom to my face the clips ended up on the cutting-room floor. I have often dreamed about making love to Julie Goodyear — hasn't everyone? — but unfortunately as I'm on the enormous king-size bed just moments away from a stupendous orgasm a giant axe appears and cuts short my pleasure.

Julie is dynamite on legs and has tremendous presence and natural beauty — she can walk into rooms and stop the conversation. If Julie walked through the middle of the worst battlefield on earth, every soldier would lay down their arms and stand to attention. She has that effect on men.

She is a very powerful woman and, as I've mentioned before, I am drawn to powerful women. But whenever I have attempted to get frisky and place a moist kiss on her cheek she has kneed me swiftly in the testicles, laughing as I fell to the floor.

Another lady with enormous presence and talent is Barbara Knox, who plays Rita Sullivan. She comes into the studios, does the business, and goes home. Her performance as the battered woman in scenes with Alan Bradley, played by Mark Eden, earned her the coveted BAFTA award and well-deserved it was too.

It was great early on in the series playing scenes with her. She is supremely confident and capable of putting enormous emotion into every scene. True professionals, we ran through all our scenes more or less word perfect without any rehearsal. A superb actress, she can play comedy followed by some of the most heart-rending scenes imaginable. Barbara must be a scriptwriter's dream — whatever they throw at her, she does with immense panache. I often said if we'd met twenty years ago we'd have been the greatest trapeze act in the business.

We were both reduced to tears in one scene that millions of TV viewers saw during the early days when Reg was romancing Rita. Reg took her to a tea dance, where a group of pensioners waltzed with them around the room. But Barbara and I wept after watching the elderly men and women dancing.

We had turned up to film on location and found this group of pensioners who we assumed were extras. When the cameras stopped rolling I asked the director, Brian Mills, where he'd hired them. He told me he had popped down to a local old folks' centre in his lunch hour and had found all these pensioners playing bingo. The star prize they all wanted to win so badly was a £1.29 box of teabags.

He was so moved by seeing them in such dire straits that he instantly offered them the chance to appear as extras — for £50 a head. I suddenly realized why all these so-called extras had looked so happy. They'd not only been given the money, but they'd been given the opportunity to appear in their favourite soap — and for a day they could all be someone special.

The story was heart-breaking for me. I walked away with a lump in my throat — I was that moved. I went and told Barbara, who was equally overcome. Both of us went back downstairs and signed autographs for the whole lot.

During those tea dances with Barbara I had to keep a tight grip on myself, because I found to my amazement I was getting frisky. I was getting aroused by Barbara, because she possesses such eroticism, style and flair. I have always responded to that and here I was being filmed for millions of viewers getting a stiffy while I was dancing with her.

But the music was romantic, and I was playing Randy Reg,

who was trying his best in the soap to rumple Rita. As the music played on, I became more and more entranced by this enchanting woman in my arms. The rest of the world didn't matter. I was waltzing with Rita and I had become Reg. His character had taken over me completely and I had stiffened with the prospect of a roll in the flat above the Kabin. It got a real grip on me and I eventually had to slip out round the back and adjust myself. If it gets hold of the actors like that, what does it do to the viewers?

There is always a moment in a really good script where you get sucked into what your character is going through, although I must confess I've never been aroused in that way before — at least not on screen. It was a combination of the skilful writing and the beautiful Barbara that brought it on.

It happened in a different way to Kevin Kennedy — no, you mucky lot, he didn't get physically excited over me. But his reaction made one short scene burst into life for all of us. Reg had walked into the Rovers and was telling Curly he had got the job of manager that he wanted so badly.

We rehearsed the scene first and when Reg broke the news Kevin followed the script, clicked his fingers and said: 'Yes.' But when it came to the real take Kev threw his arms into the air and started shouting, 'Yes, yes, yes,' in pure joy and excitement. I was stunned: it was a superb reaction and it came straight from the heart. Afterwards I turned and said: 'You really believed that, didn't you?' He grinned sheepishly and said: 'Yes, I loved it.' I knew it was genuine because that is exactly what I did when I got my *Street* role.

Another time he was delighted was when I had to adjust myself on my fiftieth birthday. It was the day when the whole cast got their revenge on me for all my awful pranks. At the mid-morning tea break I was called downstairs to take a phone call. I walked into the room and everyone else was in there. Standing in the middle was a huge busty woman in leather, wielding a huge whip. She said: 'Come here, Ken, and receive your punishment.'

She ordered me to remove my trousers and I immediately became a slave. I took the lot off. I was stood there in my underwear in front of all the *Street* legends. I was ever so thankful my undies weren't full of holes. I then was made to bend down and take my beating, which everybody loved. They all cheered when she made me pull off her clothes with my teeth.

I have, as I've mentioned, been called into the boss Carolyn Reynolds' office for bits of discipline after being seen to have overstepped the mark. But I must confess I enjoyed my public flogging far more than any of the private ones in the *Street* boss's office. Kevin, who had ordered the strippogram, was beside himself with laughter as were the rest of my colleagues in the cast.

When his birthday came along Kevin spent the whole day on edge — waiting for somebody to jump out on him. He was a bit surprised when I gave him a watch. It was something he'd wanted, but it should also tell him .... there's still plenty of time for me to get my revenge!

14

Reggiemania

Everybody's heard of Beatlemania and nowadays everyone's heard of the pop group Take That. A phenomenon on a similarly colossal scale is Reggiemania, the unadulterated adoration of British soap's strangest superstar ... Reg, not me, but him. Women clamour for a squeeze of the bulging tum, or a wisp of the thinning hair — how else do you think a stud like me could go bald?

It is the constant pawing by the fans, the bared boobs for me to autograph, the inner thighs requiring the signature Reg. All these things can lead to premature reaction ... whether it be hair-loss, ageing or ejaculation. At its peak Reggiemania was a monster — a bit like the man himself. The Reg Holdsworth tee-shirt, emblazoned with the slogan 'Knowledge is Power', outsold sales of tee-shirts by all the pop bands in 1993, including Take That. A staggering 160,000 of those particular Reg tee-shirts were sold.

The term Reggiemania for the baying mobs of female fans that turned up at my personal appearances was conceived on a wringing-wet day in Grimsby. Yes, home to the fishing trawler, seagull droppings and the stench of stale skate. In this once thriving port the women are man-mad after packing their sailor husbands off to sea for a month at a time.

I was caught up in the middle of this madness. Women, and some blokes for that matter, began to scream like banshees. 'Reggie, Reggie, Reggie,' the chant went up, rising in a crescendo as I stepped from the stretch Lincoln Continental for the supermarket opening. Pete was driving and said he hadn't seen anything like it since the day Billy Fury visited Preston and the town stood still. That was the 1960s, but here we were in the 1990s and I was the marvel of the moment.

Time indeed stood still for us as we struggled through the heaving bosoms and the pouting lips — and that was just the sailors on shore leave. Take it from me, it was mayhem. A frenzied throng with only one thing on their minds: touching or even taking home a piece of Reggie. The latent sexuality of the fat bastard was making the women go faint. The crush was making me go dizzy as somebody slipped another knocker under my nose for signing, simply, 'Reg'.

The man was a magnet, a real animal. A cross somewhere between a slippery snake, a horny bunny and a Manx kipper. Reg was a reptile and they loved to watch him slither. Some sharp-eyed journalist on the *Grimsby Evening Telegraph* brought the scene to life with the simple headline: 'REGGIEMANIA'. It was 27 March 1993 — a day in history that put Grimsby high up on the Reg Holdsworth map.

This had been happening to me for months away from the Granada Studios. My personal appearances were in demand everywhere from St Ives to Inverness, and across the Irish Sea it was much the same. I was shuttling round Britain in my American cars like a pop star on tour. The sexual offers were remarkable — I'd never have had the energy to supply all their demands. Anyhow, I'm married and my physical philandering is behind me, although just like the next man I can still enjoy a good old-fashioned grope.

Reg Holdsworth had by this stage become a cult figure. Thousands of pirate tee-shirts featuring yours truly were being flogged at pop concerts throughout Britain. The gaffe for the pirates was blown when trendy adult comic *Viz* started advertising on the back: 'Get your Reggie tee-shirts, only £10.99'. One of the pirates even went on local radio in Leeds bragging how he'd sold 11,000 of them in one month alone. Granada's response to such blatant money-making was to slap injunctions on the manufacturers. But that ain't easy if they are illegal back-street businesses.

Fed up with the attitude of the *Street*'s management when it came to marketing the nation's number-one soap, I minced upstairs to have it out with the boss. I was going to say some pretty unsavoury things, like: 'Why don't Granada make some money out of this?' 'Why can't the actors get a share?' and 'Do we have a proper marketing department?' Now Granada TV had been used to making loot out of TV and to that degree it made lots of it. But I thought the business needed bringing into the 1990s, where there was a tidy shilling to be made out of marketing products based on the TV shows.

Reg had proved that a character could sell. A short time after this showdown meeting, a London-based agency called Wood Collins were appointed to the marketing arm of Granada TV. The company was about to start making serious cash — and why not? What's good enough for Warner Brothers and Walt Disney should be good enough for Granada.

Carolyn Reynolds, now an executive producer, even addressed a trade gathering at Birmingham's National Exhibition Centre as Granada honed its marketing skills in time for a big push before the thirty-fifth anniversary celebrations for *Coronation Street*. I am happy and proud to say I was in the vanguard of this marketing philosophy.

My personal appearances were an individual way of selling on the product that the people loved on screen. The supermarkets, nightclubs, or wherever, were paying £2,000 or £3,000 a time for actor Ken Morley, but the fans who packed the venues out on every appearance were chanting for Reggie. They loved him and he loved them and the wonga they helped him make.

In 1993, after just three years in the show, I was given the ultimate accolade by fans throughout Britain ... the title of the Best Actor Ever in Soap. Thousands upon thousands of *Street* fans need thanking for handing the title over by voting for me in the *TV Times*'s biggest ever poll. The magazine was celebrating its twenty-fifth birthday. I got Best Actor Ever, a remarkable achievement after such a short space of time. And Julie Goodyear was rightly given the other top gong for being the Best Actress in Soap History. We were crowned the King and Queen of Soap. My award hangs at home in the lounge; I look at it and think of the fans who made it possible. From the bottom of my soul I owe them an ever so big thank-you.

I may appear a blundering barmpot in the role of Reg, but under the bluster I'm really a big softie. I am a very emotional human being. Sue cites my tears after our Lancashire heeler Fritzi died as the side of my personality that the hundreds of thousands of fans never see. It was November 1993, when poor Fritzi was mown down outside our home in Chorley. I cradled him in my arms and was in a state of shock after he was hit by a car. The driver slammed the brakes on and I shouted, but it was still too late for Fritzi. I was absolutely devastated: I was cuddling him and saying over and over again: 'My dog, he killed my dog.'

I felt responsible for his death, because I'd taken him out for a walk. I was sobbing and the sight of me made Sue cry as well. The next day we buried Fritzi in the garden and planted a lovely shrub on his grave. Sue said that it is this loving and tender side, that nobody else sees, that she likes most in me.

But that's not the side the fans know and love. They want the raunchy, the raving Randy Reg, so I give him to them by the bucketload. One recent whistlestop tour of Ireland was a fine example of the Reggie roadshow in action. My big pink Cadillac covered 1,200 miles in five countries in just four days. It was wild and I was wicked. The car started off at Whittle-le-Woods in the morning, travelled north and crossed the border into Scotland. The motor, with Pete at the wheel, was en route to Stranraer to catch the ferry to Larne, from where he headed down to Belfast. I jetted into Northern Ireland at eight o'clock that Friday evening after a full day on the *Street* at Granada Studios.

I teamed up with Pete at the city's Europa Hotel and he

whisked me over the road for a date on a BBC TV chat show hosted by a chap called Gerry Anderson. He didn't do a lot for me, but his guests included former top model Paula Hamilton and sexy ex-*Sun* Page Three stunner Samantha Fox. I got a peck on the cheek off Paula, but fancied far more with Sam. *The Sun*'s vastly experienced photographer Ray Bradbury got a great exclusive picture of me cuddling Samantha. Ray then persuaded Sam to give me a big kiss — it was obviously something she'd been dying to do since she first set eyes on me. It was instant ecstasy for me and Ray wasn't far behind.

Later she invited me across to her table at the after-show party — the Randy Reg reputation was ready to go to work. I returned the compliment by requesting her company for a champagne nightcap at the Europa. We glugged a bottle in the bar in the style of true stars. And so to bed. We turned a few heads as we strolled nonchalantly into the lift together at around 3 a.m. We went up and whether or not I did is a private matter. As fans of Sam know, she may be small, but she's perfectly formed. I hope she says the same about me these days. She's delightful and has the singing voice of an angel as well as that heavenly body.

Sam was due to jet off at dawn to help some Romanian orphans, but she got a later flight. She was no doubt tired and emotional from the rigours of the night before. The next morning I woke refreshed ... in bed alone. I really fancied feeling shagged out with Samantha in bed beside me, perhaps next time we meet that'll happen. I've got a lot further than most fellas who fantasize about her, at least I've kissed her and given her a squeeze. In its day this would have been enough ammunition for about 20,000 hand shandies, but these days I just don't have the time.

After tucking into a figure-filling, full fried Irish breakfast I had my first personal appearance of the day down the Shankill Road. The crowds were out in force — they even got the Union Jack out — but from previous visits I realized the bunting wasn't for me. It's just a sign of the awful religious divide in Northern Ireland. I had visited the North during the Troubles and noticed the difference peace had made. The army checkpoints had all gone, the guns had vanished from every street corner. I am glad for the people that peace has broken out at last. An RUC man, originally from Sunderland, was in charge of the detachment dealing with crowd control during my visit.

When my visits to a supermarket and a leisure centre were completed, I headed off for a quick autograph-signing session on the Falls Road. The people there were just as friendly. I was on the other side of the peace line, an enormous graffiti-covered wall that stretches between the Catholic and Protestant parts of the city. At about 5 p.m. I had to hit the road for the three-hour drive to Dublin. That night I met up with Sherrie Hewson for a late-night slot on the popular Irish TV show hosted by the ever-youthful-looking Pat Kenny. There was no time for dinner, which is often the case. After the show it was back to the bar in the exclusive Berkeley Court Hotel, near Dublin's famous Lansdowne Road sports stadium.

As soon as Sherrie and I arrived back at the hotel we were invited into a posh wedding; a couple of Garda — Irish police officers — had got hitched. All the cameras were pointed our way and the flashes went off. But before long we were ushered out, because the bride was a bit upset that we were stealing her limelight. We left and retired to the residents' bar to sample a famous local stout — the Guinness was good and after a few pints I was feeling stouter as well. It is a brilliant brew, but it really does pile on the pounds. A charming Dublin-based Garda inspector, Edmund Finucane, joined our company. Pete, an expert on aviation warfare, regaled us all with tales about Edmund's famous ancestor Paddy Finucane, an Irish-born fighter pilot renowned for his heroic exploits before his death in World War II. We all had a giggle before heading up to bed. The Irish are a wonderful, friendly people.

The next morning we faced a four-hour drive to the Londonderry International Air Show, a massive event with thousands of people. En route, Pete and I talked about old times. He recounted how his father, an RAF navigator, died in the Second World War when Pete was just a babe. His father's whole squadron of Beaufighters trained for eighteen months before setting off to strafe the U-boat pens. Inside a fortnight they had all perished. All those brave young men dead in just twelve days, leaving lots of widows to bring up little ones, like Pete, alone. His dad was shot down over Holland, the plane crashed into the sea and two months later his body was surrendered by the waves.

We remembered his father and heroes like him again at the show when we clambered into the B-17 bomber used in the movie *Memphis Belle*. The body of the plane seemed so thin; there was virtually nothing to protect those lads from the bullets the Germans fired their way. I sat in the cockpit and appreciated the nerves of steel those flyers must have had. I also imagined the terror those young men must have gone through on every engagement, as their pals got shot to pieces as they went on their daring bombing runs.

When we arrived at Derry airport I was greeted by the Mayor, Councillor James Guy, before I went on to open the show. I posed for pictures with him and, Reggie-style, offered him £20 if I could wear his chain for the day. He didn't let me. The show's organizer was that human dynamo from Leeds, the legendary events manager Jeff Brownhut, who never gave me a moment's rest as he made sure I ran like clockwork to fulfil my hectic schedule of radio interviews and live broadcasts. Along the way I signed several hundred autographs.

After a very busy afternoon the Cadillac headed south to Galway. We arrived at 10 p.m. and enjoyed a pint in the bar of the Great Southern Hotel and chatted about the 1960s with a high-flying computer expert who remembered mass orgies in his youth in beer gardens round Norwich. Tragically, our drinking pal told us he was dying of cancer, but he looked to have plenty of fight in him and I happily signed photographs for his daughters and secretary.

Early the next morning I had another personal appearance at a new cash-and-carry store. In the afternoon we had to drive across the country to Dublin, but the radiator sprung a leak. Pete was despatched to get the repairs done during the morning PA and I nipped in afterwards. Even the visit to the garage in Galway turned into another personal appearance as I signed snaps for the lads who'd fixed the car. At one stage there were fifteen of them peering under the bonnet — now that's what I call service.

By this time Sherrie and I had decided to fly ahead to the Musgrave's cash-and-carry store near Dun Laoghaire on the outskirts of Dublin. When we arrived the crowds, as ever, were massive. Afterwards she jetted back to Manchester and I rejoined Peter for a catamaran trip across to Anglesey, through Wales and back to Whittle-le-Woods. Just thirty miles from our destination the Cadillac broke down on the M56 near Altrincham. It was 1.30 a.m. when I called for breakdown assistance. At 6 a.m. I arrived home, weary. Another weekend on the road was over and the bank account boosted by about £8,000. I could earn more in a week doing personal appearances than I could in a month acting on *Coronation Street*.

Reg, the fornicator and the fool, was in demand everywhere. Women in particular wanted to get their hands on him. One woman, who got her arms round me and squeezed my bum in one of the hen-party-type crowds, shouted out to her friends: 'Getting hold of this is better than a trip to Lourdes.'

Another time I was doing a nightclub with the front rows full of panting females. One of these shameless hussies got hold of my plums in the palm of her hand and said: 'You don't get many of these to the pound.' Realizing she needed to be put in her place, immediately I responded: 'Any more of that, love, and it'll be the end of the show.' I was feigning indignation, before I added swiftly: 'I'll be going straight home and taking you with me.' With a loving tweak she left them to dangle. I always tell the ladies I'm not a gynaecologist, but I'm willing to have a good look at anything they want to show me.

It was always great fun doing personal appearances with Sherrie. We've done gigs in all sorts of clubs, clubs for the young, clubs for the old from Edinburgh to London and beyond. But one I'll never forget was a Valentine's Eve night at the trendy gay nightclub LA2 in London's Charing Cross Road. The *Street* has a massive following among the gay community.

Well, Pete pulled up outside the club and the manager told him to drop me off in the middle of this football-match-size crowd. We told him that wasn't a good idea, but he insisted. I've never seen a man sweat so much in the space of five seconds, because that was all it took for me to be lost in a mob of men dressed in all sorts of bizarre costumes, from full leather, through rubber and down to bicycle shorts. Others were in feathered boas, sequins and pearls and on a couple of occasions the drag queens had the dreaded five o'clock shadow.

Sherrie arrived soon after and is never one to be outdone. She was wearing the shortest of short black leather skirts, black high-heel shoes, black fishnet stockings and a shameless dress with a plunging neckline. My first remark to her was: 'I see you've been in my wardrobe again, haven't you?' The queens loved it, but her husband Ken, who had brought her, didn't see the show. I can't think why, but he preferred to wait outside.

I followed up with the lyrics of that well-known ditty: 'I kissed you on your legs and on your thighs, I went a little higher and got something in my eyes, it looked just like cream, but tasted something like glue — I only hope that glue came from you.' This had the gay audience rolling in the aisles. I had them in the palm of my hand, metaphorically speaking, of course. It gave them all a sense of what was to follow. It was real no-holds-barred stuff and they lapped it up. The gay community has always appreciated a good joke and for the same reason the sight of Sherrie's knickers seemed to drive them wild. I offered to throw them to the audience, saying there was enough for everybody.

They took Sherrie's side and started chanting: 'You fat bastard, you fat bastard.' This has somehow become a sort of signature tune of mine in nightclubs; the punters love swearing at me. Imagine my horror the next day when the newspaper headline read: 'REG'S GAY DATE'. I thought it was that chap from Peckham telling the world how I almost singed his member. I knew mother would be none too pleased if she saw it.

As it was, it was simply a review of our personal appearance at this nightclub. The event had featured a gay version of TV's *Blind Date* and was obviously rather near the knuckle, if you'll pardon the phrase. MPs rapped my performance for giving 'credence to the sleazy gay world'.

One bloke who certainly isn't that way inclined, however, is the Marquis of Bath, otherwise known as the Loins of Longleat. Not a lot of people know this, but the Loins once escorted me round his baronial pile, near Swindon, showing off his rather risqué murals, or muriels as Hilda Ogden would say. The paintings leave little to the imagination and are a work of art. He was a very entertaining chap to be around and, like myself, quite a womanizer.

He believed in having lots of women, quite a forward-thinking individual. Randy Reg certainly admires his principles, but Maud would have got in his way if he'd planned having more wifelets than Maureen. I put in an appearance at his nightclub, Oscars in Swindon, before I popped into his fabulous stately home. It was a surreal experience.

Yet experiences like that are not unusual when Pete is around. He has an uncanny knack of turning many often quite normal events into abnormal happenings. 'Home again, home again, jiggity, jig', is his catchphrase. Every time we pass through the gold-coloured Elvis Presley-style gates at the top of my drive, Pete churns out his little ditty. We do hundreds of trips together and it's driving me barmy. I've told him the next time he says that I'll throttle him. But Pete is talentless in other directions as well. He is to map-reading what bricks are to buoyancy. The number of times his navigational skills have circumnavigated our destination are too numerous to mention.

He also has the uncanny knack of saying the wrong thing at the wrong time. Pete puts his foot in his mouth as many times as most people eat breakfast. Every trip I bite my bottom lip as I wait for his next pearl of wisdom. He was hired by myself as chauffeur, confidant and fall guy as a result of our friendship, spanning nearly fifty years.

He also does a remarkable Elvis-style left-leg wiggle, which has been used on stages up and down the land to break the ice. Being called up to perform also embarrasses him slightly, so it's my form of revenge for his frequent faux pas. But his big mouth has almost got him the bullet on more than one occasion.

A classic Pete quip came very early on when he'd driven me to a club up near Middlesbrough in the North East for a public appearance. We were staying in a nearby hotel and after the show the clubowner offered us a pint of his fine North Eastern ale. Peter, being a Philistine, declined the offer, informing the man, who'd just paid his wages: 'We call that paupers' footwash in Lancashire — nobody in their right mind would drink it.' I decided to order him to return to the car forthwith. I didn't want him saying anything else that might upset our generous host. He was dangerously close to a knuckle sandwich. Even worse, the motor might have got damaged.

Outside I gave him the rocket he deserved: just what did he mean, saying that? Unrepentant, he said he didn't like the beer. I told him if he was getting it for nowt he ought to like it. We let the matter drop there, well at least for ten minutes or so, because throughout the rest of the trip I berated him Reggie-style for his slip-up. He lapped it up, because Peter is the master of the foot in the mouth.

Another gem from his one-liners collection that can put a dampener on any good day happened in the pleasant town of Knutsford, Cheshire, on 9 April 1993. It was a Friday and I was opening a conservatory centre. The crowds turned out in force despite the day being full of drizzle. After jumping out on my arrival I asked Pete to get an umbrella out. He immediately asked: 'Who for?' I was stood there getting soaked, so I just glowered at him. The brolly arrived shortly.

I had a feeling it was one of those days. The appearance was busy, busy, busy, but in the background I could see Pete kicking his heels by the Cadillac. I thought to myself as I signed the hundredth autograph: 'He hasn't put his foot in it for days.' I knew he wasn't cured. It was just a temporary remission. The day finished on a good note; the man who owned the business was shaking my hand and was obviously delighted with the turnout. It was grand, particularly considering the grey clouds and inclement weather. People were still braving the elements.

This chap reached into his pocket and said: 'I'd like to give you a few pounds more towards expenses. It's been a good day.' That was Pete's cue. He said straight away: 'A pity the rain ruined it.' The words carried on the crisp spring air. I thought: 'He didn't say that, you're dreaming, wake up man.' I pinched myself — he had said it. I wanted to punch him. I refrained, but once more I sharpened Reg's rapier tongue on the blithering idiot. Can you believe it ... there we were standing to make an extra few bob and old Pete was poised ready to sink us with another verbal atom bomb.

One of his most memorable moments came on 7 December 1992, shortly after we rolled up at the Central TV Studios in Nottingham where I was to film *Celebrity Squares* with Bob Monkhouse. Pete was instructed to nip in and find out where the dressing room was. A simple enough task, which a trained parrot could have managed. Pete came out, having completed the task to his satisfaction. He was beaming, because they had said they'd send a couple of people up from costume to help carry the cases.

He proceeded to unload the car, and sure enough a couple of people came to give him a hand. Suits and shirts were handed over. A third chap then walked up and Peter offered him a rack of clothes, as my witless driver reached back into the car. The gentleman in question didn't take them, so Peter turned round and offered him them again. The chap who had asked him if he needed any help was in fact the head of Carlton TV. After witnessing this pantomime, with Peter trying to get a senior TV executive to hump my shirts, I went over and had a quiet word with Pete. I asked: 'Do you know who that was?' The predicted reply followed: 'No.' The rollicking began: 'Well, you daft prat, you've just asked the head of Carlton TV to act as a gofer.' But not perturbed in the slightest, Peter returned to the task in hand.

Talking of tasks in hand reminds me of his wife Monica's witty tricks with our sandwiches. She always makes up a marvellous packed lunch for our expeditions to personal appearances. This day I opened up the lunch box to find a French stick with a shrivelled black hand attached to it. The butty made me burst out laughing — it was too good to eat. Monica had stuffed a black velvet glove and coloured it to give the impression it was a decomposing hand. I decided to take it into the studios and surprise some of the cast by sticking it in the fridge. It worked a treat. Lynne Perrie opened the door and saw what looked like a rotting human hand holding a sandwich and she let out a scream ... oh how I laughed.

After this successful trick Monica started spicing up packed lunches with lots of little extras. Another that proved a winner was a highly phallic garlic sausage. Now at the time I had blackened windows on my stretch Lincoln and other cars would drive past with people peering in trying to guess who was inside. We were on the way to Hull along the M62 when a car full of girls started buzzing along beside us. These girls were paying extra attention to the machine and, with a series of cards placed at the window with scribbled names on, managed to guess who was in the back. When my thumb emerged as they wrote 'Reg', the girls started to strip off their shirts and bras, baring their breasts in my direction. It was a very horny sight as these women were all well endowed.

I had to show my appreciation in some way. The only thing for it was the giant pink garlic sausage. Using the switch, I lowered the electric window and to howls of delight from the girls let them have the garlic sausage inch by inch over the darkened glass. They were too far away to touch it, but I'd given them a taste of one of my favourite on-the-road pranks. It has been adapted since to emerge glistening above the glass with a pair of my Reg specs attached to the top. It has the girth and meat inside it to make many a girl smile. And, like myself, it has done just that.

One prop I never really fancied getting too close to was a shovel full of steaming horse droppings. This heap of manure was handed to me by a cheeky photographer during a personal appearance I put in on the first Sunday horse race meeting ever held in Britain, at Doncaster on 26 July 1992. The caption for his picture read: 'Reg says the best way to follow the horses is with a bucket and spade.' The snap must have been a pile of crap as well, because it never made the newspaper.

Another picture that never made the newspaper, but made Roger regard his daddy Reg as a real superhero, was when I appeared on the *Sooty Show*. At home I'm Ken, his dad, and on TV I am Reg, his dad; that is how four-year-old Roger sees things. He has a mummy, Sue, and his dad Reg has a wife, Maureen. Now whatever else I may have achieved in my career paled into insignificance in Roger's eyes when he saw a photo of me with Sooty. He asked me all sorts of questions about the meeting, like where did you put your hands when you held Sooty and so on. I know there will be a time when he sees a photo of me with Sam Fox and asks all sorts of questions. Like, where did you put your hands, Daddy? But at the moment he's more interested in glove puppets than girls.

Another TV appearance that I quite enjoyed was on the Channel 4 *Big Breakfast Show* in 1995 when they had me compete in one of their barmy contests alongside motorcycle daredevil Eddie Kidd. We both had to run around with our trousers round our ankles and grab balls and put them in a box. Now after the show I said to Eddie: 'I've heard about your spectacular jumps, can I tell you about some of mine?' He didn't hear me, but I was going to tell him about the screamer and the woman whose wig fell off before we started.

One television appearance that turned into a right fun do was down in Wolverhampton, where I took part in the Telethon. TV tough guy Lewis Collins was there with his wife and their new baby. We had a very enjoyable time and some great fun. *Dr Who* star Jon Pertwee and William Russell, who played Ted Sullivan in *Coronation Street*, were also there. Not too long after, William left the Street when his character turned into dead Ted. He was a smashing bloke and after he was killed off in the soap he flew out to join up with his Brazilian wife, who was working as a doctor doing research for the World Health Organization out there.

As part of the Telethon fundraising we were all given three-wheel electric bikes called Trikes, which were invented by Sir Clive Sinclair, famed for his Sinclair C5 and the Spectrum computer. We were expected to complete a complex circuit, which looked as if it required a fair amount of energy. I managed to cheat by grabbing hold of a police motorcyclist's arm and getting a tow, but poor Lewis had to more or less run round, having had the pedals on his machine drop off. I finished way in front of him and couldn't resist saying to Pete as he struggled in nearer last than first: 'He Who Dares Wins, eh?', a reference to the famous SAS motto, the title of one of his action-adventure films.

But Pete and I have on occasion had to leg it ourselves. One memorable time when we legged it for dear life was down at Trecco Bay, near Porthcawl, in South Wales.

We'd just arrived at the Sea Bank Hotel and decided to have a stroll through the town. We were walking along the road when all of a sudden four coaches pulled up and screaming fans started jumping out. We were expecting the madness and mayhem the next day on Sunday, 2 May 1993, at the sprawling Trecco Bay caravan park, but after a long day on the road we desperately needed a break. So the pair of us, looking like a couple of puddings on legs, set off down a side street. With the excess weight each of us was carrying we didn't get too far, so we decided to hide behind a pile of dustbins.

There we were down a back alley in Wales, cowering among a mountain of rubbish, fearful a bunch of brazen young women would run up and lay their hands on us. When we were younger we'd have both given our right hands for this kind of attention off the ladies. Pete gets groped on PAs as well as me. I've explained to him that it's what is known as a perk of the job, but he never ceases to be amazed when it happens. Women on numerous occasions have said: 'You're with Reggie and we can't reach him, so we'll have to make do with you.' He pretends to push them away, but I know deep down he's a dirty little beast, like myself, and he really loves it.

Another in the same mould as Pete and myself is Kevin Kennedy. He is quite happy to be groped by women fans, in fact he's quite happy to be groped by anybody. We've done some belting appearances together, but some of the best have been in Ireland. Kevin has his roots in the Emerald Isle and absolutely adores the people over there. He also enjoys Guinness and, despite drinking gallons of the stuff, retains his pencil-thin physique.

We've done dozens of personal appearances in Ireland and every time you are virtually guaranteed to bring the traffic to a standstill. We did one together in Letterkenny and they went completely wild — frenzy wouldn't be too strong a word for it. They were jumping on one another, pushing, shoving and doing anything just to touch us. We'd arrived in style in 'Chitty Chitty Bang Bang' and pandemonium broke out. Now when Reggiemania was born in Grimsby shelves and displays went flying, and the same was happening in Ireland. The Garda couldn't keep them back and they were literally ripping the clothes off our backs.

After about forty minutes we had to cut the visit short, because people were being trampled in the street. There we were, the quintessential prat brothers, and people were nearly being crushed to death just trying to touch us. It just goes absolutely mad — it is spooky sometimes just how insane the hordes can be. I must have done about six or seven hundred personal appearances since joining the *Street* and I never fail to be amazed at just how popular the character of Reg and the other characters in the cast are.

I worked out the other week that in the last four-and-a-half years I've covered 190,000 miles. At an average of fifteen miles per gallon, that is 12,000 gallons of fuel — a whopping £30,000 worth of petrol. I've also given away over 40,000 signed photographs to fans. That's a hell of a lot of people to shake hands with.

And on occasions it can be just like a presidential cavalcade, with police outriders escorting the pink Cadillac through the crowds as people lean from shop and office windows, camera flashes firing everywhere and proud mums wanting pictures of Reg kissing both them and their babies. Politicians and presidents only tend to get to kiss the babies and that's usually only at election times. It happens to me at every PA. No wonder they sold over 160,000 tee-shirts with the logo 'Knowledge is Power' and Marks and Spencer look like clearing 60,000 pairs of Reggie socks in their first six months on sale. My karaoke video sold £90,000 worth inside two days.

top: Hair wig go! My first wig. I liked it so much I bought the company. They only ever made the one in frizzy red afro.

above left: On the beach at Clacton – before 'care in the community'.

above right: Kenny the eagle – my daredevil days on a moped.

Opposite: The King Thing. I put on Presley gear to pay a TV tribute to Elvis. I've been into rock 'n' roll since the 1950s and love it just as much today.

Top: The two degrees – me and Sue on graduation day. Our relationship was a meeting of minds.

Above: Fat's my boy. I display my Mr Blobby physique on holiday in Ibiza in 1987. Sadly, I've put on a bit of weight since then.

Fan-tastic! I'm mobbed during a personal appearance in Ireland, but even on this side of the Irish Sea it's bedlam when Reggie hits town.

op left: Arthur Brown – he was like my second dad.

op right: My mum, Phyllis, 81 years young.

bove: Confess thee – wearing this red cardinal's hat I burst into a local hotel bedroom alf-naked and woke up the wrong bloke.

Top: Chord blimey – Kenny the keyboard king shows young Roger how to tinkle the ivories.

Above: Rub-a-dub-dub, soap star by the tub. I give Roger a scrub and brush up, but leave the nappies to Sue.

op: Bride and groom – Sherrie Hewson looked a picture but I was worn out. The
hole cast put on the Ritz. Lynne Perrie is by my side showing off her first lip implant;
e second lip inflation saw her leaving the show.

bove left: The other Phyllis in my life, played by actress Jill Summers – she's a scream.

bove right: The King and Queen of *Coronation Street* – Julie Goodyear and I both
llected awards as the Best Actor and Actress Ever in a soap.

Emma Wray was my co-star in the hit comedy *Watching*. I played the part of bird-watcher Eric. This performance landed me my *Street* role.

Pete and I, like the Lone Ranger and Tonto, have gone out night after night, day after day, and dodged the crowds to escape personal appearances. Sue and Roger couldn't believe it when they joined us on a trip to reopen Blackpool's three piers for First Leisure. There were thousands upon thousands of fans and holidaymakers on the promenade clamouring to clutch Reggie to their bosoms. Some swine even stole the Lincoln badge off the boot of the car as Sue and Roger waited inside.

Once we did a gig at the Paradise Club in Derby and the manager said: 'I can't believe it. This is the biggest crowd I've ever scene — when Jason Donovan appeared here he didn't get this.' They were all chanting: 'Reggie, Reggie.' I let them have him. Another time, on 13 June 1993, we pulled into the Post House Hotel, Reading, in the early hours of the morning and popped into the bar for a pint before bedtime. The only other people in there were quite a large number of young people and an adult couple. We didn't know them from Adam, but they came over and introduced themselves as Britain's top rap band at the time and asked for my autograph. I was extremely flattered, but as I'd never heard of them I never asked for their signatures.

One of the biggest crowds I've experienced was in Bradford, West Yorks. It was there, in front of at least 10,000 people on Thursday, 25 November 1993, that I switched the city's Christmas lights on. I called Peter up to the stage just so he could see for himself what a crowd of that size looked like. The following year, I switched the lights on at Batley, also in West Yorks, and once again the streets were at a standstill.

The Christmas lights switch-on in November 1993 came in my busiest week for personal appearances ever. I did fifteen from Cullompton in Devon to Edinburgh and a lot of points in between. It was damned hard work, but the loot made it all worthwhile.

On 19 May 1994, I met Ernie Wise again at London's Carlton Hotel in Cadogan Square, where we'd both been invited to the Tie-Wearer of the Year awards. The last time he'd seen me I'd had a cockatoo on my shoulder in the gents at the Beeb, so I didn't remind him of that. It was Pete who insisted I go over and have a chat. He knew that Eric and Ernie were early comic heroes of mine. He told me, 'If you don't chat with Ernie Wise you'll regret it for the rest of your life.' I went up and said hello. He chatted with Pete and me for a fair while. He is a fantastic bloke and still retains that inspirational sense of humour.

Pete stunned me into silence on another occasion when we were at an American Classic Car Show at Tamworth in Staffs. He dragged me away from signing autographs and said, 'There's someone you have to meet.' He pulled me to this corner, where a bloke stood with a trilby and a mac on. He turned to face me and said: 'Of all the bars in all the world — you had to come into this place.' It was a Bogart double, and I stared open-mouthed, he looked that much like the real thing. Then he smiled and I burst out laughing. The date was 25 September 1994, and I'd just been suckered.

Another impersonator Pete and I had a laugh with was Jimmy Jemain, who is billed as the Shadow of Cliff. We met up with him at Gateshead's Paramount Club on 23 November during that hectic week in 1993. We had a few jars and a chat and enjoyed ourselves a little. We bumped into his name again on 5 June 1994, during a PA up in Morecambe, Lancs, and decided to go and give him a surprise. We nipped into the club he was starring at and crept up to his dressing room. Then outside, at the top of our voices, we started crooning 'Living Doll'. He burst through the door thinking it was somebody taking the mickey, but when he saw us he just doubled up laughing. We wished him luck and were on our way.

The *Street*'s Johnny Briggs, who plays Mike Baldwin, used to do personal appearances. He has also come up the hard way, doing lots of jobs, and has been the itinerant jobbing actor in his day. He is a master at playing the villainous boss. He is one of the few actors who can smile as he slips the knife in — a rare talent. His philosophy is the same as mine: 'Work it hard, make it pay and take what comes your way.'

Bill Roache, who plays Ken Barlow, is the *Street*'s sole surviving cast member from day one and in his time had done his share of personal appearances. But when he went on the campaign trail for the Tory Party he swiftly noticed the difference between a personal appearance for political ends and one for charity. He visited Bury and Oldham with this rosette on his chest and people booed him. When I saw him with it on I said: 'Here Mother, there's that bloke from *Coronation Street* shoving the Tory Party down folks' throats.' There he was on the box as a working-class chap from *Coronation Street*, but in real life he was pushing the toffs' party. This was my reaction as a punter watching Ken Barlow — I really believed this struggling schoolteacher would have been a socialist, but that's the power of the *Street*. On Wednesday nights twenty million people tune in and they believe what they see on that screen.

Of course, in those days, we had Lord Home and Anthony Eden and we know what school they'd been to. How things have changed — who would have thought the son of a circus juggler would one day be juggling the books for Britain?

I wasn't in the soap at the time, but now I know that Bill, politics aside, is a smashing guy. It just backs up the old adage that actors should never be seen with politicians, whores or Royalty. Remember Peter Sellers getting stick for rubbing shoulders with the Royals? Bill and I have only recently chatted. He is a very private person who spends much of his time in the studios inside his dressing room, which he uses as an office. Our chats have been mainly on the subject of our spreading girths. But he also told me how he'd cleaned his teeth up. They had gone terribly brown from smoking, but for two weeks he slapped a slimy mould over them at night and they've come up almost as white as those of that ex-US President, Jimmy Carter.

I asked him if he knew anybody who could make hair grow, but sadly he didn't. He is sixty-one or sixty-two, so he's not done too bad fending off the old middle-age spread. Although I've told him: if I had his hair and his looks I wouldn't worry about the stomach.

With middle-age spread in mind, I displayed mine not so long ago after a charity appearance at a police and army long-distance walk up near Kirkby Stephen in Cumbria. I'd popped into the town with Peter for a greasy fry-up when I noticed a haberdashery store. I went inside and had a rummage round and found a fantastic red hat like the one worn by cardinals, very similar to the one Oliver Reed wore in the movie *The Devils*.

The pair of us were going on from this charity day to a reunion of about a dozen old college pals in the Yorkshire Dales beauty spot of Reeth. I took the hat and we had a grand night, recalling all the lusty adventures from the 1960s and catching up on old times. At 3.30 a.m. a coachload of local nightclubbers were dropped off outside the pub and after spotting the pink Cadillac started chanting: 'Reggie, Reggie'. I got up and waved from the window in order to quieten them down and soon after we all nipped to bed.

In the morning Pete and I were up early to tuck into the full Yorkshire breakfast. Other old chums couldn't face their fruit juices. After breakfast I smuggled a wooden ladle and a silver spoon up to the room to make a crucifix. I donned my red hat and took off my shirt and dived into Peter's room using the witchfinder general's line from *The Devils*: 'Confess thee, confess thee, man, I have come to confess thee.' He chortled — it worked a treat.

So I burst into the room next door, belly hanging over my jogging bottoms, and jumped on the bed shouting: 'I have come to confess thee, man.' Imagine my horror when I realized that the bloke I'd just woken up in the bed had nothing to do with our group. He looked at me, horrified, and pulled the covers over his head. What would his pals think? He'd had a half-naked *Coronation Street* star jump on his bed. I made a hasty retreat, but couldn't resist telling Pete what had happened. He laughed all the way home and when we got there ... he said it: 'Home again, home again, jiggity, jig.' I swear I'll strangle him.

15

Reg's Rewards

When you dream of fame you imagine the glitter, the glamour and the good life. It's all a million miles removed from the dreary two-up-two-down terraces of *Coronation Street*. But that cobbled street set me on the road to fortune and travels far beyond my wildest imaginings.

Brushing up the scraps in the yard at Hill's Bakery I'd never even leant on my broom to fantasize that one day someone would be sweeping up the table in front of me. I came from humble roots and hadn't even heard of silver-service waiters, let alone realized that they used a tiny brush and a silver shovel to clean the crumbs off the table between courses.

As I picked up my £4-a-week wages, I dreamed of seeing the palm trees in the most exotic spot on earth ... Cornwall. Up until then, the only holiday destination I'd been to was Blackpool. I'd never have believed I'd one day be sipping champagne cocktails on a cruise ship in the Caribbean.

That happened to other people. The folk with the cash. When I repaired tellies for Radio Relay, I saw the celebrities on the screen and dreamed they had a better life than me. I experienced through television and books many foreign fields that I never thought I'd witness at first hand.

On Pathé newsreels Pete and I watched Elvis Presley perform and saw his magnificent mansion home at Gracelands, Memphis. We'd leave the cinema with less than a shilling in our pockets and pray that one day we'd go there together. It was a dream, nothing more.

But then I became Reg Holdsworth and overnight he made Ken Morley famous. All those far-flung places suddenly became accessible and dreams started to come true. Is there anything wrong in striving towards a goal that could give you more than you ever imagined possible? Reg Holdsworth helped make my fantasies into realities.

However, it didn't happen without some hiccups along the way. The Granada TV press office caused the problems, as far as I could see. It had been standard practice down through the ages for newspapers to take *Coronation Street* stars off on jaunts round the world in exchange for stories that would titillate their readers.

Now the editors know, as I do, that the man in the street loves to see stars getting the full treatment. This is because the average working person loves to live out his or her own dreams through glossy photos of far-off spots they reckon they'll never reach. When I was brushing up in Hill's Bakery, a snap of Elvis in a pink Cadillac could transport me via my imagination to another place and time. So if one of your favourite TV characters or pop stars experiences the sumptuous side of life, you think, 'Good on them. That's what stars do all the time.' It isn't what stars do all the time, but you like to think it is.

When you pick up a pittance, you want to believe there is an escape route from the drudgery for you, your children, or your grandchildren. And stardom is one of those pathways out of poverty. Look at all the young lads who want to be football stars, or boxers ... they put their bodies through all that physical punishment to escape the drab existence they could otherwise face in a factory or office. Manchester United's star striker Ryan Giggs earns a reported one million pounds a year — now that's something to work towards.

But there was a chap in a position of authority at the Granada press office who apparently didn't understand this dream. Despite titters from all and sundry, he attempted to impose a strict regime where stars were prevented from picking up the perks of the job, such as free foreign holidays. I thought it was a load of twaddle and I told him so. I was told it was unacceptable to go on holiday to any destination with a newspaper. Even a trip to Rhyl would have been ruled offside.

I was told in no uncertain terms that it was unsavoury to give the impression to the average viewer that the cast of *Coronation Street* were living the life of Riley. Compared to a chap on the factory floor, we were. The *Street* workload is mentally demanding and the six-day-a-week schedule is severe, but still, it's a lot better than working in a sausage factory.

I asked him: 'Where should we go on holiday? Cleethorpes, Skeggy or Blackpool?' I told him that people who tuned into the programme had no objection to seeing Reg sat on a beach in the Bahamas. They expected it. That was, and still is, my argument and it is true. I love the British resorts and still take regular day trips to the Golden Mile at Blackpool, but variety is the spice of life.

I mentioned offers of trips to Russia and Italy. But he said: 'No, no.' It was one of his favourite words. I found this a bit annoying, not because I am on an ego trip, but because I have always been a freelance, a maverick with the philosophy of being an easy rider. The freelance mentality is that you can do with your life what you want. This is in direct contrast to the corporate mentality. When actors have been with a show for twenty-five years they become part of the company.

But I have never regarded myself as part of *Coronation Street* or part of the Royal Shakespeare Company. I am just a visiting jobbing actor. Being told that I couldn't do something like visit the Caribbean or Russia was extremely irritating. It went completely against the philosophy by which I had run my life.

At the same time as I was getting these bans, other things were being refused. I asked if I could do a joke book about the life and times of Kenny Morley, the world's greatest lover. The answer was 'No'. I asked if I could bring out a Christmas rap record entitled *The Supermarket King*. It had some very funny lyrics which included the phrases 'jack your body' and 'bet I'm not a gambling man'. I thought I had a potential Number One hit. But that was rejected, because the lines were deemed to be references to characters in the soap. Harmless *double-entendres* to me, but apparently bad news to them.

So I jetted off to Moscow. I'd already been to Chicago to the Ford and Cadillac museums there. The trip to Russia was for a visit to the Zil car factory outside the capital. I was told not to visit supermarkets and I accepted that. When I jetted in, the temperature was twelve degrees below freezing. The proverbial brass monkey would have lost his balls and a whole lot more besides. We were staying in a hotel that was the last word in luxury. It might have been inside, but outside there was unimaginable poverty. You have to see it to believe it.

There were people standing outside who looked as if they hadn't eaten for a week. They were trying to sell cups, old shirts and lots of other rubbish. It was astonishing to see these elderly folk on the verge of starvation. It made me think of Mr Rochford, my old teacher, with his heart-breaking stories about India.

Until that day in January 1993 when I arrived in Moscow, I had never witnessed real poverty. I knew then what he meant about the starving natives. Couple poverty with sub-freezing temperatures and you have an atrocious situation.

The next day, my English journalist guides were met by members of the Russian press corps who were taking us on the trip to the Zil factory. Driving there we passed grey street upon grey street filled with cold grey people. There were no shops that you'd notice, no neon lights, no bright colours. It was like a painting by Lowry of matchstick men brought to life. En route, I asked one of the Russians where the advertising billboards were. He answered, smiling, with a question: 'What is there to sell?'

I wasn't prepared for the Zil works. It was like a town in its own right. We were escorted into the director's office and greeted. From there we walked through a door and were confronted by the most massive factory imaginable. It beggared belief. An astonishing 63,000 people worked in this one place.

During Granada TV's heyday, the company still only employed 3,500 people.

It was like a scene from something in the 1920s, all these rows upon rows of workers dressed in khaki uniforms. The production lines stretched into the distance. It was an immense place. They were producing huge, earth-moving lorries, which were on a colossal scale. It was like something out of *Gulliver's Travels*: the workers looked Lilliputian by comparison with the machinery and the building.

When we got back to Moscow for a spot of sightseeing, I noticed the hundreds of armed soldiers and policemen that seemed to be everywhere. It was a beautiful city. We went into Lenin's tomb, which was empty. The photographer said the body looked like a dummy. Fortunately, the army guard were outside doing their high-stepping march. After we got out, the photographer Boyd Milligan persuaded me, against my better judgement, to pose in the graveyard at St Basil's Cathedral. This attracted some very stern looks from the guards, some of whom had just come off duty at the Kremlin.

After four days we returned to the airport at Moscow, which reminded me very much of a 1950s bus station. For me, visiting Russia was like going into a time-warp. People were queueing everywhere for stuff. It was a far cry from Chicago, which I'd visited the year before. It was my first trip to the States and I immediately warmed to the place.

I am a big fan of American cars. I've owned a number of different makes in my time, but now the triple garage at my home is stocked with a pink Cadillac Coup De Ville, another pink Cadillac, a Buick Roadmaster and the obligatory Rolls-Royce. Cars have been a passion since I had a collection of Dinky toys as a boy. The models have just got bigger and bigger and Reg Holdsworth has helped me indulge myself.

Not long after I joined the *Street*, I was nipping about in a Lada estate I bought for £300. I'll never forget running into one star-struck policeman, who booked me for reversing on a motorway slip road — then asked me to sign an autograph for him. I can't remember the precise language I used, but it was a definite refusal. Then, in 1993, I saw him again at a road accident, where he was taking pictures of an overturned RAC van on the motorway.

I was walking on a bridge with the dogs when he shouted over to me, 'Remember me? I booked you.' He then passed the camera to one of his colleagues, ran over to me and put his arm round me and said: 'Just one for the album.' He now drinks in my local, and I've told the story in there frequently, to his eternal shame.

I loaned the Lada to my uncle when he came to visit from Australia. It was a good car; it did the job. I've always enjoyed conversations with people who know their cars. Now at Granada one day I was absent-mindedly leaning on a BMW, wearing a flak jacket with a lot of zips on. This young chap came over and asked: 'Do you like the car?' I replied: 'Yes.' Then he said: 'Well it won't look so bloody good if you scratch it with that zip, so get off it.' Very abrasive, but he had a point. He thought I was an extra in need of a rollicking.

The next time I saw him was at Bettabuys — his job was supplying cars for the filming on *Coronation Street*. This time he realized I was one of the cast. He was extremely edgy and I tortured him by shooting across surly looks. But soon after, he discovered I was a car fan and we became friendly. I regularly came over to inspect the Bentleys, the Turbo Esprits and the Aston Martins that he turned up in. We chortled together about that first meeting. His name was Bob Whitehead, and we had many a good laugh together.

It was a great shock when I discovered that this marvellous bloke, who was so full of life, had been tragically killed in a car crash along with another young lad in March 1995. Kevin Kennedy told me about the tragic accident when I asked after Bob, having noticed he hadn't been about for months. Poor old Bob was dead, but I can still see his face now, smiling with a twinkle in his eye as he told me the latest joke.

Being a car fanatic he would always inspect my latest purchase. In the early days on the *Street*, my machine was a black Pontiac Le Mans Special. One memorable incident with this car was when I parked it unwittingly on some Ministry of Defence land and went rambling as I learnt my lines. Inside the hour, Sue had the police knocking at the door in London asking after a Kenneth William Morley. She told them I was up in Lancashire and probably learning my lines on the moors. A racy Pontiac Le Mans Special is hardly the inconspicuous kind of car a terrorist would choose. Needless to say, I never went back to that bit of moorland. The headlines could have been awful: 'STREET STAR RANDY REG SHOT DEAD ON RIFLE RANGE'.

After the Pontiac Le Mans, I lashed out on a succession of other big American motor cars during my traipse down the golden road to success. I forked out for a Lincoln Continental Stretch, a Lincoln Continental Coupé, a Pontiac Trans-Am and a Cadillac Fleetwood. And I even ended up not doing all the driving myself after Pete accepted his redundancy from the TV rental firm and accepted my invitation to act as a chauffeur.

Our boyhood dream came true, thanks to a nice newspaper editor who happily splashed out on an all-expenses-paid trip for us to fly to Memphis. That was a marvellous experience and Pete was entranced as we entered Gracelands. On the day Elvis died, I was driving my car through London when I heard the news on the radio. I immediately pulled over to a phone box to ring Pete in Chorley. It was 16 August 1977, and everything just stopped. We were both shocked and could not believe it. Pete was the first of us to make it on the stage in our youth ... he was the singer with a rock band. But the hefty burden of fame was later to fall on my shoulders.

The death of Presley at the age of forty-two ended everyone's youth. We had taken for granted that our generation's star would grow old gracefully in Gracelands with us. When he died we felt robbed and thwarted. It was so awful. We both wanted to go to the States to pay our respects at the King's grave. He was the one and only — an irreplaceable star. When the opportunity to go to Memphis came up it wasn't clear that I would go. I couldn't go without Pete, because it was something we had intended to do together. So I flexed the famous superstar muscles and got him included in the freebie.

We toured Elvis Presley Boulevard, saw the Sun Records Studios at 706 Union Avenue and visited Gracelands. Pete put on a dark-green velvet shirt Monica had made him for a fiftieth-birthday present. I insisted he wear it as we toured Gracelands — he ended up stripping half naked in the road in Tennessee. Not a pretty sight, but if he hadn't worn it he would have regretted it for the rest of his life. We both gawped in amazement at the Grand Ole Opry building, the original home of country and western music.

We enjoyed a beer or two in B.B. King's bar and chatted about all the great stars who had appeared on the Sun Records label. As well as Elvis there was a whole multitude of greats, including Johnny Cash, Jerry Lee Lewis, Roy Orbison, Carl Perkins, Charlie Rich, Rufus Thomas and, of course, B.B. King. After he'd had a few beers, I insisted Pete get on the stage in that bar and give us his left-leg wiggle. He knocked them dead. An American barmaid drawled: 'We ain't seen anybody do that since the boy himself.'

Pete was walking on air. We both were after such a fantastic once-in-a-lifetime experience at someone else's expense. Granada appeared to view trips like this with a mixture of suspicion and disdain, but they were deemed just about acceptable. Still, it was very much a borderline issue. On my return, though, I was brought down to earth with a bump when I was summoned into the office and it was indicated to me that all these freebies had to come to an end.

It was explained to me that a new philosophy was in place and the old lax attitude, which allowed stars to trot off hither and thither at some newspaper or other's expense, was over. This was greeted with a mixture of scorn and incredulity by the entire cast. All the actors and actresses had for years been enjoying the hospitality of various newspapers. There was a time when people were carted all over the globe at no cost to Granada. *Coronation Street*'s popularity was such that I've no doubt that had trips to the moon been on the agenda, then the stars would have been flown there.

The newspaper which flew us to Memphis carried a picture of me dressed as Elvis on 23 May 1993, but all the shenanigans had taken the shine off it for me. The proof of the pudding was there before their eyes: a positive *Coronation Street* story in the newspaper, firing the viewers' imaginations.

As a conclusion to the series on car plants round the world, I asked the office if I would be permitted to travel to Rome for a shot of me dressed as Nero fiddling in a convertible Ferrari. This was refused on the grounds that it was a promotional advert. I could just see lots of the *Street*'s twenty million viewers rushing off down to Northern Italy to buy the next £400,000 model off the production line. All this would happen, of course, after they'd seen Randy Reg piddling about in one ... I don't think so.

Last year they allowed me to bring out a *Party Time Karaoke*, featuring *Jailhouse Rock, All Shook Up, Summer Holiday* and *Rock Around The Clock*, to name but a few. It did a roaring trade, selling a remarkable £90,000 worth of the £10.99 tapes in the first two days alone.

But enough of that unadulterated bragging and back to the holidays. In 1992 Sue and I joined Barbara Knox and Liz Dawn on a four-day cruise to Lisbon on the magnificent Cunard ship the QE2. The only problem was the weather, which was terribly rough. Sue had the sea-sickness injection and was right as rain afterwards. The trip was her first meeting with Barbara, who played the other woman in my life. I never confessed to Sue that Barbara had turned me on during those tea-dance scenes. It would have been a bit difficult to explain. Show me a man who tells his wife about every erection he gets. I, like Reggie, was simply born with hormones that just won't lie down.

We had a superb short break. The holiday was a regular freebie for *Street* stars. On the trips you were expected literally to sing for your supper. I still remember Barbara and Liz serenading me in the magnificent ballroom on the ship. Both did excellent cabaret routines — they were obviously born to be stars no matter what they did. The cruise was something else, the service second to none. Sue was bowled over by both of my female colleagues. As a *Street* fan, she'd known them for years, but it was a rare treat meeting them in the flesh.

The only boats we'd been on before this were *The Rubber* and rowing boats on park lakes. To have travelled on the world's most famous luxury liner was wondrous. But stardom was going to transport us off on yet another floating fantasy ...

a Cunard Princess cruise of the Caribbean. We were to set sail for a fortnight through azure waters, under cloudless skies, seeing spectacular sunsets, eating exquisite food and all in sumptuous surroundings.

But this cruise led to more bother. It was okayed for *The Sun* to go on the cruise with myself, Sue and Kevin Kennedy and his gorgeous girlfriend Clare. Everything was set until the *News of the World* indulged in a little high-seas piracy and had Cunard kick *The Sun* men off the ship before they even got there. Not to be outdone, *The Sun* sent two journalists to the other side of the earth to shadow our every move. It was hell out there for them. The baking sun, the endless supply of first-class cuisine and the scrupulously clean quarters.

Each time either Kevin or myself dived into the crystal-clear Caribbean, a photographer would pop out from behind a palm tree, capturing our beer bellies on celluloid. We soon cottoned on to the undercover team, but by this time they had a mountain of snaps.

One evening at the bar we told our new-found chum, a Costa del Crime-based Cockney heavy, about these two chaps who were on our trail. He was horrified that we were being pursued with such vigour. Obviously thoughts of Slipper of the Yard on the trail of Ronnie Biggs flitted through his mind. In an instant he'd decided to step into the fray. He immediately bounded over to two blokes on the other side of the bar who had been staring over at us. He started lambasting them: 'You are just filth. What are you doing following these people round? You are filth and you make me sick.' He pointed his finger at them again before storming off. We hoped he wasn't off to his cabin for a sawn-off shotgun, because he'd got the wrong guys.

These chaps were quaking in their boots. They came over and apologized. They were from a chocolate factory and had splashed out on the holiday from their divorce settlements. They had only been staring because they had never been so close to TV stars in their lives. Nobby and his friend were introduced to the aggressive Cockney when he returned. We didn't want them getting thumped on our behalf.

Meanwhile, the culprits from the newspaper were watching with interest from across the bar. After several days cruising through the islands, these chaps had obviously got all the material they needed. They very properly came across and introduced themselves. The taller headmaster figure described himself as Alastair Taylor and his photographer friend was a chap called Simon Wilkinson. We nicknamed them Crystal Tips and Alastair after the kiddies' cartoon characters from the 1960s and 1970s. Having done the job, these fearless seekers of truth were both raring to fly home out of the heat and the five-star luxury, so they could get on with their next nightmare assignment. Such dedication.

The cruise had started off in San Juan on the paradise isle of Puerto Rico. It had taken in St Kitts, Nevis, Antigua, Guadeloupe, Martinique, St Lucia, Barbados, St Vincent, Grenada and St Thomas. The *News of the World* team arrived as *The Sun* squad jetted home.

Granada's former press-office photographer, Stuart Darby, and reporter Alan Hart were looking forward to their mission. On the first night we joined them for some lip-lubricating liqueurs. But on the way to bed one of them got badly lost. He wandered into a cabin he believed to be his own and went straight into the loo. A short while later a lady screamed and a burly, bearded man in his pyjamas asked the errant hack how he happened to be there. He'd stumbled by mistake into the captain's quarters.

The next morning the journalists were summoned to see the captain, who was in a furious mood. He tore them off a strip or two and told them in no uncertain terms that he didn't want any similar slip-ups during the remainder of the voyage. They were, after all, guests of Cunard. Sheepishly they returned to our company and explained how they'd just escaped being keelhauled, or forced to walk the plank, or maybe even both.

Then they got down to the serious business of interviewing and photographing us for days on end. Just like *The Sun* men, they were seasoned professionals and knew just how demanding the job was going to be before they were despatched. They never set a foot out of line for the rest of the journey. It must have been murder for them. As we were enjoying ourselves with gay abandon, they sat there with their lemonade shandies watching as we quaffed gallons of tropical punch.

It was certainly a holiday with a difference and a far cry from my early breaks in the Blackpool boarding-house. Kevin and I did a few turns to entertain the Brits on board. We gave them our favourite Blues Brothers impersonation, first aired on Irish TV to much applause. We also belted out some rock 'n' roll classics for the pleasure of the people on board.

The Americans on the ship had obesity off to a fine art. There was one couple who sat eating non-stop all day. Sandwich after sandwich, chicken leg after turkey leg, pig's trotter after cow's heel, crab after lobster ... it was just like a rerun of the loading of Noah's ark, only this time all the animals were dead. You name it, they ate it.

An enormous American lady, who looked as if she'd eaten several other people, engaged us in conversation. She explained: 'The doctors have told me to cut down on my food intake or die. I've decided to eat while I can and die happy.' She was another marathon muncher. In their company I looked sylph-like. At every opportunity I sat near the fabulously fat Americans. They made me look like a lath — Kevin looked like a splinter.

He is one of Britain's most nervous men. Seeing him trying to consume a cup of coffee is hilarious. He's the only man I know who can turn an espresso into a cappuccino — he shakes that much it ends up with a froth on top. I often sneak up behind him and give him a tweak and that sets him twitching at top speed for a good thirty seconds. He doesn't have a washing machine at home — he just throws the soap powder and his clothes in the bath, then jumps in and has a twitching fit. We can both be very cruel about the other.

On board we did a chat show one evening and Kevin was asked what his first impression was of me. The heartless swine said: 'I thought they were extinct.' Another one he enjoys telling is how I'd even turn up at the opening of an envelope, but I always insist I'd only do it if the price was right. Anytime

Cunard want to open a supermarket on one of their ships, I've told them I'd do it for free. Those boats are five-star luxury that has to be seen to be believed. Fortunately, thanks to Reggie and *Coronation Street,* I got to see it for free, which made it all doubly sweet.

Another absolutely mind-blowing trip made possible through the popularity of Reggie was a jaunt to Canada, where *Coronation Street* is very big indeed. On that trip I recall they played their national anthem and everyone stood up. It took me back to my youth and the Bughouse in Chorley, where we all stood to attention for 'God Save the Queen'. I didn't want to stand up, but I thought I best had, being a guest and all. I remembered getting thrown out by that usherette for eating my ice cream as the music played, and smiled to myself. If only the boys in the Bughouse could see me now. Not only rubbing shoulders with the rich and famous, but actually being one of them.

Yet there is a downside to the glamour and glitter: with them you get the jealousy and the idiocy from a tiny minority who try to make your life a nightmare on fame street. I've lost count of the number of times the cars have been damaged or some plonker has scrawled 'Reggie' or 'Reg's car' down the side of a Cadillac or the Lincolns when I had them. Drunken yobs and jokers forced us from our last home. In the early hours of the morning, after a skinful, they would target us for late-night abuse.

We had clowns dropping their trousers and exposing themselves. Others pee through your gates. I've also had bottles and bricks thrown over the wall. Other prats wandered up the drive chanting: 'Reggie, Reggie, Reggie.' On another occasion I was watching TV in the living room when I got this feeling I was being watched. I looked at the window and there was this face pressed right up to the glass looking in. I dashed outside to ask what he was up to and the chap said: 'You're the fellow off *Coronation Street.* I just thought I'd come and have a look at you.' What do you say to somebody who has trespassed on your premises to stick their face up against your window? I was lost for words and he just wandered off.

I also got fed up with people driving past beeping their horns and chanting: 'Reggie, Reggie.' The local fire-engine even went through a phase of putting its siren on, and the lads on board shouted, 'Reg!' The same thing has happened with ambulances. As a result of all the unwanted attention I started turning the house into a fortress, because it does get to worry you. I was developing a siege mentality and that was no good, so we had to move.

Now I've got a sprawling bungalow home set in two acres of secluded grounds with a fish pool, trees and a bit more privacy. I plan a swimming pool and have just splashed out on an extension, so there is more room for when guests stay. I've also got a new room for my office and a massive games room for Roger and myself. You must remember that, like most blokes, I am still a big kid at heart.

Anyway, I always keep 50p in my pocket for luck. If things don't work out, I can always gas myself.

16

Fun at Firmans Freezers

Toupee or not toupee? That was the question. I most definitely wanted Reg to wear a hairpiece to add some hilarity to his life under the new American bosses. I'd seen and heard horror stories of blokes getting the bullet simply because they weren't considered young and virile enough to hold the reins of industry.

I wondered what a fifty-something, or forty-something for that matter, could do to stay in a post and protect himself from the old golden wheelbarrow that comes out round about the same time as most middle managers' hair. I thought the follically challenged could always slip on a syrup to hide their disappearing crowning glory. I imagined the high comedy that was sure to follow in the wake of a balding individual who tried to carry on as normal in a wig. You can't suddenly fool friends and staff into believing you've sprouted hair overnight.

And for Reggie at Firmans Freezers his new hairpiece has been laughs all the way, right from the very first fitting. The scriptwriters excelled and my colleagues in the cast have been equally witty about the wig. Those readers who've never had one fitted don't know what they're missing. At Sue Pritchard's instruction, Reg was to have his hairpiece created by Roy Marsden of Covent Garden — renowned as Britain's finest theatre and film wig maker. Roy travelled up to Manchester and measured Reg's noble bonce for a fitting.

Deftly pulling a plastic sheet over Reg's head, he then encased that with sticky tape to make a mould of the skull. Then he took it away to London and made a net to the exact shape of my head and threaded real hair through it. He supplied me with three rugs, a short, a medium and a monstrously long.

After they had been delivered, I had to go to a wig fitter in Manchester. The chap who adjusted and trimmed them was ever so jumpy. My telling him I wanted to look like Andy Warhol did nothing for his nerves, although one of the crew joked: 'The only difference between you and Andy Warhol is that he's been dead for ten years longer than you have.' The master wig fitter said to the director, Brian Mills, with a hint of trepidation in his voice: 'I have to make a living out of this when you've gone. I still haven't got over what you did to trade when you gave Fred Gee that ridiculous wig ten years ago.'

But in this day and age, with all the paranoia over ageing, I'm sure he does a roaring trade. Lots of people certainly roar with laughter in my experience when you slide a syrup on. But I see Labour leader Tony Blair is trying to outlaw age bias at work. Now there's a smart man, elected as leader on the youth ticket, realizes he's going to grow old, so wants to introduce some legislation to prevent younger men getting his job. Old Reg would be proud of a move like that.

Yet I do think Mr Blair has the right idea if he can prevent employers discriminating against workers just because they are old. Some of the giant B&Q DIY stores even started advertising for greying staff after discovering that they treated customers better and often knew how to do some of the jobs the clients were trying to tackle. Better an old head advising you on fitting a new door lock than a strip of a lad in the local Botch-It-and-Bungle DIY store who's never seen the lock out of the packet.

Anyway, back to that wonderful wig. Shortly after the fitting, I took the syrup home to give Sue a surprise. I walked into the kitchen and she screamed as soon as she saw it. But then Sue really shocked me when she asked me to wear it that evening in the boudoir. I said: 'Won't that be like doing it with somebody else?' She replied: 'Yes, that's exactly it.' Well, it worked wonders. Although, since she said that, I've been keeping a closer eye on my young wife, because if you take that comment further you know what will happen? Yep, I'll come home and catch her on the kitchen table with the wig and the milkman.

At one stage Sue even said she was jealous of Sherrie Hewson, because she was seeing more of me with the wig on than her. But despite my magnetic personality as far as women are concerned and the gallons of sexual charisma exuding from my every pore, the lovely Sherrie still doesn't fancy me. She once told a newspaper she hated snogging with me, because I had a 'squidgy' face. If she'd been kissing my bottom, yes, because ladies have called that squidgy in the past. Sherrie went on in this article about not liking the squashy, squiggly feeling she got when she kissed me. After it appeared in the newspaper, tens of thousands of women came up to me to try it out, because let's face it, nobody could understand what she was on about.

But the wig did pull the rug out from under one guy, a smashing chap called Jon Eaton, from Mansfield, Notts, who was one of the best doubles about of old Reg. He'd planned to venture out as a Holdsworth clone after getting made redundant as a colliery electrician. But just after the nation's top lookalikes agency got in touch with him, Reg got the rug and that was his promising new career nipped in the bud. I told him it was a cruel world and that he'd got the looks, but I'd got all the loot. I also mused that my father must have been doing a spot of work across the Pennines, because surely blond blue-eyed sex machines like myself don't grow on trees. Amazingly enough, not so long ago I was up at a personal appearance in Kendal in the Lake District when I spotted a local assistant bank manager who was a dead ringer for Reg.

These guys must have phenomenal success with the ladies, because everywhere I go, I get women slipping notes with their telephone numbers on into my pocket. If I took up all the offers I had to get between the sheets, I'd be awfully busy. One newspaper even interviewed my fans after a gig at a nightclub in Doncaster and the reporter got quite a surprise that all these gorgeous young women were after my body. The headline read: 'IT'S GIRLS, GIRLS, GIRLS ON THE ROAD WITH RANDY REG'. When they asked me how I dealt with the propositions I joked: 'I just use Castrol GTX.'

But Sue knows I haven't got time to stray and now I'm leaving the *Street*, she's bought me a little Vietnamese pot-bellied pig to keep me company. It won't be long now before some smart photographer gets a picture of me together with the new family pet and has it published as a competition under the heading: 'SPOT THE DIFFERENCE'. For a share of the tenner prize money, I can tell you I'm the one with the glasses.

But back to the good times behind the scenes of the *Street*. I bet you've always wondered what actors do in the spare time during breaks in filming. Well, let me tell you: all entertainers, and particularly male actors, often get twitchy and bored while waiting to rehearse a performance. Conversation invariably revolves round 'the business', sports, politics, music and, of course, sexual matters. During these languid periods, insults are usually directed at each other's performances and appearance. Football and cricket will be practised around several very valuable company awards and *objets d'art*. The odd guitar is also strummed, often accompanied by obscene lyrics.

Sexual matters are talked about explicitly. This is done often in a bold attempt to amuse the female members of the cast, who, likely as not, have seen and heard it all before. A gaggle of actors — in the *Street* green room often myself, Kevin and Philip — assisted by others with less expertise, will give a mimed performance of the various sexual positions tried and tested over the years.

In fact, on one such occasion we had a surprise visit when Kevin and myself were demonstrating the pleasure of the old soixante-neuf — that's 69 for the plebs among you. None other than the previous managing director of Granada Television, accompanied by his wife and daughter, walked into the green room midway through our performance. Blissfully unaware of their presence, we both added the coital grunts and moans one hopes for en route to orgasm. Our visitors, in a state of shock, were ushered from the room as quickly as they'd arrived by the *Street*'s stalwart stage manager Gordon McKellar.

Meanwhile, Kevin and I, having completed our virtuoso performance, received a standing ovation from our colleagues in the cast. I even went round with the hat! It was only afterwards that we discovered just why they'd been so ecstatic — they thought we'd both dropped ourselves right in it. Fancy them not telling us — actors can be so cruel.

But the moral of the story is simple ... the green room is the actors' room and you step into it at your peril. If you can't abide strong language and sexual stories of the most explicit variety then never enter that room. Most actors are unshockable. In fact, up to the late 1800s actors were classified by law as vagrants and had been since Elizabethan times. The reason for this goes back to Greek times when Plato said that men were the imitation of gods and that actors were the imitation of men. In other words all actors are imitations of real life, they are fraudulent, fakes, tricksters and definitely not to be taken too seriously. Shocking an actor is like getting a pig to fly. By the age of eighteen many are so far gone that the only way to shock them would be to stick their finger in a plug socket.

Actors can be animals. I remember a pair once exchanging heated comments in a theatre's green room. One of the actors then left and had a poo in the sink inside the other fellow's dressing room. Later, the outraged individual came in berating the beast who'd done it in his basin when the other bloke, who loathed him, said: 'Sorry about that, old boy, the loos were locked. I dropped it in your sink, but I did try to poke it down with a pencil.'

A crude lot, the acting profession, at times. Another famous actor, who shall remain nameless, frequently brought upstairs plates of food, so he could play an odious trick on other stars. Taking a plate of tomatoes, lettuce, chips and sausage, he would lay his member by the bangers to see if it would be noticed. This wheeze never failed to have a huge result, with the food and plates going in all directions. He would ask: 'Not enough sauce for you, darling?' One person you couldn't try that trick on would be Lynne Perrie — as she revealed in her autobiography, she was never slow at stepping forward for an extra serving.

I'll never forget her appearance on *The Word*, the late-night Channel 4 show, now axed. Lynne had an interview with Chris Quinten, who played her son Brian Tilsley on the *Street*, in which she uttered the immortal line: 'Man, boy or dog, throw it on the bed.' My only regret was that she didn't include Reggie Holdsworth in that. I thought: 'What a fitting epitaph.' Her crooning of *My Way* warmed the cockles of my heart. I found the whole episode great entertainment and tremendously funny. But down on *Coronation Street* her old pals were shocked rigid, because they had known her much longer than I and had known another side of Lynne. In her day she was vivacious, talented and possessed a great singing voice.

Mark Eden was another star who left the show infamous as a result of his character's antics. He played Alan Bradley, who battered poor Rita Fairclough, and as a result of his fantastic portrayal of this monster, he got singled out for aggravation wherever he went. Whenever he went out he'd keep his collar up and a hat on to hide his face. Apparently he went round taking extra care after getting thumped by one irate fan, who had taken his attack on Rita for real.

Johnny Briggs is another who can tell tales of how the fans can react strangely as a result of what they've witnessed on TV. He told me how he got off a train at Euston and jumped into the back of a cab. The cabbie set off, but after a couple of minutes looked in the mirror and said: 'Hang on, I know you, don't I?' Johnny said: 'I suppose you might do.' The cabbie said: 'Yep, you're that Mike Baldwin.' Johnny nodded, at which the cabbie stamped on the brakes, leapt out and opened the door beside the famous star. He said: 'Go on, get out, the way you treat that Alma you should be ashamed of your bloody self.' Johnny was left standing on the pavement, scratching his head as the angry cabbie drove off.

I had a strange thing happen to me at one of my personal appearances. A smartly dressed chap approached and said: 'Can I have a word with you, Mr Morley?' I tilted my head to listen as he said: 'I've heard that, in order to extend Manchester airport, they're going to knock down the Rovers. I think it's disgusting. You should do something about that.' I'd have made a joke, but this guy was deadly serious. I couldn't believe it, but he was stood there straight-faced talking about a fictional pub in a city-centre studio as if it was his local.

That the fans believe so strongly in the characters is a tribute to the true professionalism of the whole *Coronation Street* team. Lots of fans expect Jack to live with Vera in real life. It is very odd. I had an old aunt who used to say good night to the newsreader every night. When we asked her who she was talking to, she'd say, 'That nice chap on the telly who just said good night to me.' I suppose in a way he was. If you go into people's living rooms three nights a week you can become like a family friend.

I have fans who write to Reg as if he's a long-lost pal. In fact, I got one letter from a chap in the Lake District who'd been a pupil of mine at a school in Houghton, near Preston. He asked: 'P.S. Do you remember me?' I replied:

I do indeed remember you. Mostly for your flatulence, which on several occasions nearly removed the headmaster's wig. I also remember your endless nose-picking and your astounding inability to remember anything for more than five minutes ... I'm surprised you remembered me! However, I wish you well in your chosen profession, but why a man should choose to live surrounded by 40,000 sheep is beyond me.

Yours,
Reginald Eisenhower Holdsworth

Another fan from Cambridge once sent me a pound for a signed photograph and asked where he could get a similar wig. I replied:

Thank you for the £1. It has enabled my wife and I to have

meat for the first time in a fortnight. The wigs were made by
Baz of Hyde, but only two were produced. I got one and the
other went to a John Major, of 10 Downing Street, London.
If you have another pound I suggest you send it to him,
because he has been looking somewhat downtrodden of late
and obviously needs the money. Alternatively, write to Baz
and he'll do you a wig that will get everybody laughing.
After all, it's worked for me and John.

Yours,
Reginald Bosanquet Holdsworth

Fans like these two would be amazed at the curious way
filming is done for their favourite soap. The cast are never told
what the storyline is in advance, they only find out when they
get the script a week or ten days before filming. Then, because
we film the outside scenes on Sundays and Mondays, we end
up having to learn lines out of sequence. For example, if there
is an argument in the Rovers followed by a fight outside, we'd
film the fight first in the street on the Monday, then three days
later the argument is recorded in the studio at the Rovers on the
Thursday. The effect this can have on people is that you really
can begin to wonder not only *where* you are, but *who* you are.
If it's a heavy script, then some days you won't know if you're
coming or going.

Then on the Wednesday, we all have a technical rehearsal,
which is done after you've had the scripts for just a couple of
days. The producer and all the executives turn out to watch the
cast giving a rendition of their scenes in a semi-lit studio. It is
nerve-wracking stuff — just like a first night in a theatre,
except you get one every week. Some people say it is
unnecessary making the actors suffer all those nerves. And
people with that argument do have a point, because all the stuff
we did in Bettabuys, and later in Firmans Freezers, was done
without a rehearsal.

But Wednesday is regarded as a big day and all the women
dress up for this premiére performance. The producer turns up
in something bright, maybe a red or a yellow outfit. The ladies
in the cast look equally elegant. I have often found myself

sitting, or standing, there doing my lines and looking at these tasty, well-dressed female executives. As I stared at them I started thinking: 'My God! I could give you a good seeing-to, darling. Just lean against the bar over there and I'll show you where my reputation comes from.' The left-hand side of my brain is doing the lines and the right-hand side is giving me a mental hand shandy.

It's true, the *Coronation Street* production office is a place of fantasy for me. It is now staffed entirely by women, which has been a source of great pleasure. I imagine getting locked in there and it drives me wild. I only hope that now I've gone, they've found a way of getting the stains out of the carpets.

Talking of fabulous women, one of the great *Street* legends was Pat Phoenix. I never met her myself, but I've heard some wonderful stories. One of them involved that other *Street* sex siren, Julie Goodyear. In her early days, Julie used to go to the studios from her home at Heywood on the bus. Anyway, one day Julie was stood there in her leopard-skin mini-skirt and high heels, having missed the bus, so she decided to hitch-hike. A bloke driving a huge concrete mixer couldn't believe his eyes and stopped to offer the shapely blonde TV star a lift. As they pulled up at Granada Studios and Julie jumped out of the cab, Pat Phoenix, wearing an extremely expensive designer gown and lavish fur coat, had just stepped out of a Rolls-Royce but all eyes were on Julie and the cement mixer. As the two women strolled into the studios together, Pat turned to Julie and said with a smile: 'Don't ever try to upstage me again, luv.'

Oh! How I'll miss them all, with their endearing little ways! In the business you know you've made it when the bookies start offering odds about how you're going to be got rid of. William Hill offered 100–1 that Reg would end up suffocated by his wig, 66–1 that he'd drown in a waterbed accident, 50–1 that he'd be murdered by mother-in-law Maud, 33–1 that he runs off with Curly, 20–1 that he runs off with shopgirl Tricia and evens-favourite that he goes off to a new job. Well, we all know now what's happened.

And that ending spoiled my favourite gamble, which was William Hill's 500–1 against Reg and Bet going out together in a suicide pact. Not long after making my announcement, I joked that I'd like Reg to turn into a real stiff by being frozen solid during a naughty nookie session in one of Firmans Freezers. Sadly, the flood of money that poured in on that prediction might as well have been thrown down a drain. Or better still, slipped into my pocket.

17

Life After Reggie

I hope that, by now, you will understand why I had to leave Reggie behind. In discussing my life, I've given you an insight into the type of person I am, a bloke who can stuff a daft wig on his head and entertain twenty million people. You can't do that successfully without having a wealth of experience of life itself.

Being Reggie has been a very, very happy period and has had an enormous effect on my life. I've met thousands upon thousands of wonderful people who tell me they love Reggie in the show. I've also made a great deal of money, for which I am extremely grateful.

There have been hiccups along the way, which I've highlighted for you. The idea that a star lives in a cocoon of happiness is absolute rubbish. We live in the real world, as does any person who has ever worked in an office, a bank, a factory, or out on the road, or wherever.

Throughout the years I have met lots of interesting people and have learned that life is a challenge. I'm now moving on to my next challenge. Long live the independent spirit, long live Granada and long live *Coronation Street*! However, at the end of the day it has always been a job to me — it may be well paid, but it is work.

There have been emotional moments. When Reg Holdsworth handed over the keys to Curly Watts, I walked slowly away from the supermarket, past the rolling cameras and I cried. Leaving Bettabuys was the end of an era. The scene had to be very emotional anyway, but it came straight from my heart. I actually lived every moment of it.

I was swallowing back a huge lump in my throat all the way through. When I walked off camera the tears spilled over. As I passed the cameras, there was total silence. There was none of the normal clatter and chatter from the crew — even the hardened cameramen felt for Reg. He'd been promoted and moved on as area manager, and everybody knew it was the end of his reign as the Beast of Bettabuys. He had made us all laugh for four years. Now he was making us cry, but the viewers never saw it.

The supermarket was Reg's kingdom. It was full of memories — a week later one of the camera crew said to me: 'We can still all hear your voice barking orders down the aisles.' But I still managed to say bye-bye to Bettabuys.

Now I've said bye-bye to Reg, and yes, the old waterworks went on again. He'd given me such a lot of fun. He had also earned me a fortune and the fame I craved. But within an hour of walking out of the studios, he was in the past and I never, ever worry about what has been. Life is too short for that.

Yet I'm already on course for other things. I've produced this autobiography in double-quick time. I've got a belting part playing a dame and a dope in the panto *Sleeping Beauty* at the Sunderland Empire — get your tickets from the box office now! You are all welcome. It is the theatre where the comedian Sid James collapsed on stage on 26 April 1976, and died in hospital soon after at the age of sixty-two. They say it's haunted and I don't fancy meeting the ghost — strangely enough, he was starring in *The Mating Game* at the time. But before that panto starts in December, I am doing a theatre tour with dates from Basingstoke to Barnsley and all points in between. The personal appearances are also pouring in, so I could be opening a shop down your street one day. Bring the book along and I'll sign it for you.

But next year I plan a long family holiday, probably to the States. I don't know what will happen after that. Granada TV may still want to do a pilot for a series about a photographer entitled *Flash Harry*, but who knows? Other scripts are dropping on the mat and life has always had a habit of taking me off in unexpected directions.

Just before I left Granada I went to see a clairvoyant. He told me that I would leave the *Street* and go to Australia to work. He predicted that I would become a big, big star and make lots of money. I took it with a pinch of salt, just like we did when that old gipsy foresaw fame and fortune for young Kenneth.

But then the spiritualist startled me by saying his vision was coming from a guide who looked like Dracula with long, grey hair. He said the chap, who hadn't been dead long, was carrying a bag brimming with cash and he was holding a violin. His description was of an old pal, Ken Divine, a talented violinist from Wigan. He had been diagnosed as suffering from cancer of the pancreas and had died two days before my visit. This clairvoyant could never have known he was a pal of mine, so perhaps his prediction may prove correct. Only time will tell.

One thing I do know is that next year I'll be sitting at home with my feet up, a pint in my hand, with the wife — or somebody else's — on my knee, as the Rovers Return appears and the theme tune starts and I'll say: 'Good God, I used to be in that, didn't I?'

Anybody who requires autographs should write to Reginald Holdsworth, care of *Coronation Street*, Granada TV, Manchester. And if you ever go down the *Street* and see him, give him all my best wishes. Reggie — I loved ya, baby, but it's 'Tara, chuck, until the next time.'

Not everyone who leaves *Coronation Street* achieves oblivion. I have been likened to that other famous late starter, Arthur Lowe. He was in his forties before he got anywhere and had been working for peanuts on the stage. It was only when he joined *Coronation Street* in the 1960s, as Gamma Garments boss Leonard Swindley, that he began to make his name. Yet when he left the *Street* he did the old quick-shoe shuffle and joined the BBC. As we all know, he went on to become one of the best-loved actors on TV, with his tremendous portrayal of Captain Mainwaring in the David Croft and Jeremy Lloyd comedy series *Dad's Army*.

My lesson in life for others is simply that, no matter how low you are at the beginning, with determination and a little luck you can reach the top and turn yourself into a success. I started off as an overweight £4-a-week apprentice and I've ended up an overweight, bald millionaire!

But seriously, the biggest job of my life is already under way ... being a parent. It is tough, and it is important that Sue and I give Roger a good start in life. He needs the knowledge to know what's right and what's wrong. With that behind him, he can go on and make a success of his own life. He'll be brought up aware that knowledge is power. But power can be used for good or evil. If he uses his power to good effect, then I'll be a proud dad and the happiest man in the world. Here's to success for everyone. And by the way, if there's anyone out there, 'Gizza job.'